Democracy

Upside

Down

With contributions by:

Michael W. Apple
Alan Draper
Richard Guarasci
Douglas M. Kellner
Kenneth Teitelbaum

Democracy
Upside
Down

Public Opinion and Cultural Hegemony in the United States

Edited by
Calvin F. Exoo

New York
Westport, Connecticut
London

Grateful acknowledgement is made to the following persons and organizations for permission to reprint previously published material:

A passage from *Tropic of Cancer* by Henry Miller is reprinted with permission of Grove Press, copyright 1961.

Lines from "Bryan, Bryan, Bryan, Bryan" are reprinted with permission of Macmillan Publishing Company from *Collected Poems* of Vachel Lindsay. Copyright 1920 by Macmillan Publishing Company, renewed, 1948 by Elizabeth C. Lindsay.

Lines from "Editor Whedon" are reprinted with permission of Ellen C. Masters, from *Spoon River Anthology* by Edgar Lee Masters, Macmillan Publishing Company, copyright 1916.

Excerpts from *The Myth of Sisyphus and Other Essays* by Albert Camus, translated by Justin O'Brien, are reprinted with permission of Alfred A. Knopf, Inc., copyright 1955.

Library of Congress Cataloging-in-Publication Data

Democracy upside down.

Includes index.
1. United States—Popular culture. 2. National characteristics, American. 3. Public opinion—United States. 4. Political socialization—United States. I. Exoo, Calvin F.
E169.1.D44   1987   306'.4'0923   87-2380
ISBN 0-275-92453-X (alk. paper)

Library of Congress Catalog Card Number: 87-2380
ISBN: 0-275-92453-X

First published in 1987.

Praeger Publishers, One Madison Avenue, New York, NY 10010
A division of Greenwood Press, Inc.

Printed in the United States of America

The paper used in this book complies with the Permanent Paper Standard issued by the National Information Standards Organization (Z39.48-1984).

10 9 8 7 6 5 4 3 2 1

Contents

Preface

If this book has a virtue, it is modesty. It is no more and, we hope, not much less than a drawing together of some of the better empirical work bearing on the matter of cultural hegemony in the U.S.

We hope it will be of interest to scholars who may have tilled in one of the fields herein reviewed—let us say, hegemony in the news media—and would like to step across a neighbor's fence and see how the work is going on in the schools, the workplace, political parties, or the entertainment media. Are the questions there parallel? Are the answers?

We also hope it will be of interest to scholars and students at work in larger fields, fields of which cultural hegemony is a parcel. Fields like public opinion, political socialization, political behavior, political sociology. We hope that those who are mainly acquainted (due to the nature of the available texts) with the mainstream account of these subjects will want to know more about an important alternative to the prevalent way of seeing.

We hope it will be of interest to any socialist scholar who has ever spent a star-filled night wrestling with the Jacob's angel of the Left: the question "Why not?"

About all those things, as I say, we can only hope. But there is one thing about this book of which I am sure and will boast, shamelessly and at length. That is the aid and comfort of the mentors, colleagues, and friends who nurtured this book like an extended family.

They include my teachers at the University of Wisconsin–Madison, who showed me that critical thinking begins at home, with one's own work: Peter Eisinger, Leon Epstein, Booth Fowler, Patrick Riley, Richard Merelman, and Fred Hayward. The hardest questions my mind's ear still hears are echoes of their supportive interrogations.

They include my beloved colleagues in the Government Department at St. Lawrence University: Sandy Hinchman, Alan Draper, Bob Wells, Ansil Ramsay, Rick Guarasci, Bernie Lammers, Laura O'Shaughnessy, Larry Frank, Phil Neisser, Joe Kling, Brad Klein, and Ahmed Samatar. The testament of their work reeducates me every day about commitment to what we do, to scholarship and teaching.

They include all the other rabble-rousing, troublemaking, unresigned, unassimilated rebels in Canton, New York, and at SLU: people like Liz Kahn, Bob Schwartz, Lew Hinchman, Laurie Baron, Dick Perry, Stu Hills, Steve Papson, Kerry and Rachel Grant, Pat Alden, John Barthelme, who see, as Gramsci did, that it is not "possible to *know* without . . . feeling and passion."

They include my first "haven from a heartless world," my mother, my late father, my brothers and sisters, Henry, Patty, Alan, Gay, and Marge, whose "mere enveloping love" (as an other-directed critic of the inner-directed family will call it in Chapter 7) taught me about the *caritas* that "seeketh not her own," but "beareth all things, believeth all things, hopeth all things, endureth all things."

They include Gail Colvin and Laurie Olmstead, who transformed my primitive scribblings into something miraculously machine-readable, and did it with infinite patience. And Sheila Murphy, who has been such a valuable secretary, such an invaluable friend.

They include my beamish boys, Joshua and Christian. In a time that is right for "pessimism of the mind," their infinite hearts are my font of "optimism of the heart."

Above all, this list includes my co-conspirator, yokemate, best friend, love of a lifetime: the pilgrim soul to whom this book is dedicated.

1

Cultural Hegemony in the United States

Calvin F. Exoo

In all ideology men and their circumstances appear upside down, as in a *camera obscura*.

Karl Marx

TRAGEDY IN A MASK OF TRIUMPH

At the memorial service, we are told, the president found "the right words" to "make it easier," "and he delivered them eloquently" (Magnuson 1986, p. 31). But the children there cried anyway. Maybe they were too young to know that the president had found the right words. Then again, maybe they were young enough to know better.

Quickly, it came to be called the "space shuttle tragedy." It's a good word, "tragedy," with its nod to the Greek stage, where human pride and weakness are always in the leading roles and the Fates are always in the wings, waiting. The indelible image of the explosion itself is not of a bang, but a whimper—those wispy plumes of human frailty, set against a cold and empty sky, trailing into the sea.

But just as quickly, the tragedy of it was forgotten, hidden—dressed in a mask of triumph. With amazing rapidity and precision, the nation's idea factories were retooled to mass-produce a perfectly uniform new line: *the* meaning of the shuttle explosion. It was a message of the America that the challenge of the last frontier so perfectly epitomized, where enterprise, freedom, and bravery had combined to produce the explorers, competitors, dreamers, doers—men and women of the right stuff.

Their accomplishments were not diminished, but dramatized by the deaths of the seven crew members. Fittingly, the nation's president set the tone:

The future is not free; the story of all human progress is one of a struggle against all odds. We learned again that this America was built on heroism and noble sacrifice. It was built by men and women like our seven star voyagers, who answered a call beyond duty (in Magnuson 1986, p. 31).

That tone resounded in the stories and editorials of the news media:

"It's all part of the process of exploration and discovery—it's all part of taking a chance and expanding man's horizons," President Reagan explained to school children yesterday.... He has offered the right solace, not despair and not withdrawal, but more missions, even more school teachers in space. In this moment, the country mourns; in the next, the task will be to honor the dead by again turning tragedy into triumph (New York *Times*, January 29, 1986).

Within a few short weeks, the entertainment media had readied its first contribution. A popular network television show saw its child star, Punky Brewster, through the tragedy. In a lesson similar to one taught in an elementary school just after the explosion and aired on network news, Punky's teacher asks the pupils whether the astronauts were "brave explorers," and whether we should be proud of them. They affirm these things in unison, and hope out loud that the space program won't be stopped. After the additional comfort and counsel of former astronaut Buzz Aldren, who likens the shuttle crew to "explorers...all through history," Punky has adjusted well: "I still feel bad about the shuttle," she concludes, "but you've gotta take risks if you're doing something nobody's ever done before.... 'If' is a word smack in the middle of life."

The labor movement joined the chorus, led by the president of one of the country's largest teacher's unions, whose weekly newspaper column praised those "risk takers" prepared to "meet the challenges and crises that inevitably face every nation. In time of need there have to be those who are prepared to step forward" (Shanker 1986, p. E7).

Among its numerous contributions to this hymn, the advertising industry produced and sponsored a "special section" of *Time* magazine on May 19 for such clients as Rockwell International and McDonnell Douglas. Entitled "Man in Space: A Celebration of 25 Years of Space Exploration," its story began with a "bristling, world-leading, headstrong America...locked in a cold war"; with a "young President brimming with enthusiasm" but beset by "Soviet challenges in Cuba, Soviet technological feats, and aggressive Soviet foreign, economic and military policies.... Kennedy became determined to use the space program to symbolize his vision of a technologically and politically preeminent America." The ensuing "story of danger, risks, heroism, even death" has produced a program that "has been the envy of the world" (Stafford 1986).

But nowhere was the point pressed more fervently than in the schools. The New York State Commissioner of Education, for example, sent a memo to every school district in the state calling on "our schools, colleges, and cultural institutions... to teach the lesson of the astronauts' aspiration, diligence, courage, and knowledge." "They were a team trying to press the frontiers of knowledge on behalf of all of us.... Each had earned a place in the Challenger through hard work and sacrifice.... That is the lesson we must carry from this tragic event and imbed in the education of all people" (Ambach 1986).

In all of this, no one asked whether there might be another lesson to be learned from the tragedy. No one asked whether the presence of "the first teacher in space" might have been a "pseudo-event," designed to shed the warm glow of favorable publicity on the space agency or on the president, who had conceived the idea. No one asked how far the program had in fact pushed "the frontier of knowledge on behalf of all of us" through its main mission, the placement of corporate and military satellites in orbit. Or why the shuttle flights had been manned, since the placement of satellites rarely requires the risk of astronauts' presence. No one asked whether competition and ambition might have spurred NASA or its contractors to push those "frontiers" too far, too fast.

No one asked, in those first days, but history had ripped the underbelly of an American Dream, and soon the guts came spilling out. Investigators determined that the explosion had been caused by ruptures of both the primary and backup seals on one of the shuttle's booster rockets. A document not released until four months after the explosion showed that, six months prior to the disaster, NASA had results of a test showing failure of the seals at temperatures of less than 50 degrees. The Challenger was launched in 36-degree weather. Seventy-four seconds later, it disintegrated. Asked why the test results did not prompt further studies, the NASA official in charge of the booster-rocket program replied, with typical right-stuff understatement, "In hindsight, someone might certainly conclude that the data wasn't being properly dealt with" (New York *Times*, May 13, 1986, p. 1).

On January 27, the night before the launch, a team of engineers at Morton-Thiokol, the company that built the booster rockets, unanimously agreed that, because of the cold, the shuttle should not be launched. In teleconference, the NASA administrator in charge of the booster-rocket program fumed at the idea of delay: "My God, Thiokol, when do you want me to launch, April?" Delays were awkward for several reasons. For one, corporate clients whose satellites NASA was launching had made it clear that long delays would jeopardize their contracts. And rumors later circulated that the White House had pressured NASA to launch Challenger in time for the president to mention "the first teacher in space" in his State of the Union address, scheduled for delivery on January 28. In fact, nine White House staff members had telephoned NASA in the eight days before the launch. Later, the White House refused to release records of those conversations to a Senate panel investigating the matter.

After two hours of questioning by NASA officials, the Thiokol vice-president in charge of the booster program took his team into caucus. The engineers remained unanimous against the launch. But Thiokol's senior vice-president told the other administrators present, "We have to make a management decision." He asked the vice-president in charge of the engineering team to "take off his engineering hat and put on his management hat." Although the engineers remained unanimously opposed, the Thiokol managers present relented and agreed to recommend a launch. The rest, as they say, is history.

THE ARGUMENT IN BRIEF

Most books about U.S. public opinion seem implicitly to agree with James Madison that "Authority [in our society is] derived from and dependent on [the people]." Ultimately, it is their culture, their attitudes, arrived at autonomously and spontaneously, that will govern (Dahl 1956, pp. 132–33). This is democracy as we would like it to be and, we rest assured, as it is in the United States—sovereignty from the bottom up.

This book demurs. Animated as it is by the theory of cultural hegemony, it wonders whether the formation of public opinion may in fact be a "top-down" process: to what extent can "haves" impose their ideology on "have nots"[1] by dominating such sources of political ideas as the media, the schools, the workplace, political parties, and interest groups?

On this view the space shuttle tragedy is, in miniature, the American tragedy. The nation's idea factories took that shameful occasion to celebrate the very "American Way" that had led to the disaster. Ambition, competition, commercial success—together they were a one-way ticket to oblivion, words to die by. But in fact, our cultural institutions take every occasion to celebrate an ethos[2] that their owners and managers can bank on, but that is a dispiriting, debilitating tragedy for millions of poor and working class Americans. As a later section will argue, the American Way of freedom is cold comfort to those it has left free only to live the slow death of poverty, drudgery, powerlessness, and indignity. Even for those enriched by it, a culture that counsels avarice has taken its inevitable toll—the withering of what Kant called the Moral Will, the nobler self.

This book is about that American tragedy. "The right salve" for the wrong system; words that work, for a regime that does not. Democracy upside down.

WHAT IS CULTURAL HEGEMONY?

Already in 1927, as Antonio Gramsci began his *Prison Notebooks*, the rooftree of history had fallen in upon the notion of "inevitability": working class men and women had not, as a matter of course, seen the injustice of modern life, or banded together to change that life. Already it was clear there was to be no "of course" about history. Amid the rubble of the Marxian prediction, Gramsci wondered why not.

The basis for what sometimes seems Marx's cavalier optimism was his assumption that our culture—ways of thinking, believing, and behaving—are determined by our material circumstances (Marx 1970, preface).[3] Thus, for a while, a property-owning class would be able to command the compliance of working class people, browbeating them with the coercive powers of government and the implacable demands of making a living. But ineluctably, the tensions of working class life—of losing control over the fruits of one's labor, of how one worked and for what—would draw the working class to consciousness of its plight, to resistance and revolt. And, argued many Marxists in the 1920s, wasn't the proof in the historical pudding? Hadn't Marx's scenario just been acted out in Russia?

But as Gramsci looked around him, he saw a Western world very different from Lenin's Russia. There, a State that had lived by the sword, died by it—force was undone by force. But here, in the West, nations were stronger than coercion alone could make them; here, they rested as well on the consent of the governed. To achieve that consent, a ruling class had to deploy more than police. It had to man the barricades of "civil society"—the schools, the mass media, political parties, churches, trade unions—all those places where political ideas and instincts are made and remade.[4]

The flag to be captured on this battleground of civil society is what Gramsci called the "common sense"—the usually uncritical, often unconscious way in which most people perceive the world (Gramsci 1971, p. 419). It is what we take for granted. Gramsci called the conquest of these heart habits *egemonia*, hegemony.

The great genius of Gramsci's account of this struggle is that it is full of healthy respect for all the combatants. That is not true of some accounts of "false consciousness," which seem to ascribe only self interest to the dominant, and stupidity to the dominated. In Gramsci, to be sure, the common sense does protect ruling class power and privilege. But the propertied class has only succeeded in capturing the common sense by wrapping its ideology around a core of "good sense"—a set of genuinely worthy ideals.[5] For example, one might argue that the ideal of freedom, which figures so prominently in the American common sense, ought to—it is a real *desideratum*. But somehow, propertied-class ideology has conquered that word, wrapped it in a particular meaning (freedom to do as I please with my property; free enterprise; free markets). That meaning, of course, tends to exclude other meanings more favorable to working and lower class people (freedom from poverty; freedom of a people to choose its civic destiny, even if the choice is to abrogate property). In our society, says Herbert Marcuse, "speech moves in synonyms and tautologies" (1964, p. 88). Words that should begin debates end them. Words whose meanings should be argued over are instead invariably defined by the status quo, where the haves have and the ruling class rules. The "free world" is our world. Never mind that U.S. workers expect to take orders most of their waking lives, at work, while Yugoslav workers run their own factories (Pateman 1970). The "free press" is our press. Never mind that it is bound wrist and ankles by commercial imperatives and by the dominant ideology (as Chapter 3 will argue). "Success" is commercial success. "The American Way" is the capitalists' way. "The good life" is their life. Good words, words whose only limits should be limitless imagination, are, for the moment, bound to the service of one idea, one class. But other meanings remain in them, latent, like the strength of Samson, of Prometheus.

Put another way, the capture of the common sense is not a matter of the strong hypodermically injecting their version of the truth into the weak. Human give-and-take does not work that way. Instead, the common sense is "negotiated by unequal forces in a complex process through which the subordination and resistance of the workers are created and recreated" (Simon 1982, p. 64).

Gramsci summarizes his position and hints at its implications in one of the most quoted passages of the *Prison Notebooks*:

In the East, the State was everything, civil society was primordial and gelatinous; in the West... when the State trembled a sturdy structure of civil society was at once revealed. The State was only an outer ditch, behind which there was a powerful system of fortresses and earthworks (Gramsci 1971, p. 238).

Those who would storm the Bastille in the modern West had better begin, not with a military assault, but with a "war of position" in the cultural trenches, which are now the old regime's first line of defense.

Finally, Gramsci cautions, the pattern of those trenches will differ from nation to nation. In each, capitalist ideology has been married to a unique national history and mythology, by unique "means of mental production." This of course "necessitates an accurate reconnaissance of each individual country" (Gramsci 1971, p. 238). Gramsci's charge has been ours, as we have undertaken the mapping of the cultural trenches of the United States.

WHAT IS THE DOMINANT IDEOLOGY? A CATECHISM

A cultural hegemony argument had better begin with some evidence that there is such a thing; that there is, to begin with, an ideology that best serves the interests of the "house of Have," but is accepted by the "house of Want" as well.

Basic, of course, to such an ideology is belief in the economic system under which the haves have and the have-nots don't: capitalism. In McClosky and Zaller's concise, comprehensive definition:

the values and practices associated with capitalism ... include private ownership of the means of production, the pursuit of profit by self-interested entrepreneurs, and the right to unlimited gain through economic effort. In its "ideal" formulation, capitalism also stresses competition among producers, a substantial measure of laissez-faire, and market determination of production, distribution, and economic reward. Certain notions from individualist doctrine and the so-called Protestant ethic, such as an emphasis on achievement and hard work, are also widely regarded as part of the capitalist creed (1984, p. 2).

The sheer percentage of Americans joined in this litany of capitalism is impressive, as Table 1 demonstrates. But even more striking is the fact that assent does not diminish much among working and lower class Americans, as Table 2 indicates. Even those who have not been flattered or blessed by the ideal and the real capitalism nonetheless affirm it.[6]

Capitalism's twin pillar in the edifice of American culture is liberal democracy (Hartz 1955, p. 89; McClosky and Zaller 1984). Again McClosky and Zaller's definition is a good beginning:

Both the theory and the practice of democracy rest on the notion that all people possess equal worth and have the right to share in their own governance—to rule themselves either directly or through leaders of their own choosing. The ruled, in short, must consent to their rulers, who are in turn accountable to the governed (1984, p. 2).

Logically, of course, capitalism and democracy are not so much twin pillars as twin rulers—a sort of American Romulus and Remus, with all the brotherly love that that implies. Freedom to choose, after all, includes the freedom to choose socialism. American Brahmins have always feared that the rabble could be roused to such brigandage (McClosky and Zaller 1984, pp. 130–31; Hartz 1955, pp. 128–34). But the evidence we have just reviewed suggests that these patricians underestimated their own

Table 1   Support for Capitalism and Related Values among Americans (in percentages)

1. People should place more emphasis on working hard and doing a good job than on what gives them personal satisfaction and pleasure.

agree	63
disagree	23
unsure	15

2. There is nothing wrong with a man trying to make as much money as he honestly can.

agree	95
disagree	5

3. Our freedom depends on the free enterprise system

agree	82
disagree	18

4. Some form of socialism would certainly be better than the system we have now.

agree	11
disagree	89

5. Private ownership of property:

is as important to a good society as freedom	87
has often done mankind more harm than good	4
decline to choose	9

6. The more government regulation there is, the less efficiently companies can operate.

agree	65
disagree	22
other	13

7. The most important factor in determining who gets ahead:

luck	8
hard work	68
family background	24

Sources: items 1–6, McClosky and Zaller (1984); item 7, Schlozman and Verba (1979).

cultural hegemony. When, at the turn of this century, push came to shove, they knocked much of the working class clean out of the electorate, and they leavened the meaning and danger of democracy with more than a pinch of "meritocracy" (see p.18, and Chapter 2). Today, for Americans, democracy's freedom to move about ends where capitalism's nose begins.

Even the rejection of undiluted laissez faire, which has grown up over

Table 2   Support for Capitalist Individualism, by Occupational Level and Income (in percentages)

	Occupational Level			
	Low 1	2	3	*High* 4
1. Hard work is the most important factor in getting ahead (% agreeing)	67	66	69	70

	Family Income	
2. The way property is used should mainly be decided by the:	Under $6,000	Over $35,000
Community, since the earth belongs to everyone	18	20
Individuals who own it	68	60
Decline to choose	14	20
3. Competition, whether in work, school, or business:		
Is often wasteful and destructive	9	12
Leads to better performance and a desire for excellence	77	73
Decline to choose	17	15
4. Under a fair economic system:		
All people would earn about the same	9	2
People with more ability would earn higher salaries	76	84
Decline to choose	17	14

Sources: item 1, Schlozman and Verba (1979); items 2–4, McClosky and Zaller (1984).

the course of this century, is no cause for the apocalyptic terror with which some businessmen have described it (McClosky and Zaller 1984, pp. 130–31). New Deal liberalism was offered to Americans, and accepted by them, not as the end of capitalism, but as a new beginning; not as a way of destroying entrepreneurialism, but of making it possible. This was to be done by providing a minimum level of regulation for the game's rule-breakers, and welfare services for its blameless losers—just enough, it was hoped, to allow them to get back into the game (Lipset and Schneider 1983, p. 238). Put it another way: equality of opportunity is the object (even among labor leaders, 84 percent agree), not equality of result (only 4 percent of labor leaders opt for it, say Verba and Orren 1985, p. 72). Thus the well-known finding that Americans are "operationally [New Deal] liberal" and "ideologically conservative [capitalistic]"(Free and Cantril 1968; McClosky and Zaller 1984, p. 272) is not in the least surprising or inconsistent. New Deal liberalism is a perfectly straightforward means to capitalist ends.

There may be no more compelling or startling evidence of this than the fullness with which New Deal liberals sing the anthems of capitalism. "By sizable majorities, they affirm the importance of the free enterprise system, private property, competition, and wages based on achievement rather than need" (McClosky and Zaller 1984, p. 224; see also Verba and Orren 1985, p. 72). With only a little less ardor, capitalists have acknowledged their compatibility with New Deal liberalism by embracing some State intervention into the economy. "Unregulated competition, they found, gave rise to a degree of uncertainty that made it difficult to plan their industrial activities efficiently. As a result, some of them . . . demanded that government establish laws and regulatory agencies to . . . help stabilize their markets" (McClosky and Zaller 1984, p. 149; for further evidence of New Deal liberalism among capitalists, see Dye and Zeigler 1983, pp. 111–13; Wiebe 1967, p. 297; Kolko 1963, p. 5).

This is not to say that there are no disagreements among Americans, just that our disagreements are minor, about means, and are bounded by a gentlemen's agreement on the end. That end is a land that rewards, above all else, lonely striving in a selfish game, which government tries only halfheartedly to make fair.

WHERE DOES CAPITALIST INDIVIDUALISM COME FROM?

Yes, Americans sing the anthem of capitalist individualism in unison. And other strains of the culture have been politely resonant: individualism, democracy, New Deal liberalism—none have disturbed the marching hymn with a dissonant chord.

But saying this says only that there is a pervasive, prominent ideology in the United States. And this book claims there is a hegemonic ideology, one successfully urged upon one group by another. To get from "prominent" to "dominant," we shall have to contend with one of the most imposing opponents to be found in the field of American political culture, Louis Hartz.[7]

Hartz's argument is elegance itself: since the American unison, what he calls our "liberalism," differs from the European pattern, why not look at that world we differ from, and ask how—won't this tell us why? He finds the genesis of difference in the "storybook truth" of American history: "that America was settled by men who fled from the feudal and clerical oppressions of the old world" (1955, p. 3). Americans didn't just lack the feudal tradition; we repudiated it in the glorious moment of our nativity and claimed individualism as our birthright. Then, in the next century, as the rest of the working world discovered socialism, how could we do likewise? How could Americans engage in class warfare, when we did not think of ourselves as members of a class—when we had insisted all along that ours was a classless society;[8] when we had no strong sense, no memory of class, as the European had in his history, his mythology, his language, his very bones?

Such a thesis is not called bold without reason. Its high noon has come often. Some challengers have pointed out that not all Americans were "born" into the liberal consensus, as Hartz argues. Blacks, for example, and southern European immigrants were dragged into that consensus, a process that involved some kicking and screaming. Our argument is that hegemony theory is better prepared than consensus theory to tell the sad tale of these dissonant cultures' encounter with dominant America, as Chapter 7 will try to do. Their story is a long chapter in the American tragedy.

It is also too glib to say, as Hartz sometimes does, that the American cultural outline simply remained as it had been cast in the crucible of founding (p. 89). As I will argue in this chapter, the capitalist individualism that emerged triumphant in the homestretch of recent history is not the republicanism that led at the starting gate. Nor was it "implicit from the outset," as Hartz says at other times, that the former would inherit the latter's dominance (p. 199). Philosophically, Populism has at least as much of republicanism's genes as capitalism has. But of course, our argument is that often the race was run not on philosophy's, but on politics' track, where the fix is in, where the high rollers do the handicapping, and where the best set of binoculars for viewing all the action is hegemony theory.

This is not to say that Hartz is wrong. It is to say he is only half right. The story of American comity is different from the European tale of conflict, and it cannot be understood without the historians who begin with the question of our "exceptional" consensus. Unfortunately, they also end with that question. In between they have neglected one of the primordial forces behind our dominant culture, perhaps because it happens to be at work in Europe as well: the power of capital to sell capitalism.[9] Together the missing memory of class and the powerful presence of capital are the twin roofbeams of American culture: neither explanation alone will support our singular superstructure—the completeness of capital's conquest.[10]

THE GEOLOGY OF AMERICAN POLITICAL CULTURE

The common sense of a people grows, layer on layer, over time. Gradually, the early ways are submerged and become invisible. Yet, they remain important; in a sense, the core of the culture (Gramsci 1971, p. 326). This section will describe the geology and the history of American political culture, for three reasons:

First, as we shall see, the outer layers of the culture bear the marks of the inner and cannot be understood without them.

Second, as we have already mentioned, to complete the argument, hegemony theory must argue not just *that* capitalist individualism permeates the culture but *how* capitalists helped that happen. Several of the chapters in this volume find that the critical turns were taken long ago. Because those historical arguments about "how" refer to currents of thought long since submerged, this section will try to say what those currents were and to try to bring them, for a moment, to the surface.

Third, this section will begin the rejoinder to Hartz's argument that what American culture became was "implicit" in what it had been.

Puritanism

"Winthrop stands at the beginning of our consciousness," declared the Puritans' historian, Perry Miller, and it is true, for better and for worse (Miller 1967, p. 6). The Puritans' moralism, their doctrine of the "calling" to divine mission in mundane pursuits, their self-image of a "City upon a Hill" and a "chosen people" have echoed down the halls of our history. From the fateful lightning of Abolition to the ignominy of Know-Nothingism, Manifest Destiny, Colonialism, and Nativism, Puritan zeal remains the terrible swift two-edged sword of American culture (on these connections, see Kleppner et al. 1981, pp. 120–21; Bellah 1975, ch. 2).

On the other hand, Puritanism did not spawn the big fish of American culture—capitalism. Winthrop's famous shipboard sermon could not be more clear: in the City on a Hill, God and Mammon, *caritas* and *cupiditas* cannot both be served. "If our hearts shall turn away soe that wee... shall be seduced and worship... our pleasures, and profits... wee shall surely perishe" (quoted in Bellah 1975, p. 15; see also Cotton Mather, in Bellah, p. 65).

And not only was *caritas* at odds with profit, it was collectivist. From Calvin's Geneva to the Massachusetts Bay Colony, the Puritans acted out "an understanding of man as fundamentally social... derived from... the Old Testament notion of the Covenant between God and a people held collectively responsible for its actions, and from the New Testament notion of a community based on charity or love and expressed in brotherly affection and fellow membership in one common body" (Bellah 1975, p. 18). The gulf between such an understanding and the self-interest preached by capitalism is wide indeed; a Lazarus could scarcely see across it.

Of course, Max Weber also had a point in arguing that the Puritan personality had a weakness for capitalism. The doctrine of predestination made the Calvinist's an anxious life. Calvin himself felt the elect were indistinguishable from the non-elect. How to see, to know? That question needed an answer, and one grew up around the doctrine of the calling. When one is of the elect, he becomes a tool of the Divine Will. Intense moral activity is the hallmark of God's people. Inevitably, this doctrine became a holy treadmill, an insatiable "hunger and thirst after right-eousness," a mania for moral accomplishment (Weber 1958, p. 114). Of course, such a mania made capitalism enticing to the Puritan, with its palpable "fruits" for one's unstinting labor—hard evidence of one's elec-tion. But such success could not slake the Puritan thirst until "economic accomplishment" had become a kind of "moral accomplishment." And how, given the jeremiads of Winthrop, Mather, and Edwards against "profits," did this remarkable transformation take place? How did wealth move from being the camel in the needle's eye of salvation to being the very proof of virtue? Even Weber understood that the Puritan person-ality had to be torn from its religious moorings before it could be swept away in the tide of capitalism (Abercrombie, Hill, and Turner 1980, pp. 45–46). What force could have torn and carried it? R. H. Tawney's answer is still the most compelling: naturally those Protestant preachers who were the "living word" and who looked to their wealthiest parish-ioners, quite literally, for sustenance were hard pressed to deny the emerging ideology whose central tenet held that wealth is a virtue (Taw-ney 1926). By the end of the nineteenth century, the Protestant cler-gyman, who remained "a central spokesman for American culture," was persuaded that what is good for business is good for the soul (Bellah 1975, pp. 56, 74–75). The City on a Hill had become Babylon.

Agrarian Republicanism

"The remarkable coherence of the American revolutionary movement and its successful conclusion in the constitution of a new civil order are due in considerable part to the convergence of the Puritan covenant pattern and the...republican pattern. The former was represented above all by New England, the latter by Virginia, but both were widely diffused in the consciousness of the colonial population" (Bellah 1975, p. 27).

As Americans dreamed of a land without monarchs and their armies, without dukes and lords and their rigid codes of honor, they wondered what ordering principle would replace those anachronisms. The answer that galvanized them into, through, and beyond the Revolution was republican virtue (Tocqueville 1966, p. 51; Formisano 1983, p. 57; Bel-lah 1975, p. 27). If there is to be no law from the top down, justice must emerge from the bottom up: it must come from the will of the people to act on behalf of the greater community. Happily, the end of such a society was also its means—a free and equal people would also be a virtuous people.

Republicanism, like Puritanism, was a far cry from proto-capitalism. Its hero was the "frugal independent" yeoman "ready to serve at [the] community's call" (Bellah 1975, p. 24)—a far cry himself from the wealthy, self-interested capitalist that America later learned to love. In fact, republicans saw the kind of inequalities capitalism would later produce as the seventh seal for the good society. There is no virtue in luxury, Montesquieu had argued, echoing the epic poets of the Roman republic, and the new republicans agreed. Nor can virtue live long in poverty; it leaves no "stake in society," no means to independence. Once we have lost that, said the great oracle of American republicanism, "we shall become corrupt as in Europe, and go to eating one another as they do there" (Jefferson 1973, p. 24).

Of course, Jefferson did allow that a "natural aristocracy" would emerge to head the republic, while the yeoman remained its sturdy backbone. But this natural aristocracy was antithetical to the robber barony that later captured the culture's fancy: the devotion of Jefferson's elite was to the public good, not private profit (Cawelti 1965, pp. 28–43).

This is to say again that Hartz's point needs to be supplemented. Republicanism did not become capitalist individualism, it surrendered to it—surrendered, we shall argue, only as capitalism captured the high ground of the culture. But that surrender would not have been so unconditional had Hartz not had a point: like Puritanism, republicanism had an Achilles heel, which capitalism quickly found. For the Puritans, it was anxiety. For the republicans, it was a limited vocabulary: most of the time, the terms "class," "State," and "interdependence" were not in their lexicon. Instead, they took the name Tocqueville had pejoratively called them to heart: "individualists . . . they . . . imagine that their whole destiny is in their own hands" (Tocqueville 1966, p. 508). And what a compelling theme self-reliance has remained, through Emerson's famous essay, to twentieth-century film images of the lonesome cowboy, the iconoclastic cop, and the avenging vigilante/martial artist. As a corollary, a society of self-reliant yeomen and artisans had no need of intra-class solidarity or inter-class warfare. Even after their preindustrial idyll had shattered into a world of "masters" and "laborers," the latter often repaired to the language of "commonwealth": a trust that workers and "honest employers," legally equal, could cooperate to secure the good of all (Wilentz 1983, p. 59).

Such fond hopes hint at the innocence of republicanism toward economic power (Cawelti 1965, p. 44). Instead, because heretofore the "tool of the rich" had always been the favoritism of kings, republicans feared the friend they needed most to counter the weight of wealth: State power (McClosky and Zaller 1984, p. 86; Hartz 1955, p. 135).

This is not to say that republicans never found the right words to resist capitalism. The Populists, for example, saw clearly that republican freedom and equality required that republican "community" become "solidarity" and a strong State (Goodwyn 1976). And while part of their defeat can be attributed to the newness of their words, part must be explained by the fewness of those words finding their mark, the paucity of media for conveying them, compared to the kilovolts of propaganda carried by the transmission lines of capitalist hegemony (see Chapter 2).

Liberalism

Of course, also there at the birth of the nation, close enough to republicanism to share the dais with it in the founding documents was the liberalism of Hobbes and especially of John Locke. Political society, they argued, was not a covenant, but a contract. Its basis was not civic virtue or the social impulse, but rational self-interest. Men and women came together, not to pursue the human possibility, but to escape it—to escape the *bellum omnium* and its invasions of life, liberty, and (above all) property (Locke 1969, p. 413).

Here, at last, would seem to be the embryonic capitalism that made that ideology's eventual ascendancy "natural." But even here, the outcome was not foreordained. Locke, for example, defined "property" in a way that would have made J. P. Morgan a man of limited means: as those natural resources with which a man "hath mixed his labour" (1969, p. 407).

But an early and crucial round in the American fight over the meaning of liberalism did go to capitalist individualism, when James Madison weighed in with his definition of property as the unequal fruit of "unequal capacities." Protection of these inequalities, he said, is the "first object of government" (1964, p. 18).[11] Madison and the other founders forged a constitution that suited that purpose admirably, even if it did not do as well by other purposes, such as democracy (Piven and Cloward 1982, p. 83).

Jeremy Bentham, who is often thrown in with this liberal lot, is really not at ease in their company. Can one ask that "the greatest happiness of the greatest number" be pursued without assuming some modicum of grace, of altruism, of republican virtue in man?

But Adam Smith answered, "yes," and brought the argument to its dubious conclusion: there is a way from immoral man to moral society—from personal rapacity to societal happiness. Laissez faire: let the invisible hand of the free market be, let it work its benevolent will. This individual competition will put a better mousetrap in every pantry, a chicken in every pot.

Republicans may have seen a self-serving, hedonistic snake in the grass of liberalism, but they could not always resist the apple it offered. Their own belief in independence, their fear of government power, their innocence of economic power, all gave them a taste for laissez faire. For all its republican rhetoric, Andrew Jackson's Bank War was, in the end, nothing but a crusade for Smith's doctrine. And once the apple had been tasted, as Jackson began to see in his Farewell Address, it was the independent yeoman and artisan who were banished from the garden, to toil all their days in fields owned by others, at what work, what wage, what pace those others would set.

But Jackson's story, like the nation's, is not just a story of the failure of republican vision. It is also a story of the success of capitalist hegemony, as Chapter 2 will argue. That Jackson was beset by more than vision problems is evident from a look at his republican contemporaries, who saw with the clarity of Cassandra what was happening. The Working Men's Party and the General Trades Union inveighed against the growing servitude of working men, against the enervating luxury of the rich, against the death of virtue, of *communitas*, at the hands of *cupiditas* (Wilentz 1983, p. 49). Their program, again, was not adequate to stem this tide. Mainly, they asked that their trade unions be given the right to set their hours, wages, and work conditions. It is not surprising that this trade union consciousness did not become political consciousness in Jackson's time. His moment was still too close to the hated mercantilism of a recent past, still too far from the political power of the coming capitalism.

What is more surprising is that later, when, in the Populist and socialist moments, that political consciousness did emerge, it did not grow. Part of the explanation is Hartz's: socialism was not a robust child in America; the climate was wrong. But part of the explanation is ours: socialism has been smothered in its cradle by the hands of hegemony.

Capitalist Individualism

At the crossroads of our history stands a sphinx, posing a riddle: why did the United States choose capitalism, in the very moment that Americans could first look down that road and see how tortuous a path it was. Even as the chorus of "independence through entrepreneurship" reached its crescendo, history called it a lie. Even by 1870, "between 60 and 70 percent of the Northern labor force worked in occupations where a master was the rule" (Rodgers 1978, p. 37). And not just "for a while," as Lincoln had promised, as "[the laborer] saves, then hires another . . . as he himself becomes an entrepreneur" (in Rodgers 1978, p. 36). No, "whatever the life chances of a farmer or shop hand had been in the early years of the century, it became troublingly clear that the semiskilled laborer, caught in the anonymity of a late-nineteenth century textile factory or steel mill, was trapped in his circumstances—that no amount of sheer hard work would open the way to self employment or wealth" (Rodgers 1978, p. 28). And while the poor stayed poor, the rich got richer. Capitalism kept its promise of "acres of diamonds," but only to a precious few. By 1893, 9 percent of the nation's families held 71 percent of its wealth. Twenty-five percent of all farmland was owned by .006 percent of the population (Verba and Orren 1985, p. 37).

Later chapters will argue about *how* and *why* the nation turned to capitalist individualism. But turn it did, there can be no doubt. At first, the new wine was poured into old homilies. Although Franklin had seen wealth only as a means to life's intellectual riches, and Mather saw earthly treasure as an actual impediment to the treasures of heaven, their work and self-improvement ethic was harnessed to the acquisitive way, drawing it into respectability. Wealth was desirable, argued their revisionists, not for itself alone, but also for the moral virtue won in the hard work of wealth's pursuit (Cawelti 1965, p. 53). "In the long run," wrote the Episcopal Bishop of Massachusetts in 1901, "it is only to the man of morality that wealth comes.... We know that... only by working... along the lines of right thinking and right living can the secrets and wealth of nature be revealed.... Godliness is in league with riches" (quoted in Cawelti 1965, p. 75).

The Puritan work ethic was not the only venerable mantle donned by capitalists. They also wrapped themselves in republican independence. Decades later, the National Association of Manufacturers could still refer to a linkage forged in the late nineteenth century, confident of its strength in the national mind:

At the threshold of our national existence we solemnly asserted "the right to life, liberty, and the pursuit of happiness...." We became a nation of free men not serving political masters but ourselves, free to pursue our happiness without interference from the state, with the greatest liberty of individual action ever known to man. Individuals, conscious of unbounded opportunity... turned with ... vigor to producing... goods and services in freely competitive markets.... Our "private enterprise system and our American form of government are inseparable and there can be no compromise between a free economy and a governmentally dictated economy without endangering our political as well as our economic freedom" (quoted in Bellah 1975, p. 115.)[12]

All of this is perfectly familiar and seems to sustain Hartz's claim that the "supplementing" of the early ethics by capitalism was "bound to" happen (Hartz, 1955, p. 89). But by the end of the nineteenth century, the old orders and the new were anything but supplementary. Instead, capitalism had begun to leave the earlier ethics, like so much dead weight, at the side of the road. Partly, they were the weight of contradiction: between Puritan community and the carnage of competition; between the sturdy independent yeoman and the literally beaten factory worker; between the ideal of democracy and the rapidly emerging reality of plutocracy (see Chapter 2).

Partly, the gilded life of the industrial captains that was everywhere on display—in the news, the ads, the stores, the movies—made wealth an irresistible end in itself (Trachtenberg 1982, pp. 121–34). No one beholding the lavish palaces of Vanderbilt or Rockefeller would have supposed there was anything virtuous about them, but they were not less dreamed of on account of it. "The people had *desired* money before his day," said Mark Twain of Jay Gould, "but *he* taught them to fall down and worship it" (quoted in Miller 1968, p. 257).

Partly, the fight for the new order was waged and won from a philosophical battlement. The intellectual myth capitalism took up to explain itself, to replace Winthrop's worn-out City and Jefferson's old-fashioned farm, was Darwin's jungle. The law of "natural selection," no less at work on Manhattan than on the Galapagos Islands, was competition in which the fittest would survive and prosper; the unfit would take their place as the dregs, the mudsill class, of society. Even as empirical analysis, Social Darwinism was less scientific theory than dubious analogy. But its proponents wanted it to be even more than science: they made the law of the jungle a moral imperative. Not only *is* survival of the fittest the way of things, but it *ought* to be. Government action, for example, should not tamper with nature's assignations, however ruthless they may seem, lest the evolution, the progress of society be retarded. "A drunkard in the gutter is just where he ought to be. Nature is working away at him to get him out of the way, just as she sets up her processes of dissolution to remove whatever is a failure in its line," was the tearless verdict of the theory's most famous apologist, Yale's William Graham Sumner (1934, vol. 1, p. 481).

While Social Darwinism defined the terms of intellectual discourse, the "success literature" of the period brought capitalist individualism to the people, and captured their imagination. These biographies, popular journals, and novels by Cornwell, Hubbard, and Woodbridge[13] were more optimistic than the dour Sumner. They did not accept that only the able would ascend, but preferred to believe that "where there's a will, there's a way" (Cawelti 1965, p. 173). And they occasionally paid lip service to some old verities—that wealth should be made honestly, and was not complete without the "inward satisfaction" that usually accompanied it (Cawelti 1965, p. 185). But the force of their message was unmistakably at one with Social Darwinism: now, to be a success was to be a commercial success. The yeoman/artisan was no longer a hero, no longer enough. He had been replaced by the entrepreneur, the self-made man, the captain of industry.

In other ways as well, Social Darwinism and the doctrine of success were better suited to capitalism's needs than the old ethics had been. Now, ruthless competition; enormous inequalities; *de jure* and *de facto* disfranchisement of blacks, "ethnics," and the "lower classes"; even wage slavery were no longer embarrassments. They were the ebb and flow, the is and ought of nature. Gone too were the dysfunctional virtues of the old ethics. As self-improvement gave way to self-preservation, piety, humility, and civic concern were replaced by assets better adapted to the corporate jungle. Hard work remained, of course, but it too was no longer enough. The new hero of the success literature, the organization man also needed confidence, "personality," salesmanship, the art of conversation, of fashion, the will to win (Cawelti 1965, pp. 181–182; Rodgers 1978, p. 38). Virtue gave way to "ability."

It has often been argued that the corporate success ideal triumphed because of the paucity and poverty of alternatives to it. U.S. radicals, it is said, never outgrew their Jeffersonian fears of interdependence and State power (Hartz 1955, p. 123; Kolko 1963, p. 304). And it is true that the goal of, for example, the Populists was a society where men and women might have control over their own lives, where "individual human striving might be fairly respected" (Goodwyn 1976, p. xv). But they also saw that that could not be achieved except through a "cooperative commonwealth—constant grass-roots organization directed toward the use of State power to fundamentally restructure the economic order (Goodwyn 1976, pp. xi–xv). The Populists' defeat in the 1890s, like that of the socialists two decades later, cannot be blamed solely on their philosophical weakness. To do so is to ignore their political weakness, and the strength, the fearsome strength of their opponents (see Chapter 2).

As that strength flexed, almost unchallenged after 1896, working men and women continued to resist (Gutman 1976). Of course they did. The broken promises of the work ethic lay all around them: hard work, it had been said, would bring the fulfillment of independence, craftsmanship, mobility. All of it was mocked by their servile, mechanized, static work lives. But as their resistances failed, working people gradually retreated, making their peace with freedom and dignity on terms set by their employers (Rodgers 1978, pp. 30–64). One of those treaties, for example, promised the "freedom to set one's own pace and pay" under the piecework schemes of Frederick Taylor—schemes that left employers far more free than workers to set pace and pay (Rodgers 1978, ch. 2). A similar strategy involved choosing the "freedom" to sacrifice oneself—to longer hours, a second job—so the children might see the promise kept—another delusion that would mock the worker even into the third and fourth generations (Sennett and Cobb 1973, pp. 125–30; 155). But the most alluring compensation offered the worker was to be found outside the workplace. As structured by capitalists battling the problem of overproduction, that after-hours freedom became the freedom to consume (see Chapter 4; also Lasch 1978, ch. 4; Rodgers 1978, ch. 3). Sennett and Cobb have argued that working class consumerism is not the hedonism most have taken it to be. It is rather, like the Protestant ethic it replaces, a way "to heal a doubt about the self." For a man who spends his days under the cool appraising eye of a boss, the point of owning a big, expensive, gas-guzzling car that is more consumed by rust than by its owner is not luxury, but to drive something he "won't get pushed around in" (1973, p. 171). But whatever else it was, consumerism was the bribe the working class took to leave the beloved Jefferson behind and answer the altar call of the new gospel: capitalist individualism.

The final nail in Jefferson's coffin was bureaucratic expertise. It was another of the "mandates" elites assumed after the Icarian fall of Populism. Advancing capitalism, "progress," they said, had complicated things beyond the ken of ordinary Americans. The measure of the new social, economic, and political problems could be taken only by a new cadre of specialists. In government, that meant the moving of important decisions out of popular control, out of "politics" and into "nonpartisan," "independent" agencies. The quotation marks mean that these were independent in the sense that one may be independent of locks on one's doors, or independent of a watchdog. It was an independence corporations took full advantage of in their new "partnership" with government (Kolko 1963).

At about the same time, all the institutions of civil society began to wrap themselves in the mantle of "professional expertise." In the schools, in the workplace, in the newsroom, in the offices of social workers, psychologists, and lawyers, the message was the same: Our specialized knowledge is beyond you. We are the new clergy. Accept the host as we offer it, the gospel as we interpret it, the truth as we varnish it. And as in government, so in civil society: corporate elites had much to do with defining this orthodoxy, as later chapters will try to show. Before it was over, the limbs of the sturdy yeoman would be unstrung. His sure faith in his right and capacity to forge his destiny was undone. Now, so much of life is "best left to the experts" (Wiebe 1967; Lustig 1982).

New Deal Individualism

By the third decade of this century, "success," "the good life," "the American Way" had lost all their meanings but one. The spectrum of national possibilities had faded to a drab monopoly.

But America would come to a second crossroads, a second chance to discover an alternative to competitive individualism, when in 1929 an economy based on that ethos crashed. This time, America turned. But the man to whom it turned was not an alternative to capitalism, he was its savior. Now, to be sure, Roosevelt did trample all over the garden of laissez faire. The New Deal was, after all, a series of government programs designed to regulate the economy and provide welfare-like services to some of its orphans. But the import of those programs is simply this: they were designed not to bring down capitalism, but to make it work; not to critique the rags to riches story, but to create it. Roosevelt staunchly defended the programs in individualistic terms. His argument, repeated incessantly, was simple:

1. The old system of "completely unrestrained individualism" was no longer adequate to modern, interdependent society:

   It is worth remembering, for example, that the business corporation, as we know it, did not exist in the days of Washington...and Jefferson. Private businesses were conducted solely by individuals or by partnerships in which every member was...wholly responsible for success or failure. Facts are relentless. We must adjust our ideas to the facts of today.

2. Now, government action is necessary to provide a "minimum level" of regulation of the economy's outlaws and security for its orphans.

3. But *cui bono?* To what end, this government action? How do we know when to start, when to stop? Roosevelt's answer was clear. The goal is a system where *individual enterprise will be rewarded*:

   Let me emphasize that serious as have been the errors of unrestrained individualism, I do not believe in abandoning the system of individual enterprise. The freedom and opportunity that have characterized American development in the past can be maintained if we recognize the fact that the individual system of our day calls for the collaboration of all of us....Any paternalistic system which tries to provide security for everyone from above only calls for an impossible task and a regimentation utterly uncongenial to the spirit of our people. But government cooperation to help make the system of free enterprise work, to provide that minimum security without which the competitive system cannot function, to restrain the kind of individual action which in the past has been harmful to the community—that kind of governmental cooperation is entirely consistent with the best tradition of America (Roosevelt 1938, pp. 339–42).

The New Deal program was scrupulously congruent with that philosophy. Its largest income maintenance program, Social Security, was a "self-supporting program of social insurance," as was unemployment compensation. Non-insured welfare programs were carefully limited to the "deserving poor"—dependent children, the blind, the disabled (Leuchtenberg 1963, p. 132). All others, of course, were to fend for themselves, except for emergency relief measures. The act that addressed the rights of workers was concerned with "the inequality of bargaining power between employees who do not possess full freedom of association or actual liberty of contract and employers who are organized in the corporate or other forms of association" (in Verba and Orren 1985, p. 42). And this New Deal variant of capitalist individualism did not die with Franklin Roosevelt. In fact, his long shadow has fallen over the programs of every subsequent Democratic president. The most notable expansion of the welfare state since the New Deal, Lyndon Johnson's Great Society, was simply a "continuation of the later New Deal that had been interrupted... by World War II" (quoted in Leuchtenberg 1983, p. 138). This time, the very names of the programs bespoke their self-help philosophy: Head Start, A Better Chance, Educational Opportunities, Operation Bootstrap. Andrew Carnegie himself, who had said, "help those who will help themselves," would have nodded as Johnson explained his vision: "The War on Poverty is not a struggle simply to support [culturally deprived] people, to make them dependent on the generosity of others. ...It is a struggle to give [them] a chance" (Johnson 1965, p. 376). "President Johnson insisted that the Great Society had nothing to do with welfare programs," adds a former staffer. "It was an education and training program designed to equip everyone to earn a decent living on their own in the private economy" (Thurow 1981).

The difference between this and the modern Republican position is one of means, not ends. It is a disagreement over how much government interference in the economy is the "minimum level" necessary to allow individual opportunity. A mere matter of degree.

Other voices, other moods remain absent from our public discourse.[14] There is no faint echo of the socialists' prophetic judgment in either party. There is no hint of Debs, who said, "While there is a lower class, I am of it." Class lines, everyone agrees, are not to be razed, but risen through. There is no hint of Spargo, who said, "From each according to his ability, to each according to his need." Instead, ubiquitously, the formula is reversed, and its meaning restricted: "To each according to his ability—to produce what is marketable." America remains in unison, without a fundamental debate over the purpose of politics, holding the truth of competitive individualism self-evident.

Recent Trends: Narcissism and the New Conservatism

The New Deal had made its course corrections, but hadn't changed our destination. It had not replaced the lost *communitas* of republicanism or Puritanism. In fact, it had reaffirmed *cupiditas*. And so, after an uncertain caesura of depression and war, capitalist individualism reasserted itself. More than ever, its promise was the "complete satisfaction guaranteed" by consumption. As Chapter 4 will show, that message was driven by powerful new engines of hegemony: an increasingly formidable advertising industry and the "new parent," television. The way of "making it" to the Nirvana of "having it all," still untethered by any old or new ideas of obligation, continued its subtle, insidious evolution, as the gospels of success began to attest in the 1950s:

They praised the love of money, officially condemned even by the crudest of Gilded Age materialists. . . . "You can never have riches in great quantities," wrote [one of them], "unless you can work yourself into a white heat of *desire* for money." The pursuit of wealth lost the few shreds of moral meaning that still clung to it . . . [it] appeared as an end in its own right (Lasch 1979, p. 58).

Nor is there anything resembling criticism of the structure or practice of enterprise in America, something which even earlier proponents of success . . . indulged in occasionally (Cawelti 1965, pp. 216–17).

The final chapter of this unlovely literature is being written in our time. Its bald titles come quickly to the point: *Power, Winning at Work, Winning through Intimidation, Look Out for Number One, Rich is Better, Unlimited Power, Go For It!*, and so on, instruct readers in such not-so fine arts as how to establish "momentum," a "winning image," or a pecking order with a "power stare" or a deliberate rudeness, with the "use of" a mentor or the "leaving behind" of one, when the right time comes. "[These] latest manuals differ from earlier ones . . . in their frank acceptance of the need to exploit and intimidate others, in their lack of interest in the substance of success, and in the candor with which they insist that appearances—'winning images'—count for more than performance" (Lasch 1978, p. 59).

Their advice has not fallen on deaf ears. A study of 250 managers from 12 major companies describes the new corporate leader as one who wants above all to "be known as a winner, and his deepest fear is to be labeled a loser." He has little time for "personal intimacy and social commitment." He is "open to new ideas, but he lacks convictions" (Maccoby 1976 pp. 100–06). In short, his "view of the world . . . is that of the narcissist, who sees the world as a mirror of himself and has no interest in external events except as they throw back a reflection of his own image" (Lasch 1978, p. 47).

Here is the "apotheosis of individualism" (Lasch 1978, p. 66). Capitalism, cut loose from the Protestant and republican ethics, has come to its logical conclusion. Over the course of this century, self-improvement became self-aggrandizement and self-preservation, reason became calculation, image became all. If you've made it, flaunt it, in unapologetic impulse gratification (Lasch 1978, pp. 69–70). Liberalism has come full circle, a self-fulfilling prophesy. The *bellum omnium* is back, with a vengeance.

At the same time, working class Americans, who do not often find themselves "winning at work," have been offered their own brand of new conservatism. The New Right is commonly interpreted as a reaction against the pace of social change of the 1960s and early 1970s. "Status politics," Max Weber called it, a wounded prestige, lashing back against the unfamiliarity of the civil rights, anti-poverty, and women's movements (Phillips 1983, pp. xix–xx; Reichley 1985, p. 316). Others have countered that working class Americans were not hostile to these movements until *they* were handed the check. Policymakers did not pay for this "passive revolution"[15] out of their own pockets, or out of those of their wealthiest constituents, but out of working people's: it was their children who were bused; their neighborhoods were bulldozed to make way for urban renewal; their taxes were disproportionately increased to pay for new social services; their applications for jobs or promotions were sacrificed to the exigency of affirmative action (Rieder 1985).

But whatever else it is, the New Right is also a paid political announcement, brought to us by corporate seed money, as Chapter 2 will argue. This makes it less surprising that the movement's agenda includes laissez faire doctrines that do not serve its working class constituency well. "Without religious and moral issues front and center, many of these voters tend toward the more liberal or populist side of economics" (Phillips 1983, p. 97). So the God hucksters of the New Right have adroitly played the "social issues" card: "busing, abortion, pornography, education, traditional biblical moral values, and quotas" (George C. Higgins, quoted in Reichley 1985, p. 319). But they have also married these anxieties of threatened status to the interests of a dominant class. While mainline Protestant, Catholic, and Jewish groups protested Reagan administration cuts in domestic social services, "the religious right praised the president's efforts to give freer rein to the private sector. Falwell found the free enterprise system 'clearly outlined in the book of Proverbs in the Bible' " (Reichley 1985, p. 325).

Analyzing data gathered by the University of Michigan's 1980 election survey, Arthur Miller and Martin Wattenberg concluded, "the conservative Christians represent an emerging political force in U.S. politics.... The cohesiveness evident in their political attitudes and voter behavior suggests a unique impact attributed to shared religious interests and the mobilizing influence of the new Christian right leadership" (quoted in Reichley 1985, p. 324). Pollster Louis Harris estimates that "white, fundamentalist, moral-majority-type voters accounted for two thirds of Ronald Reagan's surprise ten-point margin over Jimmy Carter" (Phillips 1983, p. 191). Thus, in our time, "class and ideology have been turned on their heads.... Conservatism shifted gears and moved toward the populist constituencies of East Texas and South Boston" (Phillips 1983, p. xxiii). Like the Puritans and republicans before them, the sons and daughters of Populism and the New Deal have begun to lose the faith of their fathers to the tender shepherding of capitalist hegemony.

SO WHAT: WHY WORRY ABOUT AMERICAN UNISON?

But surely the space shuttle analogy is wrong. While that experiment failed, surely the American experiment has succeeded brilliantly. While the culture industry's triumphant eulogies to the shuttle mission may have been lies, surely its odes to the American system are not. Perhaps the workings of the cultural machine have left us with only one American Way. Isn't it manifestly the best way? Isn't ours "the greatest nation in the only world we know," as a prominent contender for the presidency recently put it? Isn't our dearth of ideological debate, in fact, the "genius of American politics," allowing us to unite around a healthy pragmatism, to be the nation that works (Boorstin 1958; Hartz 1955)? Hasn't our free enterprise economy made our standard of living the envy of the world?

By some measures, the answer is yes. But then there are some curious anomalies. For example, the United States has towered above the world on measures of wealth for most of the years since World War II. And as one might expect in such a land of plenty, the United States has, for example, more doctors per capita than any other nation on earth. And they are better paid here than anywhere else. But here we find one of those anomalies. Despite all those doctors and dollars, the rate at which babies die is higher in the United States than in Denmark, Belgium, the Netherlands, Norway, Finland, England, and 15 other countries. Our record for life expectancy of males is no better: the United States trails 19 other countries—including every industrialized nation on earth. Other measures of the quality of life in areas like housing, nutrition, employment, occupational health and safety show the United States in a similarly poor performance. Why?

Obviously, the flow of milk and honey has not reached everyone. Instead, our ethos of self-reliance, laissez faire, and survival of the fittest has made us a great nation on another index: inequality. For one thing, the absence of a socialist alternative to that ethos has worked to preclude working and lower class Americans from political participation and power (as Chapter 2 will argue). It has made of us a plutocracy in the mask of democracy. That political inequality has, in turn, exacerbated the economic inequality implicit in the dominant ethos. Today, the top 0.5 percent of U.S. families own about half of all corporate stocks and about 35 percent of the nation's total wealth. Meanwhile, about one out of seven Americans is officially classified as living in poverty. (A more realistic definition of poverty would find almost one of every three Americans living in that cold state.) That is far more poverty than is found in most of Western Europe, where capitalist individualism has been, not a civic religion, but one side of a healthy debate. In Sweden, for example, the poorest 5 percent of the population enjoys a higher standard of living than fully 25 percent of the U.S. population.

In non-response, the United States has chosen to spend a smaller proportion of national income on social welfare than any other industrialized nation. More than 40 percent of our families living below the poverty line receive no food stamps, Medicaid, housing subsidies, or low-price school lunches. And the Social Darwinist argument that this inaction and inequality are the necessary cost of doing business—that our productivity is a function of our inequality—can no longer be sustained. The industrial nations that have outstripped the United States recently in productivity are generally characterized by less income inequality, more progressive tax structures, and more developed welfare systems than our own (Cohen and Rogers 1983, p. 24; Thurow 1981).

The harvest of our stingy sowing has been bleak indeed: inner-city infant mortality and illiteracy rates that would shame a Third World country; chronic high unemployment, unaddressed by government jobs or training programs, carrying mental illness, suicide, alcoholism, divorce, murder, wife and child abuse in its wake. Eighteen percent of our low-income preschoolers show signs of malnutrition; about 2 million Americans are homeless; about 80,000 are permanently disabled by workplace accidents each year; each year more than 100,000 die of job-related diseases; about 500,000 Americans—most of them poor—are heroin addicts; because of the high rate in low-income areas, death by homicide is eight to nine times more likely in the United States than in other advanced industrial states; 1 in every 21 young black men is murdered (Cohen and Rogers 1983, ch. 2; Morganthau 1984; *U.S. News* 1986a; *U.S. News* 1986b; Edsall 1984, p. 232). That, as they say, is life, in "the greatest nation in the only world we know."

And those are just the visible hurts of capitalist individualism. Even more pervasive are the "hidden injuries" of the American Way. In free-floating interviews with working class men and women, Sennett and Cobb found themes of "powerlessness and adequacy recur[ring] again and again" (1973, p. 41). How could they not be so obsessed in a land that denies them dignity at every turn? About 40 million Americans have been thrown out of work over the past decade by corporate disinvestment decisions—and often blamed themselves for it (Bluestone and Harrison 1982; Feldman 1982). How could they fail to inflict that pain on themselves in a land that demands that each "take responsibility for himself"? A recent study of mobility in the United States makes clear that the best way to get ahead is with a head start—"those who do well economically owe almost half of their occupational advantage and 55 to 85 percent of their earnings advantage to family background" (Jencks et al. 1979, p. 81). But how can those who do not advance respect themselves in a land where one is expected to "make something of himself"? What pride can one take in the advances his union makes, advances made only with others? How can a man who is bossed have dignity, in a land where he is supposed to "stand on his own feet," "be his own man" (Sennett and Cobb 1973, pp. 33–41)?

No one has answered the plaintive, unformed questions of the men and women caught in these contradictions better than the brilliantly vituperative Henry Miller. During the 1920s, Miller worked as personnel manager for the telegraph company in New York City. One day while the vice-president was bawling him out he suggested to Miller that he write a sort of Horatio Alger book about the messengers.

I thought to myself [said Miller]—you poor old futzer, you, just wait until I get it off my chest. . . . I'll give you an Horatio Alger book. . . . My head was in a whirl to leave his office. I saw the army of men, women and children that had passed through my hands, saw them weeping, begging, beseeching, imploring, cursing, spitting, fuming, threatening. I saw the tracks they left on the highways, lying on the floor of freight trains, the parents in rags, the coal box empty, the sink running over, the walls sweating and between the cold beads of sweat the cockroaches running like mad; I saw them hobbling along like twisted gnomes or falling backwards in the epileptic frenzy. . . . I saw the walls giving way and the pest pouring out like a winged fluid, and the men higher up with their ironclad logic, waiting for it to blow over, waiting for everything to be patched up, waiting, waiting contentedly . . . saying that things were temporarily out of order. I saw the Horatio Alger hero, the dream of a sick America, mounting higher and higher, first messenger, then operator, then manager, then chief, then superintendent, then vice-president, then president, then trust magnate, then beer baron, then Lord of all the Americas, the money god, the god of gods, the clay of clay, nullity on high, zero with ninety-seven thousand decimals fore and aft. . . . I will give you Horatio Alger as he looks the day after the Apocalypse, when all the stink has cleared away (Miller 1961, pp. viii–ix).

No, America is not El Dorado. The monotonous ethos we are left with today was not "implicit" from the outset, not the only possible outcome. It has not made ours "the best of all possible worlds." And yet, somehow, the verbal alchemy of our cultural institutions has found "the right words" to make it seem so. It has made the land of inequality, the land of opportunity; the sin of luxury, the sweet smell of success; the tragedy of plutocracy, the triumph of democracy; cupidity and rapacity, the American Way.

How?

The answer is a long story. So long, in fact, that it will take the rest of this book to begin to tell it.

NOTES

1. For a review of how these classes have been defined, see Domhoff (1978, pp. 12–13). Here, "dominant" and "dominated," "propertied class" and "working class" are understood as places on a continuum in which some people have much power, even over the lives of others. Others have little, even over their own lives. Some people are bosses; others are bossed. Some people have much wealth, and buy and sell. Others have little, and are bought and sold (see Pareto, in Bottomore 1964). Our argument is that those who have more than their share of economic power will have commensurate power over culture, and will be proportionately anxious to use that power to sustain their position.

2. This ethos, our political culture, is that which is "prior to" public opinion, "beneath it, enveloping it, restricting it, conditioning it, ... the underlying consensus" (Dahl 1956, p. 132). We define it, paraphrasing Clyde Kluckhohn, as a widely shared "system of related designs for carrying out all the acts" of our political and social lives; those of our ways of thinking, believing, behaving, and feeling that are related to politics and society (Kluckhohn 1962).

3. In fairness, although determinism is certainly on display in some of Marx's writings, the whole body of his work is more balanced. This economism/inevitabilism becomes categorical only later, in some of Marx's disciples (Abercrombie, Hill, and Turner 1980, p. 9).

4. Of course, Marx himself sometimes seems to have planted the seedling of this idea, which would grow to challenge both economic determinism and inevitabilism. The most famous passage is from *The German Ideology*: "The class which has the means of material production at its disposal, has control at the same time over the means of mental production, so that ... the ideas of those who lack the means of mental production are subject to it" (1964, p. 61). The fact that the first two generations of Marx's intellectual progeny never saw *The German Ideology* may well account for their failure to cultivate the notion of ideological hegemony. Gramsci didn't see the book either, but found passages akin to it in Marx's other writings, and took the position that Marx's "genuine doctrine" understood the importance of ideology, and that Marx's frequent stress on the predominance of material over ideological forces were lapses "from his own insight" (Genovese 1967, p. 292).

5. Is there "good sense" in the dominant ideology? As is often the case, Gramsci is ambiguous here. Clearly, good sense involves a philosophical, critical mind-set as opposed to an unreflective one (Gramsci 1971, p. 328). But the conclusions such a mind will come to are not defined in the passages defining "good sense." Abercrombie, Hill, and Turner take the "good sense" to be only that part of the "common sense" that opposes the dominant ideology (1980, pp. 14–15). But Gramsci described his own argument as one that began by trying to find, in his bourgeois adversaries, that which "should be incorporated, if only as a subordinate aspect, in his own construction" (1971, p. 344). And in the passage that most compels a finding of good sense in the dominant ideology, he allows that his own Marxism "presupposes all this cultural past: Renaissance and Reformation, German philosophy and the French Revolution, Calvinism and English classical economics, secular liberalism. ... The philosophy of *praxis*

is the crowning point of this entire movement of intellectual and moral reformation" (1971, p. 395).

6. This pattern grows even more astonishing when compared to the Western European. For example, 68 percent of blue-collar Swedes support equal pay for all occupations; 11 percent of blue-collar Americans support it (Verba and Orren 1985, p. 255). It is this European pattern that has prompted Abercrombie and his associates (1980) to argue that there is no definable "dominant ideology." As is evident from the data presented here, their argument has much more relevance to the European than to the U.S. case.

7. There are others, besides Hartz, who argue that our pervasive ideology is not the work of a dominant class, and have offered their own rival hypotheses. See, for example, Boorstin (1958), Turner (1921), Sombart (1984), and Epstein (1967). Some of these arguments are rejoined in Katznelson (1981, ch. 1), some are referred to in Chapter 2. Among these, Hartz's explanation remains the most formidable.

8. Whether Americans have in fact been class unconscious "all along" will be debated in this book. But there is little doubt that Americans insist today that ours is not a class-divided society, in marked contrast to Europeans (Schlozman and Verba 1979, p. 114–17).

9. Since this "primordial force" has been at work in Europe as well, how do we account for the success of European socialism? Eric Foner has argued that European socialism is "successful" only as compared to U.S. socialism. In most meaningful senses, there is no socialism in Europe either (1984).

10. Nor would we deny the importance of such other explanations for American exceptionalism as the difficulty of ethnic divisions or the early "gift" of the franchise (see Chapters 6 and 7). This volume does not pretend that hegemony theory explains everything about U.S. culture and opinion, only that it explains something and has been neglected by mainstream theorists.

11. Even Madison added that one may accumulate property, only "so long as his action leaves the same chance to everyone else." It is hard to know what Madison would have made of corporate capitalism, with its limited rates of mobility—limited "chances"—and its tendency to concentrate power and to preclude competition—to preclude others' having "the same chance."

12. Of course, "what is striking in the statement is the assertion of individual freedom against the interference of a . . . state, while such freedom is not asserted against the interference of vast hierarchical, bureaucratic corporations . . . that operate largely outside the . . . democratic political process and are under even less popular restraint than state power" (Bellah 1975, p. 115).

13. Curiously, the novels often cited as definitive of this genre don't really fit into it. Horatio Alger's are not really stories of "rags to riches," but of "rags to respectability." His heroes were not marked by any raging "will to win," but by more old fashioned virtues: honesty, fidelity, courtesy, and so on. They succeed not in the corporation, but in small partnerships, small shops. In short, the success of the Alger stories may have been more a longing for the republican past than for the capitalist future (Cawelti 1965, pp. 101–24).

14. For recent elaborations of what such other voices might say, see Dolbeare 1984; Cohen and Rogers 1983; Harrington 1972; Carnoy and Shearer 1980; Green 1985.

15. The phrase is Gramsci's. It refers to an unusually large package of concessions, made in a time of ferment—enough to mollify the lower class, although not enough, of course, to fundamentally alter the distribution of power and perquisites. In fact, the gap in real income level between the bottom quintile of U.S. families and the top 5 percent has nearly doubled during the past 30 years, a period including the "social revolution" of the 1960s and 70s (Cohen and Rogers 1983, p. 30).

REFERENCES

Abercrombie, Nicholas, Stephen Hill, and Bryan S. Turner. 1980. *The Dominant Ideology Thesis*. London: George Allen and Unwin.

Ambach, Gordon M. 1986. "Message from the Commissioner of Education." Unpublished memorandum, January 29.

Anderson, Perry. 1976–77. "The Antinomies of Antonio Gramsci." *New Left Review* 100:5–80.

Bellah, Robert N. 1975. *The Broken Covenant*. New York: Seabury Press.

Bluestone, Barry, and Bennett Harrison. 1982. *The Deindustrialization of America*. New York: Basic Books.

Boorstin, Daniel. 1958. *The Genius of American Politics*. Chicago: University of Chicago Press.

Bottomore, Thomas B. 1964. *Elites and Society*. Harmondsworth, Eng.: Penguin Books.

Carnoy, Martin, and Derek Shearer. 1980. *Economic Democracy*. White Plains, N.Y.: M. E. Sharpe.

Cawelti, John G. 1965. *Apostles of the Self-Made Man*. Chicago: University of Chicago Press.

Cohen, Joshua, and Joel Rogers. 1983. *On Democracy*. New York: Penguin Books.

Dahl, Robert A. 1956. *A Preface to Democratic Theory*. Chicago: University of Chicago Press.

Dolbeare, Kenneth M. 1984. *Democracy at Risk*. Chatham, N.J.: Chatham House.

Domhoff, G. William. 1978. *The Powers That Be*. New York: Random House.

Dye, Thomas R., and L. Harmon Zeigler. 1983. *The Irony of Democracy*. Monterey, Calif.: Brooks-Cole.

Edsall, Thomas Byrne. 1984. *The New Politics of Inequality*. New York: W. W. Norton.

Epstein, Leon D. 1967. *Political Parties in Western Democracies*. New York: Praeger.

Feldman, Stanley. 1982. "Economic Self Interest and Political Behavior." *American Journal of Political Science* 26:446–66.

Foner, Eric. 1984. "Why Is There No Socialism in the United States?" *History Workshop Journal* 17:57–73.

Formisano, Ronald P. 1983. *The Transformation of Political Culture*. New York: Oxford University Press.

Free, Lloyd A., and Hadley Cantril. 1968. *The Political Beliefs of Americans*. New York: Simon and Schuster.

Genovese, Eugene D. 1967. "On Antonio Gramsci." *Studies on the Left* VII:284–316.

Goodwyn, Lawrence. 1976. *Democratic Promise*. New York: Oxford University Press.

Gramsci, Antonio. 1971. *Selections from the Prison Notebooks*. Edited and translated by Quintin Hoare and Geoffrey N. Smith. New York: International Publishers.

Green, Philip. 1985. *Retrieving Democracy*. Totawa, N.J.: Rowman and Allanheld.

Gutman, Herbert G. 1976. *Work, Culture, and Society in Industrializing America*. New York: Random House.

Harrington, Michael. 1972. *Socialism*. New York: Saturday Review Press.

Hartz, Louis. 1955. *The Liberal Tradition in America*. New York: Harcourt, Brace.

Jefferson, Thomas. 1973. "Jefferson to James Madison, December 20, 1787." In *The Political Thought of American Statesmen*, edited by Morton J. Frisch and Richard G. Stevens, pp. 21–24. Itasca, Ill.: F. E. Peacock.

Jencks, Christopher, et al. 1979. *Who Gets Ahead?* New York: Basic Books.

Johnson, Lyndon B. 1965. *Public Papers of the Presidents: Lyndon B. Johnson*, 1963–64, vol. 1. Washington, D.C.: Government Printing Office.

Katznelson, Ira. 1981. *City Trenches*. New York: Pantheon Books.

Kleppner, Paul, Walter Dean Burnham, Ronald P. Formisano, Samuel P. Hays, Richard Jensen, and William G. Shade. 1981. *The Evolution of American Electoral Systems*. Westport, Conn.: Greenwood Press.

Kluckhohn, Clyde. 1962. "The Concept of Culture." In *Culture and Behavior*, edited by Richard Kluckhohn. New York: Macmillan.

Kolko, Gabriel. 1963. *The Triumph of Conservatism*. London: The Free Press of Glencoe.

Lasch, Christopher. 1978. *The Culture of Narcissism*. New York: W. W. Norton.

Leuchtenberg, William E. 1983. *In the Shadow of FDR*. Ithaca, N.Y.: Cornell University Press.

———. 1963. *Franklin D. Roosevelt and the New Deal*. New York: Harper and Row.

Lipset, Seymour Martin, and William Schneider. 1983. *The Confidence Gap*. New York: The Free Press.

Locke, John. 1969. Selections from *Two Treatises of Government*. In *Great Political Thinkers*, edited by William Ebenstein, pp. 390–421. New York: Holt, Rinehart, and Winston.

Lustig, R. Jeffrey. 1982. *Corporate Liberalism*. Berkeley: University of California Press.

McClosky, Herbert, and John Zaller. 1984. *The American Ethos*. Cambridge, Mass.: Harvard University Press.

Maccoby, Michael. 1976. *The Gamesman: The New Corporate Leaders*. New York: Simon and Schuster.

Madison, James. 1964. "Federalist Number 10." In *The Federalist Papers*, by James Madison, Alexander Hamilton, and John Jay. Edited by Andrew Hacker. New York: Simon and Schuster.

Magnuson, Ed. 1986. "They slipped the surly bonds of earth to touch the face of God." *Time*, February 10, pp. 24–31.

Marcuse, Herbert. 1964. *One Dimensional Man*. Boston: Beacon Press.

Marx, Karl. 1970. *A Contribution to the Critique of Political Economy*. Edited by Maurice Dobb. New York: International Publishers.

Marx, Karl, and Frederick Engels. 1964. *The German Ideology*. Edited by S. Ryazanskaya. Moscow: Progress Publishers.

Miller, Henry. 1961. *Tropic of Cancer*. New York: Grove Press.

Miller, Perry. 1967. *Nature's Nation.* Cambridge, Mass.: Harvard University Press.

Miller, William. 1968. *A New History of the United States.* New York: Dell.

Mills, C. Wright. 1956. *The Power Elite.* New York: Oxford University Press.

Morganthau, Tom. 1984. "Homeless in America." *Newsweek,* January 2, pp. 20–30.

New York Times. 1986. "The Death of a Schoolteacher." January 29, p. A22.

———. 1986. "Warnings 'Ignored' by NASA." May 14, p. A1.

Newsweek. 1984. "Hunger: A New Study, An Opposite Finding." February 20, p. 54.

Pateman, Carole. 1970. *Participation and Democratic Theory.* New York: Cambridge University Press.

Phillips, Kevin P. 1983. *Post-Conservative America.* New York: Vintage Books.

Piven, Frances Fox, and Richard A. Cloward. 1982. *The New Class War.* New York: Pantheon Books.

Reichley, A. James. 1985. *Religion in American Public Life.* Washington, D.C.: The Brookings Institution.

Rieder, Jonathan. 1985. *Canarsie.* Cambridge, Mass.: Harvard University Press.

Rodgers, Daniel T. 1978. *The Work Ethic in Industrial America 1850–1920.* Chicago: University of Chicago Press.

Roosevelt, Franklin D. 1938. "A Radio Address to the Young Democratic Clubs of America." In *The Public Papers and Addresses of Franklin D. Roosevelt,* vol. 4, compiled by Samuel I. Rosenman. New York: Random House.

Schlozman, Kay, and Sidney Verba. 1979. *Injury to Insult.* Cambridge, Mass.: Harvard University Press.

Sennett, Richard, and Jonathan Cobb. 1973. *The Hidden Injuries of Class.* New York: Vintage Books.

Shanker, Albert. 1986. "Risk Takers Are a National Asset." New York *Times,* February 2, 1986, p. E7.

Simon, Roger. 1982. *Gramsci's Political Thought.* London: Lawrence and Wishart.

Sombart, Werner. 1984. "American Capitalism's Economic Rewards." In *Failure of a Dream,* rev. ed., edited by John H. M. Laslett and Seymour M. Lipset, pp. 452–67. Berkeley: University of California Press.

Stafford, Thomas P. 1986. "Man in Space." *Time,* May 19.

Sumner, William Graham. 1934. *Essays of William Graham Sumner.* Edited by Albert G. Keller and Maurice R. Davie. New Haven: Yale University Press.

Tawney, R. H. 1926. *Religion and the Rise of Capitalism.* New York: Harcourt, Brace.

Thurow, Lester C. 1981. "A Liberal Looks at Income Distribution." New York *Times,* August 23.

Tocqueville, Alexis. 1966. *Democracy in America.* Translated by J. P. Mayer. Garden City, N.Y.: Doubleday.

Trachtenberg, Alan. 1982. *The Incorporation of America.* New York: Hill and Wang.

Turner, Frederick J. 1921. *The Frontier in American History.* New York: H. Holt.

U.S. News and World Report. 1986a. "The New World of Health Care." April 14, pp. 60–67.

———. 1986b. "A Nation Apart." March 17, pp. 18–28.

Verba, Sidney, and Gary R. Orren. 1985. *Equality in America*. Cambridge, Mass.: Harvard University Press.

Weber, Max. 1958. *The Protestant Ethic and the Spirit of Capitalism*. Translated by Talcott Parsons. New York: Charles Scribner's Sons.

Wiebe, Robert H. 1967. *The Search for Order 1877–1920*. New York: Hill and Wang.

Wilentz, Sean. 1983. "Artisan Republican Festivals and the Rise of Class Conflict in New York City, 1788–1837." In *Working Class America*, edited by Michael H. Frisch and Daniel J. Walkowitz. Urbana: University of Illinois Press.

2

The Broken Promise of Democracy

Calvin F. Exoo

Political parties are the beating heart of a democracy. Ours has a murmur. A deep one, strong enough to be fatal. Listen:

On November 6, 1984, the United States held a national election—52.9 percent of the voters came. Only three presidential elections have seen such low turnout since the advent of mass suffrage. One of them was in 1980.

Recent polls have found that about 70 percent of Americans think government is run for the benefit of "a few big interests." Twenty-five years ago, only 29 percent thought so (Lipset and Schneider 1983a, p. 17).

Barely half of all Americans now think having elections "makes the government pay [a good deal of] attention to what people think." Only 18 percent think political parties help in that regard (Lipset and Schneider 1983a, p. 25).

Americans are split about evenly on the question of whether "there are any important differences in what Democrats and Republicans stand for" (Shienbaum 1984, p. 30).

When asked which of four political institutions "you most often trust to do what's right," 8 percent said "none." Two percent said "parties" (Shienbaum 1984, p. 28).

When Americans are asked a fundamental political question more than once over a period of months or years, only a minority have a "sufficiently firm opinion to take the same side...in both interviews" (Erikson, Luttbeg, and Tedin 1980, p. 23).

All right, the body politic is ailing. But why the extravagant claim that parties are the heart of the matter, the *sine qua non* of popular government, that their disease has produced all the rest as "morbid symptoms"? Because even after 800 years of living in nation-states, the paltry wit of man has been able to devise just one engine capable of organizing common people for a common defense of their political interests. For better or for worse, that one engine is the political party.

Democracy's potentially tragic flaw is that politics is, for most people, a remote, mysterious arena. No one could possibly know, for example, what all the changing candidates for all the offices stand for on all the changing issues. A kaleidoscope is to be wondered at, not understood.

The job of parties is to wade in from this welter of candidates and say, "This is our insignia and it stands for you. It stands for you, working people, or for you, black people, and so on. Here's how and why we stand for you. And now you need no longer be confused by the kaleidoscope of candidates—just look for the one who's marching under our flag. And once all of us working people know that insignia, no matter how powerless we are individually, suddenly, we are an army. But an army educated to its interests. So it is an army by and for the foot soldiers. A democracy."

It is this "programmatic" function of standing for certain groups and principles, consistently, clearly, over time, up and down the *cursus honorum*, that American parties have failed to perform. Instead, they have chosen to be brokers[1] in the marketplace of votes. Interested above all in winning elections, they begin not with a clarion "here we stand," but with a chameleonic "what are you in the market for?" Whatever that turns out to be, they offer it. They are not fussy. And what, as it turns out, sells? Each party has found the formula for success in an ideologically incoherent babel of candidates who avoid issues when they can, obfuscate when they can't, and, when pressed again, offer "alternatives" so close to the middle of the road as to be indistinguishable. A marketing *tour de force*. A democratic disaster.

When the parties themselves are kaleidoscopic chaos, when they fail to answer the simple, crucial question, "Who stands for me?," when they fail to organize ordinary people into a political force to be reckoned with, then politics falls by default to those who don't need parties to be powerful. An oligarchy. And so it goes in America.

ORIGINS OF BROKERAGE PARTY BEHAVIOR

Why have our parties broken their promise to democracy? Why has no major party stood consistently for ordinary working class people, principles, and programs? There are many reasons. For example, because the vote was extended to most white males in this country before there was a working class in the modern sense, they could not be galvanized as a political force by the fight for the franchise, as European workers were in the late nineteenth century (Epstein 1967, pp. 19–26). A second argument points to the racial, ethnic, and sectional differences that sometimes balkanized the American working class, making representation by a single party impossible (Leinenweber 1984). A third combines the promise of the frontier, of "high"[2] standards of living and rates of mobility for the working class to depict a society where, it seemed, a man didn't need to rise with his class—he could rise above it (Epstein 1967, p. 28; Thernstrom 1984; Sombart 1984).

Most of these arguments seem to have little to do with propertied class control over parties.[3] This chapter will not pretend that they are unimportant, but will nonetheless concentrate on other, equally important arguments that do see the hand of hegemony in the failure of parties.

Let's begin at the beginning. "Some of the Federalist Papers," to say nothing of the Constitution they apologize, "seem to have been written by a Marx of the master class" (Harrington 1984, p. 523). With remarkable prescience, Madison described what would become of most Western societies in the century after his death: "An increase of population will . . . increase the proportion of those who will labor under all the hardships of life and secretly sigh for a more equal distribution of its blessings. These may in time outnumber those who are placed above the feelings of indigence. . . . According to the equal laws of suffrage, the power will slide into the hands of the former" (quoted in Beard 1962, pp.94–95). For men who believed that the protection of property was "the main object of government," this was a prospect devoutly to be avoided, and the framers devoted much of their Constitution to avoiding it. Their now familiar strategy was to divide society "into so many parts, interests, and classes of citizens, that the rights of individuals, or of the minority, will be in little danger from interested combinations of the majority" (Madison 1964, p. 125). The separation of powers did more than try to give veto power over the "changeableness and excess" of the people to a president and Senate elected by "men of great and established property" (quoted phrases are from Gouverneur Morris, in Beard 1962, p. 93). Its more lasting effect was to remove the main incentive parliamentary parties have for cohering over program—the maintenance of executive power (Epstein 1967, p. 35). This, of course, made possible our profoundly incoherent congressional parties.

What made incoherence more than possible was federalism. The nature of parties is to wrap themselves like pearls around grains of power. Thus, the idea of reserving "numerous and indefinite" powers to the state governments meant that there would eventually be, not two major U.S. parties, but one hundred and two. With no incentive to harmony, these far-flung party choruses attuned themselves to local prejudice and sectional interest. The result has been cacophonous candidate slates and congressional parties (Schattschneider 1960, ch. 6; Lowi 1979, p. 253). And once established, these state party fiefdoms made governmental feudalism permanent. They instructed their vassals in Congress to continue to devolve power to the states, even after the need for a centralized government was manifest and the "reserved powers" clause of the Constitution was a dead letter (Grodzins 1960).

But even as the major parties flowed into these constitutional channels, a swelling working class ideology carried some parties outside their banks, to principle and program. Unfortunately, the framework stopped them from getting far. Separate election of the president meant that even when working class parties won a sizable minority of votes, they had no hope of sharing executive power, as they might have in parliamentary systems (Thomas 1984). Similarly, single-member districts in state and congressional elections made a minority of votes like no votes at all (Rae 1967, ch. 5). For parties of principle trying to attract worthy candidates and educate the electorate, these election rules made a toehold in the system well-nigh impossible. As we shall see, parties quickly discovered that the sure way to muster the required majorities was not by standing clearly for the working class and its program, but by offering a house for all men, a shelter for none.

By 1828, republican ideology and a healthy fear of rebellion had combined to enfranchise most adult white males. In addition, most states had moved from selecting presidential electors by the state legislature, to popular selection. It was time for the debut of mass, national parties. What sort of show would it be?

Two facts of American life kept the entertainment light, kept the program from having much program. The first was federalism, which gave local parties their own power bases and thus meant that they, and not any national party organization, would run the show. Any presidential nominee acceptable to all the different-minded local barons was bound to be a bleached-out compromise, not a policy leader.

The other problem with programmatic parties was the American myth of class comity. The Revolution, now a sacred war in its still-warm afterglow, had molded Americans of all classes into a common republican language that promised a harmony of interests (Formisano 1983, ch. 3). There were, of course, issues afoot that belied that promise. A valiant Workingmen's movement militated for a laborer's right to the property that was his labor, which implied the right to join with others, to fix a price on it, or to say how many hours each day it would be provided (Wilentz 1983; Formisano 1983, ch. 10). The problem was that this movement had no long-standing sense of irreconcilable difference with the Smithian entrepreneurs who opposed it (as Thompson 1966, pp. 806–32, says was true in England during this period). In fact, both sides spoke the same republican shibboleths.

The cynical genius of the first mass parties was to find this Achilles heel of the working class: to speak the shibboleths while "transcending" the issues, stitching together a patchwork of local parties with threads of patronage, pork barrel, and personality.

Contrary to the storybook of American history, Jackson's was not the party of the common man. As Edward Pessen's painstaking review of the relevant research makes clear, Democratic leaders, like their Whig counterparts, were men of "unusual wealth and prominence [usually] in business affairs" (1969, p. 252). The Democratic constituency, like the Whig, was a hodgepodge—"the relative wealth or poverty of citizens seemed to have nothing to do with their party preferences" (Pessen 1969, p. 26; Kleppner et al. 1981, p. 100).

How could it have been otherwise? The salesman's soul of the parties offered voters no common program (Lowi 1979, p. 243). The appeal of each was itself a hodgepodge of local prejudice, personalities, republican slogans, songs, torchlight parades, and little log cabins. The candidate was "the best available hero" who could avoid "any semblance of a party platform" (McCormick 1975, p. 101; see also Formisano 1983, pp. 13–14; Rubin 1981, pp. 40–42).

But American politics has not been an unbroken string of such blandishments. Again and again, brokerage politics as usual has brought voter alienation to a flash point where urgent issues can no longer be denied and parties are forced to take a stand.[4] In the mid-nineteenth century, the powder keg packed by the parties' stifling rhetoric included the dizzying, disconcerting pace of economic growth, the Panic of 1837, what seemed to be a flood of Catholic immigration, the religious revivalism that these other forces helped inspire, and, of course, slavery.

The stand the parties finally took was, perhaps, predictable. In "classless" America, few party leaders were interested, none were successful in teaching the electorate the new language that could tell the story of the "house of Have" against the "house of Want." Instead, the Republican Party remade public discourse by repairing to an old language, one that resonated deep in the precocious consciences of latter-day Puritans. This was the language of the "calling" to duty in every sphere of life, politics included, to make of the polity a "City upon a Hill." At its best, this "political church" housed the Abolition movement. At its worst, it was xenophobic intolerance. And after the Civil War had settled the slavery question, this party system was usually at its worst, fixated on outlawing the parochial schools and the demon rum of the "heathen papists" (Kleppner et al. 1981, pp. 136–38). Catholics, along with white

Southerners and the non-Pietist churches, usually took shelter in the laissez faire of the Democratic Party.

CAPITAL'S *COUP DE GRACE*

The Campaign of 1896

Through 1892, neither of the major parties gave much notice to the increasing misery of U.S. workers and farmers. Neither proposed even regulation of, much less an alternative to, the capitalism that had produced such misery. The only question that divided the parties was whether government ought to leave the field to the process of "natural selection," or actively abet "the fittest" (Kleppner 1982, p. 144). As a result, the gay nineties were a time when industrial deaths numbered tens of thousands each year, when over 30,000 persons were "housed" in six blocks of low-rise buildings on New York's East Side, when 2 million children were full-time, 12 hour-a-day members of the labor force, when over 11,000 farm mortgages were forclosed in a five-year period in Kansas alone, and so on.

In 1892, these problems of economy and class pulled 16 percent of the electorate away from the major parties that so assiduously ignored them. Instead they voted for the Populist Party, which demanded a graduated income tax, an expanded currency, public ownership of railroads, telegraph, and telephones, and the eight-hour day for labor. The year 1893 saw the onset of what was then the worst depression in U.S. history, one that left more than 20 percent of the work force unemployed. By presidential-election year 1896, it was these class issues that could no longer be denied.

But 1896 was not the beginning for working class politics. It was the beginning of the end. In that year, the Democrats took up, however gingerly, the cause of the economy's orphans. The depression, which had begun on the Democrats' watch, handed them unprecedented losses in the congressional elections of 1894. By 1896, the "sound-money" Democrats of Grover Cleveland could no longer withstand the cry from the party's Southern and Western wings for "free silver," the expansion of the money supply that would provide some relief to the deflation-wracked farmers of those regions. Also in the platform were planks calling for an income tax, and for arbitration of labor disputes, instead of the then-fashionable use of state and federal troops to crush strikes. The party's candidate was William Jennings Bryan, whose "cross of gold" speech sketching a "silver Zion" spellbound the convention and audiences throughout the campaign.

Now to be sure, Bryan's was no radical challenge to capitalism. He and his platform were vague or silent on all the most fundamental demands the Populist platform had made, a point not lost on the Populists. "Free silver," said movement hero Tom Watson, "is but a drop in the bucket." Even as they endorsed this half a loaf, the Populists agonized over being delivered into "the lap of Wall Street Democracy" (*The Progressive Farmer*, quoted in Hollingsworth 1963, pp. 64–65). Their fears were not unrealistic. Bryan's running mate was a bank and railroad magnate, conservative on all but silver. The candidate's acceptance speech was an ode to the *ancien régime*:

Our campaign has not for its objects the reconstruction of society.... We cannot propose to transfer the rewards of industry to the lap of indolence. Property is and will remain the stimulus to endeavor and the compensation for toil (in Hollingsworth 1963, p. 85).

The year 1896 was important not because Bryan was a radical, but because the capital establishment thought he was. The Populist and related movements, together with an unprecedented wave of labor unrest had already created a superheated climate of fear among U.S. businessmen. Now, the anarchy of unsound money had been written into the platform of a major party, and its candidate was endorsed by the lunatic Populists. It was all the spark needed. The business class exploded with a vengeance that was to destroy working class parties, not just for the 1890s, but for generations to come.[5]

Their counterattack began in the newspapers, whose news slant, in those days before journalism became a profession, was whatever their owners said it was. Within days of the convention, most of the nation's major Democratic papers had renounced their party in "the most widespread shift of party allegiance in the history of presidential elections" (Hollingsworth 1963, p. 71). Thus, while his opponent sent news and editorials in pre-slated form every week to newspapers reaching at least 5 million families, Bryan had no newspaper support in such cities as Chicago, Minneapolis, and Boston (Hollingsworth 1963, p. 70). In the hysterical rhetoric of newspaper editorials, the Bryanites became "Communism and Anarchy...Jacobins...fanatics...demagogues...a mob of repudiators" (in Hollingsworth 1963, pp. 69–70).

In this climate, Bryan's opponent, William McKinley, had no trouble financing the most expensive campaign to that date in U.S. history. His $7 million total outspent Bryan by 14 to 1, a ratio that would have been larger had silver mining concerns not been generous to the Democrat.

This money and media cooperation enabled McKinley's campaign manager, industrialist Mark Hanna, to orchestrate a masterful brokerage campaign. While Bryan ran a frenzied, fraying whistle-stop marathon, McKinley calmly held forth from the front porch of his home in Canton,

Ohio, for trainloads of imported reporters and voters from across the country. Here, the set as well as the character could shine with small-town, mid-American common sense. And shine they did. McKinley's moderate, ambiguous rhetoric was a school for twentieth-century brokerage politics. The currency question was brilliantly straddled, offering farmers currency expansion through "international agreements," which money men knew could never be obtained. The tariffs that had enriched U.S. businessmen at the expense of the purchasing power of ordinary Americans became a program of "job and wage protection" for urban laborers. Daringly, McKinley even abandoned the evangelical rhetoric and issues so long cherished by his party in favor of the wide embrace of the unobjectionable slogan: "Peace, Progress, Patriotism, Prosperity" (Goodwyn 1976, p. 524).

While McKinley thus took the "high" road, "transcending" issues, his minions took the low. In the South, Bourbon conservatives raised the spectre of "Negro domination" to frighten white yeomen away from Bryanism and the Populism that was willing to slate black candidates. At the same time, these Bourbons used bribery and intimidation to enlist legions of black "supporters" in their own cause (Woodward 1955, pp. 49–95). In Northern cities, the crowbar that divided and conquered the working class was nativism. "One of the major goals of the Republican campaign strategy was to portray the Democrats as friends of foreigners and conveyers of foreign ideologies. Among the most widely used Republican campaign posters was one that pictured Bryan appealing to people of all races and nationalities" (Hollingsworth 1963, p. 96).[6]

Those workers not impressed by silken vacuities or race baiting were no doubt more impressed with another Republican tactic: intimidation. Avowed Bryanites found themselves an unwanted commodity in the job market. Businesses issued public statements threatening shutdown if Bryan were elected. Buyers made orders for material contingent on a McKinley victory (Hollingsworth 1963, p. 93). On Election night, the results were unequivocal:

> "Victory of letterfiles,
> And plutocrats in miles
> With dollar signs upon their coats,
> Diamond watchchains on their vests and spats on their feet,
> Victory of custodians, Plymouth Rock,
> And all that inbred landlord stock
> Victory of the neat" (Lindsay 1954, pp. 270–71).

Institutionalizing Hegemony: The System of 1896

McKinley's victory in 1896, together with another in 1900, discredited Bryanism and Populism and sent the Democrats scurrying back to the tried and true brokerage formula: obfuscation, incoherence, and a meeting of the other party's mind on "the cardinal principle," the rightness of capitalism (Kleppner 1982, p.148; Kleppner et al. 1981, p. 181; Hollingsworth 1963, ch. 11). What is more, the election transformed the Northeast and the Upper Midwest from areas of healthy inter-party competition into one-party Republican regions. By a different route, the South arrived at a similar destination. There, the Populists had allied themselves with local Republicans and elected a large number of candidates, including some blacks. The Bourbons who controlled the Democratic Party crucified this alliance on a cross of race, and made the South a one-party stronghold for their own brand of Democracy (Woodward 1955, pp. 49–95).

Together, the absence of competition and the absence of meaningful issues would turn much of the "house of Want" away from electoral politics for decades (Kleppner 1982, pp. 73, 81; Burnham 1982, p. 71).[7] While they were away, the "house of Have" seized its day, writing election laws that would make its temporary ascendancy permanent.

Progressivism, the banner under which these "reforms" marched, was really several very different movements (Ebner and Tobin 1977, pp. 3–12). For example, the drive for primary elections in Wisconsin was directed against the corporations that controlled the state's hegemonic Republican Party (Thelen 1972). But more often, especially when it turned its attention to political structures, Progressivism was a business and professional class strategy to vitiate working class parties and politics. For example, "the initiative for commission and manager government came consistently from Chambers of Commerce and other organized business groups" (Weinstein 1968, p. 99). Meanwhile, "lower and middle-class groups not only dominated the pre-reform governments, but vigorously opposed reform. It is significant that none of the occupational groups among them ... had important representation in reform organizations thus far examined" (Hays 1964, p. 162).

This point was obscured by the movement's own marching hymns, which celebrated "political reform" not as a class war, but a holy war. Their constant refrain was the "corruption" of the urban machine. And there is no doubt that corruption existed, although it must be added that much of what Anglo-Saxon reformers called "corruption" was merely the acting out of the familistic, paternalistic values of the machine's Irish and southern European constituents (Exoo 1983).

But *inter* these *alia*, the holy war and the cultural clash, "urban reform" was also a class war. Sometimes, even its own apologists said as much. "The electoral process ... was 'corrupt,' perhaps above all, because 'universal suffrage was but another name for a licensed mobocracy.' The one-man-one-vote principle undermined the participation of the 'intelligent portion of the community,' which simply did not 'care to waste our time bucking against a lot of cattle whose vote is just as good as ours' " (internal quotations from William L. Scruggs and E. L. Morse respectively, in Kleppner 1982, p. 59). This strain of thought was perhaps most common in the South, where the vision of reformers was one of restoring an Old South "dominated by an elite filled with *noblesse oblige* and far removed from the corruption and turmoil of fully democratic politics" (Burnham 1970, p. 78).

But perhaps the best test of whether "urban reform" was class warfare is to be found, not in the movement's membership or its words, but in its deeds. For even when its rhetoric was democratic, its accomplishments were profoundly undemocratic. The election laws it forged were a sword of Draco that drained the life not just of "corrupt machines," but of all working class parties and politics.

Those laws included the non-partisan ballot, which eliminated that simplifying cue, the party label, so important especially to the voter who is less educated, less attentive, less often cued by interest groups (Hawley 1973). Voting turnout in non-partisan cities is typically 5 to 10 percent lower than in partisan cities (Alford and Lee 1968, p. 808)—a 5 to 10 percent drawn disproportionately from among lower status voters, the "last hired-first fired" stratum of the electorate.

Another Progressive invention, electing city council members at large instead of by district, often forced working class candidates out of the citywide races they could not afford and often precluded representation for such groups as blacks, immigrants, and socialists, who were not majorities in the city, but were so in the wards where they were concentrated. "In Dayton, for example, the Socialists received twenty-five percent of the vote in the election immediately preceding the adoption of the [at-large] reform, electing two ward councilmen.... In 1913, after the [reform] charter was adopted, they received thirty-five percent of the vote and elected no one to the commission." In 1917, with 44 percent of the vote, the party again elected no candidate (Weinstein 1968, pp. 109–10; for more recent examples of the same effect, see Judd 1979, p. 98).

Together, these reforms immediately delivered the goods their proponents had promised; the election of "qualified" men to office. In all the "reformed" cities reviewed by Weinstein, businessmen either comprised or dominated their commissions (1968, pp. 103–104).

A third "reform" replaced the elected mayor, as chief city executive, with a city manager appointed by the non-partisan "men of substance" now elected at large to the city commission. This new manager would run the city according to "sound business principles," trained as he was in one of the Progressives' own schools of "scientific management" (Judd 1979, pp. 100–104). These principles, of course, stressed "civil engineering, not social engineering... economy, not service" (Weinstein 1968, p. 111), and sought cutbacks in school expenditures, special schools for the retarded, and park and recreational expenditures (Judd 1979, p.103). But programs were not the only thing reduced under city managers. Voting turnout was another. Without the high visibility of a race for the mayoralty, another 15 percent of the electorate, with the now-familiar markings of class, fell by the wayside (Alford and Lee 1968).

One of the largest swaths was cut out of the electorate by a scythe called voter registration. Again, proponents wrapped themselves in the mantle of "fighting corruption." But a look at how they did it quickly reveals a naked anti-democratic self-interest. In "practically all other developed democratic polities ... the responsibility for compiling electoral registers and keeping them up to date falls on the state, not on the individual" (Burnham 1970, p. 83). The Progressives reversed the charges, imposing the cost of registration on the citizen. It is, of course, a cost least likely to be met by those whose station in life has left them without reserves of sense of efficacy or "citizen duty" (Kleppner 1982, p. 68). In the counties where they were in force, registration laws accounted for between 30 and 40 percent of the turnout decline that occurred during the first quarter of this century (Kleppner 1982, pp. 61–62).

But the Progressives' unkindest cut to democracy was the direct primary—partly because it was so far-reaching, partly because it seemed, and still seems, so democratic to Americans. The primary has woven this paradox in several ways. First, it accelerated the regional one-partyism created by the election of 1896. Voters, party activists, and candidates who might otherwise have remained loyal to, and rebuilt, the minority party now had, in the primary, a more "viable" outlet for their frustrations and ambitions—a chance to take over the majority party. V. O. Key has demonstrated that states using the direct primary were likely to become more completely dominated by the majority party over time. Non-primary states were not (Key 1956, pp. 181–93). The damning question about one-party systems is, how can the party stand for anything, organize anyone, when everyone—liberals and conservatives, rich and poor alike—are drawn into the black hole of that one party? Key himself gave the answer in his brilliant analysis of the one-party South: it can't (Key 1949). At general elections in one-party states, which are, of course, a foregone conclusion, voting turnout rarely exceeds 40 percent of the eligible electorate (Ranney 1976, p. 71). And the primary? Most voters default from it as well, even in one-party states, where the primary is often the only seriously contested election. In the primary, there is, of course, no party label on the ballot to organize an ever-changing kaleidoscope of candidates. Making their mistakes for the befuddled dropouts is a disproportionately upper class third or so of the eligible electorate (Ranney 1976, pp. 71–72).

For the same reason that second parties withered under the direct primary, third parties all but disappeared. For example, the Socialists won 5 percent or more of the total vote in 169 congressional districts in 1912. Over the next decade, as the direct primary became pervasive, Socialist success "abruptly disappears. . . . Coupled with the harsh measures taken by state legislatures in the 1920s and 1930s to keep third parties off the ballot altogether, [the direct primary] almost certainly had a great deal to do with these changes" (Kleppner et al. 1981, pp. 189–90).

Finally, the primary has exacerbated the irresponsibility and brokerage misbehavior of candidates. Without primaries, candidates would play to a nominating audience of party activists who know something about what the party has traditionally stood for. In the primary, the audience is made up of "party identifiers" who, knowing little about party ideology (Jackson, Brown, and Bositis 1982; McClosky, Hoffman, and O'Hara 1960), have been shown smoke and mirrors instead.

Of course, the most drastic disfranchisement to occur during this period—or any other in U.S. history—took place in the South. To effect it, elites made full use of the Progressive panoply described above and then fashioned a few arms of their very own: the poll tax, the literacy test, the property requirement, and so on (Kleppner 1982, p. 66). Of course, blacks were a target of these machinations. But they were not the only target. The other was the white yeoman, who had proven himself so dangerous, so radical, in the 1880s and 90s. In fact, it might be argued that blacks were just the race-bait needed to lure poor whites to their own disfranchisement. And the affluent, well-educated gentlemen who led the movement did not blush in declaring their intentions. "The true philosophy of the movement [is] to establish restricted suffrage, and to place the power of government into the hands of the intelligent and the virtuous" (John B. Knox, president of the Alabama constitutional convention, quoted in Hollingsworth 1963, p. 115). By the time the movement had run its course, about half of all white voters, along with almost all blacks, were voters no more (Burnham 1970, p. 84). The "intelligence and virtue" of race and class privilege were secure.

Nationally, the confluence of sectional one-partyism, vacuous campaigns, and election-law "reform" was a deathblow to working class politics. By the 1920s, voting turnout had declined by 25–30 percent from its nineteenth-century levels (Burnham 1982, p. 29). Because most of those lost were low-income, less-educated voters, they could now add "poorly represented" to the list of ways in which they were deprived.

The process continued even through the 1930s, when unharnessed capitalism careened into depression, and working class people in other industrialized nations brought their socialist parties to power. In the United States, Franklin Roosevelt was too canny to repeat Bryan's "mistake" of "radicalism," and he didn't need to. This time, the Republicans were the "party of depression." So, Roosevelt "devoted most of his efforts to decrying the Depression and blaming the Republicans for it, and to setting forth general goals for the future. Much to the frustration of [his] brain trusters, Roosevelt would not spell out his recovery program, barely hinting at a federal role in relief, in planning, and in supporting farm incomes. Roosevelt was also ambiguous about other major issues" (Page 1978, p. 166). By 1936, however, it was clear how far he had wandered from the straight and narrow road of laissez faire. Then, ingeniously, ingenuously, Roosevelt won the battle and lost the war of the working class, by explaining that his program was not a challenge to competitive individualism, but an outgrowth of its principles, appropriate to an age when interdependence made necessary an umpire for the economy's rule-breakers and a temporary foster home for its orphans. The New Deal did not teach the Democratic Party the language of class. Its language was the old language of liberalism, with a slight working class accent. In 1952, after twenty years of New Deal government, only 51 percent of Americans saw the Democrats as the party of the working class (Campbell, Gurin, and Miller 1954, pp. 211–15)

This tinge of class rhetoric drew some working and lower class voters back into the electoral fray, but not enough. In fairness to the New Deal, it would have done better in this regard, had not Progressive electoral "reforms" been more prevalent, by the 1930s and 40s, than ever before (Kleppner 1982, pp. 86–87). As it was, voting turnout from 1932 to 1962 was a bit higher than it had been in the 1920s, but was actually a bit lower than it had been from 1900–18, and was nothing like its zenith in the late nineteenth century (Burnham 1982, p. 29). This "Victorian" electorate, composed disproportionately of the nation's haves, created in the three decades after 1896, and not undone by the New Deal, is an enduring, signal feature of American life.[8] As brokerage parties had helped to create it, so it reinforced the classless rhetoric of the parties, and on and on in a seamless circle of hegemony

LIFE WITHOUT PARTIES: THE TRIUMPH OF HEGEMONY IN THE SYSTEM OF THE 1980s

Beginning in the early 1960s, a bad situation grew worse. Urgent, seemingly incomprehensible, intractable issues arose. Suddenly, like an alarm in the night, there was open rebellion in our city streets. This turmoil amid the flotsam of the ghetto was unnerving enough. But then, as we sank deeper into the slough of Vietnam, ferment erupted among our white, middle class children, on college campuses. These agonies were followed, in the 1970s, by the dispiriting Watergate scandal, a decade of persistent stagflation, deindustrialization, recurrent energy crises, and a host of divisive "social issues"—abortion, ERA, busing, affirmative action, prayer in schools, and so on. Again, the job of parties is to incorporate such new issues into a coherent philosophy of politics, which the party continually sets before the people. If democracy was to be more than a word, Americans badly needed to have the available explanations of and solutions to these problems set before them. At this crucial moment, as they had done before, the parties would fail us.

The Political Language of Broker Politicians

A careful survey of campaign discourse shows that recent presidential candidates have been painfully shy of discussing all issues, especially those newly emerging. For example, Richard Nixon devoted only about 2 percent—at most, six sentences—of his most widely viewed 1968 speech, the nomination acceptance, to the burning policy issue of Vietnam. And even that count is "generous; it includes sentences promising 'action—a new policy for peace abroad'; and declaring the aim of preventing 'more Vietnams.' " His most specific statement was that " 'the first priority foreign policy objective of our next Administration will be to bring an honorable end to the war in Vietnam.' The voter could not hope to find much information here—or in the TV spots or stump speeches which echoed the acceptance speech—about what Nixon proposed to do in Vietnam: whether he would 'end the war' by massive escalation, by unilateral withdrawal, or by negotiation." In his turn, Hubert Humphrey, the Democratic candidate, gave three sentences of his acceptance speech to Vietnam policy, and was no more specific in them than Nixon had been (Page 1978, pp. 153–54).

When candidates do take specific stands on issues, it is often in obscure position papers or journals, where most people are likely to miss them (Page 1978, p. 161). What is more, the issue positions taken tend to offer voters an echo, not a choice, as each candidate hies to a centrist modal point of public opinion, which the parties' own centrism and ambiguity have at least helped to create (Page 1978, ch. 4; Kleppner 1982, pp. 160–61). When the parties' candidates do finally disagree, their disagreement is not fundamental; it is over means, not ends—over how much government intervention is necessary to supplement the capitalist economy both parties endorse (Page 1978, pp. 105–06). On the "new," non-economic issues, even these modest differences—and the choices they represent—disappear (Page 1978, p. 77).

At this point, two questions present themselves. First, why do politicians avoid issues? Any time a candidate takes a specific stand, he will, of course, alienate those voters who disagree. For parties whose aim is the promiscuous recruitment of voters, not the representation of particular groups or principles, the rational strategy is to avoid controversial issues (Page 1978, p. 178).

But how do politicians get away with avoiding the issue of who does and should get what, and how? How do they generate warmth without light? Are voters fools? We might call talk about "who gets what and how" "reality representation"—when it refers concretely and specifically to how we are doing and how we might do better in our "real" political world. Intuitively, we often assume that reality representation is the main, or even the only, function of language. That is why we are surprised that there can be so much talk, such convincing talk, with so little political reality to it. But in fact, reality representation is only one among many of what Wittgenstein called the "language games" we play, only one of the functions served by language (Pitkin 1972, ch. 3). Another, for example, used mainly by politicians, is the "mythic nation" game, which serves our deep-seated need for social location and adjustment— our need to feel that we belong somewhere (Smith, Bruner, and White 1964). In this game, politicians invoke the cherished symbols—history and values—that we share as Americans. Because we share them, affirming the speaker's incantation affirms, for each of us, that we belong in this society and culture. Intuitively, we know when we are in this mode of discourse, and we ask no more of it than that it fulfill its function. So, for example, in his nomination acceptance speech of 1980, Ronald Reagan was able to speak mainly in this vein:

It is impossible to capture in words the splendor of this vast continent which God has granted as our portion of His creation. There are no words to express the extraordinary strength and character of this breed of people we call Americans.

Everywhere we've met thousands of Democrats, Independents and Republicans from all economic conditions, walks of life bound together in that community of shared values of family, work, neighborhood, peace and freedom. They are concerned, yes, they're not frightened. They're disturbed, but not dismayed. They are the kind of men and women Tom Paine had in mind when he wrote, during the darkest days of the American Revolution, "We have it in our power to begin the world over again...."

Tonight, let us dedicate ourselves to renewing the American compact. I ask you not simply to "trust me," but to trust your values—our values—and to hold me responsible for living up to them. I ask you to trust that American spirit which knows no ethnic, religious, social, political, regional or economic boundaries; the spirit that burned with zeal in the hearts of millions of immigrants from every corner of the earth who came here in search of freedom....

Can we doubt that only a Divine Providence placed this land, this island of freedom, here as a refuge for all those people in the world who yearn to breathe free? Jews and Christians enduring persecution behind the Iron Curtain; the boat people of Southeast Asia, Cuba and of Haiti; the victims of drought and famine in Africa, the freedom fighters in Afghanistan, and our own countrymen held in savage captivity....

Can we begin our crusade joined together in a moment of silent prayer?

(Pause.)

God bless America.

Thank you.

His audience knew, of course, that Reagan was not playing the "reality representation game," where critical questions, "reality testing," are appropriate. So they did not ask whether that "American spirit which knows no ethnic, religious boundaries" was the same one that had lynched so many blacks, beaten so many Catholics, ridden so many Mormons and Jehovah's Witnesses out on rails.[9] Nor did they ask how the Reagan administration would treat the boat people of Cuba and of Haiti, or the refugees of El Salvador. Instead, sensing the mythic nation mode, the audience could relax, suspend its disbelief, and bask in the warm glow of belonging—a glow that radiated not only from, but back to, its source, Ronald Reagan.

In 1984, Reagan expanded the mythic nation theme to fill an entire, dazzling campaign. His speeches avoided issues altogether, and he refused to respond to questions about them from the press. Instead, with the flag as his "constant icon" (Lemann 1985, p. 266), "bathed in a glowing shadowless light suitable for a stage play," appearing before "backdrops coated in cerulean paint that complemented his skin tones" (Raines 1984), introduced by the unofficial campaign song, "I'm Proud to Be an American," Reagan appealed to Americans' shared patriotism and nostalgia by invoking American heroes of past and present, and themes of optimism, strength, and happiness. This "overarching message and showmanship allow[ed] him to reach across conventional boundaries of constituency support," wrote one analyst, who dubbed Reagan's "the campaign . . . of the future" (Raines 1984).

Of course, all politicians use such devices for raising support without discussing issues.[10] The danger is that U.S. politicians, unencumbered by the demands of a party to be programmatic, will rely too heavily on such unifying divergences, and not speak at all to the divisive, but crucial, questions: Who governs? Who benefits? Who ought to? Who stands for whom? As the data amply illustrate, that danger walks among us.

Flow Tide For Consultants

This vacuity on the hustings has grown worse since the 1950s, when politicians were introduced to the public relations industry (Sabato 1981, p. 12). By that time, the party organizations and their ward heelers had all but withered away in the desert of "urban reform," the assault against parties described earlier. Politicians looked for a new way to campaign. Of course, the meeting of brokerage politicians and an industry devoted to merchandising was love at first sight; here were pollsters who could divine which themes were likely to be popular,[11] and media savants who could wrap those themes in irresistible packages. Given the devotion to the bottom line that public relations people learned while serving industry, it is not surprising that the themes chosen often have little to do with issues. Jimmy Carter's media advisor was once asked, "What do you believe in?" His credo was brief: "Winning the presidency." A prominent pollster who shares that philosophy spells out its implications for campaigning: "Too many good people have been defeated because they tried to substitute substance for style" (quoted in Sabato 1981, p. 144).

Increasingly, the major product of this consulting industry is the television commercial. The most careful survey of these "spots" concludes that most of them are "carbon cop[ies]" of the "parade of symbols, flashing photographs, and easy-whistling music" used in product advertising (Patterson and McClure 1976, pp. 101, 103).[12] A more recent study adds that issue content in political "spots" has waned during the period that the influence of consultants has waxed. Recently, only about 15 percent of ads "reveal a candidate issue position that could be called specific" (Joslyn 1980, p. 96).

That figure may be permanently reduced by the stunning success of Ronald Reagan's 1984 television campaign. Prepared by a "Madison Avenue all star team," the commercials used "poignant music and soft, sun-dappled scenes of life in a small town as a way of conveying what Reagan had done for America. Footage of the candidate himself was in the same genial, nonspecific mold. The makers of the ads quite openly modeled them on successful campaigns for companies, such as Pepsi-Cola and McDonald's, that felt that identifying themselves with a happy America was more effective than making specific claims about their products" (Lemann 1985, p. 266).

A Party Abdicates

In 1968, issuelessness was exacerbated again, this time by a national party organization. In that summer, rage against the absence of alternatives visited the streets of Chicago, where the Democrats were nominating a presidential candidate:

On Monday... fighting broke out at a rally in Grant Park... near the hotels where most of the delegates were staying.... That night scores of people were beaten badly enough [by police] to require hospital treatment, including twenty newsmen.... The famous battle of Michigan Avenue was fought in front of the Hilton on Wednesday night, with mass clubbings, people shoved through broken restaurant windows, chased into the lobby of the hotel, and all of it captured on television in one of the most dramatic moments in the history of the medium (Royko 1971, pp. 187–88).

Before it was over, even the party elites assembled in the convention hall realized that somehow, those outside, in the streets, had to be brought inside the party process. The way they did it was quintessentially American. As shepherds of state and local party organizations that were autonomous, ideologically various, and sometimes still reliant on patronage, these elites were interested above all in nominating candidates with "broad appeal" who could win elections. They were not, then, in a position to decide henceforth to nominate candidates who would stand clear on the issues and distinct from the other party, even if that was exactly what was being demanded in Chicago's streets. Instead, shrewdly, they decided to "open up" the nominating process to rank and file party identifiers. In 1968, a majority of delegates to the national nominating convention was chosen by state party organizations. By 1980, 71 percent of the delegates were chosen in primary elections.[13]

Like the states' move to primary elections a half-century earlier, this move took brokerage party behavior a step further. No longer does the party organization select a candidate, which it then tries to merchandise; instead, it now offers a showroom full of candidates from which to choose. What is worse, the choice has fallen to an electorate still untutored in the party's ideology. Over half the self-designated Democrats in the country don't know the difference between the Democrats and the Republicans on the watershed question of government responsibility for insuring employment or an acceptable standard of living (Sorauf 1984, p. 404). Such nescience leaves these nominators especially susceptible to the snake oil of the image salesman.[14] Worst of all, the primary electorate is even more heavily biased toward an upper class point of view than are general-election voters. "In primaries compared to general elections, the affluent are over-represented by a margin of 41.8 percent, the better educated by...94 percent, and blacks are underrepresented by...35.6 percent" (Edsall 1984, pp. 54–55; also Polsby 1983, p. 158). This upper class primary electorate has undoubtedly moved the discourse of presidential aspirants to the Right—especially on the economic issues so vital to those left behind by the latest wave of party "reform" (Edsall 1984, p. 56).

Citizen Response to Brokerage Politics: Tune Out, Turn Off, Drop Out

Tune Out

When candidates speak clearly, voters hear and understand them. In 1972, for example, when George McGovern boldly opposed the Vietnam War, 88 percent of voters were able to label him a "dove" (Page 1978, p. 181). That is the exception. The rule is that candidates will be unclear, and so will voters. In 1968, for example, 57 percent of voters could see little or no difference between the candidates' positions on Vietnam, and those who did see a difference were badly divided about which candidate was more hawkish (Page 1978, p. 181). Again, during the 1984 campaign, a plurality of voters saw no difference between the two parties on 8 of 12 urgent issues (White and Morris 1984, p. 44).

Thus, despite the slightly more programmatic candidacies of Goldwater and McGovern,[15] despite the urgency of recent issues, voting on the basis of them remains rare. "Even dissenters of the view that voters make uninformed choices...have nonetheless found candidate image to be the most important factor in the voting decision" (Shienbaum 1984, p. 19). When asked to name the most important quality they sought in a president, 51 percent of Americans said "leadership," 43 percent said "honesty," 3 percent mentioned policy positions (Dionne 1980, p. 18). In the absence of plain talk, the frothy meringue of the image campaign has become the staple of the voting decision.

As issues failed to take the paramount place some political scientists reserved for them in the 1970s, so, of course, did ideology. The hope that the electorate was learning to bundle issues into consistent political philosophies that could guide future thinking about issues and elections seems to have been either a methodological mirage, or an ephemeral artifact of the isolated, programmatic Goldwater and McGovern candidacies. (For optimism about issues and ideology, see Miller et al. 1976, pp. 779–805; Pomper et al. 1972; for debunkers, see Shienbaum 1984, pp. 18–23; Margolis 1977; Hill and Luttbeg 1983, p. 48; Popkin et al. 1976; Sorauf 1984, pp. 402–03.)

When image is all, some amazing electoral prestidigitation becomes possible. By 1984, for example, the Reagan presidency had begun to repeal the New Deal, affecting net income losses for families with annual incomes of less than $15,000 per year, busting a major union out of existence, allowing unemployment to rise to levels unseen since the Depression, and treating workplace safety, environmental protection, and the massive deindustrialization that proceeded apace with benign neglect.

Even as this sustained assault on working and lower class people was going on, Reagan's diversionary public relations campaign kept them from voting for Democrats at the rate they had in the later Roosevelt years (Edsall 1984, p. 24). The image legerdemain we have already looked at enticed nearly half of all voters in union households, in families making less than $12,500 per year, and with less than a high school education to vote for Reagan in 1984. Almost 60 percent of those in families making between $12,500 and $25,000 voted for him (Lowi 1985, p. 291). Among these groups at least, Reagan was not so much a great communicator as he was a great illusionist. Even for those voters who somehow managed to discern the candidates' issue positions, they seemed to have ceased to matter. "At least 20 percent of those who reported voting for Reagan said they had 'important disagreements' with him on the issues" (Lowi 1985, p. 289).

Of course, an important contributor to both Reagan's victories was "economic performance," increasingly recognized by political scientists as a central criterion in voting decisions. But this too represents a triumph of illusion: for one thing, "economic performance" can be, and often is, manufactured for election years, in ways harmful to long-term economic growth (Kiewiet and Rivers 1985, p. 88). But more centrally, electoral outcomes should not have to depend on the vicissitudes of the boom and bust cycle, which will go on no matter which party is in power, but on a clear and consistent party debate over who should get what from the economy, and how. As the Reagan recovery illustrates, there is no such thing as an economy "strong" for everyone. Through it, unemployment has remained at its highest rate in 25 years, and the economic growth that occurred involved a massive dislocation of working people from high-paying, unionized jobs in manufacturing into non-unionized, lower paying jobs in the service and electronics sectors (Bluestone 1984).

Amazingly, even those left out of the recovery often accept its illusions: that a "strong leader" has produced an economy strong for everyone. If, in such "good times," in the land of opportunity, some millions fail to prosper, it must be their own fault (Feldman 1982; Schlozman and Verba 1979). Beset by such a view, the unemployed are far from taking arms against their outrageous fortune. In fact, most of them haven't the heart to vote: despite their urgent reasons for doing so, they are 15 percent less likely to vote than the employed (Schlozman and Verba 1979, p. 241). Such is the extent of the parties' failure to stand for the have not: in America, even the victim blames the victim.

Turn Off

The answer to a question posed earlier is no: voters are not fools. But they can be made fools of, and they have been. They have responded as people will when they are bested by swindlers—with inarticulate rage. The number of Americans agreeing with such statements as "The rich get richer and the poor get poorer," "What you think doesn't count very much any more," and "The government is pretty much run by a few big interests looking out for themselves" has more than doubled, going from 29 percent in the mid–1960s to about 60 percent by the 1980s (Lipset and Schneider 1983b; Miller 1983).[16] One aspect of this increased alienation has had, as we shall see, especially marked consequences: that is a decline in people's sense of political efficacy, an "estimation of their own personal capacity to comprehend and influence political events" (Lipset and Schneider 1983a, p. 19). It is measured by agreement with such statements as "I don't think public officials care what people like me think," which increased from 25 percent to 52 percent between 1960 and 1980 (Lipset and Schneider 1983a, p. 22). These alienated Americans come disproportionately from "the lower end of the socio-economic spectrum, among persons with a grade school education, and those who think of themselves as 'average working class' " (Hill and Luttbeg 1983, p. 129). Much of their frustration proceeds, as might be imagined, from a sense of being unrepresented (Hill and Luttbeg 1983, pp. 123–30).

One source of this increasing inefficacy has been the failure of political parties to take clear and different stands on the urgent issues that have arisen over the past two decades. Between 1964 and 1976, the number of Americans agreeing that political parties help to make "government pay a good deal of attention to what people think" declined from 40 to 17 percent (Shienbaum 1984, p. 29; Dennis 1980). Not surprisingly, Americans began to throw off their longstanding loyalty to the two major parties during this same period. Through 1964, about 36 percent of all Americans identified themselves as "strong" partisans. By 1982, that total had slipped to 26 percent. The proportion of Independents—those who refuse to identify with either political party—grew from 24 percent in the 1950s to 35 percent by 1980.

Drop Out

Finally, having decided that the choices parties offered were meaningless, voters stopped voting. Together, the declines in sense of efficacy and in party identification account for most of a precipitous turnout decline that began in the early 1960's, and has brought most of the nation to its lowest voting rates since mass voting began in the nineteenth century (Kleppner 1982, pp. 112, 129–30).

What is worse, this recent decline threatens to make our Victorian electorate into a Georgian electorate. Again, the voting remnant consists disproportionately of those with the educational wherewithal to see through smoke and mirrors, to their interest. It consists disproportionately of those who have reason to thank the system by laying their "civic duty" on its altar, even if they see no other reason for voting (Shienbaum 1984, p. 10).

Again, the pruned branches come disproportionately from the bottom of the tree. "The difference in presidential participation between the top and bottom income categories increased from 9.1 to 17.7 percentage points between [the pre- and post–1960] periods.... The difference between ... college attenders and those who had no more than a grade school education increased ... from 21.2 to 27.3 percentage points" (Kleppner 1982, p. 123). The disparity between white-collar professionals and blue-collar equipment operators grew from 24.2 to 33.0 percent between 1968 and 1980 (Edsall 1984, p. 185). By 1980, "the 40.3 percent of the population with incomes below $15,000 cast fewer votes...than the 29 percent of the population with incomes of $25,000 or more" (Edsall 1984, p. 181).[17]

With a Victorian electorate in place, a Dickensian society is not far behind. "People who don't vote, don't count" is one politician's blunt formulation (quoted in Kleppner 1982, p. 162), and a careful study has confirmed it: policymakers' agendas are likely to be in tune with those of citizens who are "active," not with those who are not (Verba and Nie 1972, pp. 304–08). Not surprisingly, the agenda of the upper class Americans who increasingly dominate our electorate is full of laissez faire non-responses to such problems as providing medical care, dignified work, and a decent standard of living. Working and lower class Americans, the increasingly silent majority, are more open to governmental action on these fronts (Kleppner 1982, p. 161).[18]

The results are already upon us. The first is partisan. Most of the dropouts from the electorate were supporters of that party which, heretofore, spoke capitalism with a working class accent: families with earned incomes below $10,000 are twice as likely to be Democrats as Republicans, and twice as likely to be Democrats as people whose family income is over $50,000 (Edsall 1984, p. 190).

But the more profound wages of a sinfully truncated electorate have to do with the public discourse that helps to shape public opinion. Whether or not a Republican majority is emerging, "the terms of political debate...have been fundamentally transformed" already (Chubb and Peterson 1985, p. 30). Insofar as they discuss issues and ideologies at all, politicians of both parties are now collapsing in a new center of gravity, farther than ever from the interests of working and lower class Americans.

Who Governs Public Opinion?

Without programmatic parties to organize them, ordinary citizens cannot be an electoral force. Control over politicians' deeds and words falls by default to those who don't need parties to be powerful.[19] Who are they?

The Bias of Interest Groups

The corporate elites who set out, after 1896, to save us from the dangers of democracy by wrecking parties had to find another, less dangerous way of holding officeholders responsible—not, this time, to the irrational hordes, but to those men of substance whose sound judgment should by rights prevail—*videlicet*, themselves. The horse they mounted and rode to power was the interest group (Kleppner et al. 1981, p. 141).

Later, a Panglossian school of political scientists called pluralists would see interest groups not as an alternative, but as a means to democracy. Not just "men of substance," but all citizens with urgent interests in common would coalesce to pursue them through interest group lobbying, bloc voting, campaign contributions, and so on (Bentley 1949; Truman 1958; Dahl 1956). In this way, people's interests would be represented, without all the nasty class conflict that programmatic parties entail.

The rooftree of history has fallen in upon this sanguineness. The party-wreckers were right when they supposed that interest groups would be made up mainly of moguls like themselves. While 80 percent of upper status Americans are members of some kind of organization, only 45 percent of lower status Americans are, and most of them are not active members (Verba and Nie 1972, p. 204). Fifty-eight percent of all registered lobbyists in the American states represent business, and business lobbyists are "far and away the most likely to be identified as powerful by legislators" (Zeigler and van Dalen 1976, pp. 110–11).

Mancur Olson's landmark book *The Logic of Collective Action* shows the error of the pluralist way. The pluralists' basic assumption is that, ordinarily, political behavior will be motivated by material self-interest (Olson 1971, p. 8). But if the pluralist assumption is right, then pluralism, as a political system, is wrong: groups with common political interests will not spontaneously coalesce to pursue them. That is especially true if the group is large and the resources of each member are small. In that case, the rationally self-interested will say to themselves:

1. My widow's mite will not "make" the group's efforts, or break them if I withhold it.
2. Because the group is interested in *political* prizes ("collective goods"), I cannot be excluded from the benefit (of the tax break, the public park, or whatever our common interest is) even if I choose not to help secure it.
3. Therefore, the rational thing to be is a "free rider": I should withhold my contribution, let others work to secure a benefit, which will then accrue to me as well.

This logic of collective inaction explains why only a tiny fraction of the public supports public interest groups: only a "chemical trace" of blacks support the NAACP, of environment lovers support the Wilderness Society; of consumers support the Nader organization, and so on (the metaphor is Schattschneider's 1960, p. 13).

This logic does not explain of course, how some private interests have managed to become ominously well organized. "The large and powerful economic lobbies are ... by-products of organizations that obtain their strength and support because they perform some function in addition to lobbying for collective goals" (Olson 1971, p. 132). The definitive case is the business corporation, which, of course, commands the resources of stockholders by promising private profit and, then, in pursuit of that profit, uses those enormous resources to seek corporate political objectives. More than 500 corporations now operate Washington lobbies. The Ford Motor Company alone, for example, now has about 40 lobbyists at work in Washington (*Time* 1978, p. 15). Similarly, trade and professional associations have grown gargantuan by offering private benefits such as a trade or professional journal to attract members and then using members' resources to pursue their political interests. The American Medical Association and the National Automobile Dealer's Association, for example, are among the most formidable lobbies in the country.

In general, this logic of interest group formation tends to include the "haves" and exclude the "have-nots." The exception to the rule is, of course, labor unions, which try to address the free-rider problem by making membership compulsory, via the "union shop."

But unions remain an exception, a footnote to the rule that interest groups are dominated by the upper class. In part, this is a tribute to the power of business lobbying against union organization and against the union shop (Olson 1971, p. 78). Today, only about 18 percent of the U.S. work force is unionized.

The Harvest of Bias: Money Talks

Together, the organization and affluence of upper class Americans, along with their propensity to vote, have made them heirs to the throne that parties might have filled with the *popularis*. Instead, a patrician class now presides, not only over public policy, but over public discourse and over the public opinion that discourse helps to create.

Evidence of this oligarchy abounds. For example, almost 75 percent of all interest group contributions to federal candidates now come from a conservative or pro-business point of view;[20] 24 percent come from labor (Jacobson 1985, p. 148). And this disparity is rapidly worsening. Because of restrictions in federal campaign finance laws, corporations came late to setting up the political action committees through which interest groups now make contributions. The current disparity reflects a situation in which many corporations still do not have PACs—and in which many corporate PACs are not yet running at full steam (Jacobson 1983, p. 59). That is why there is no leveling off in sight of a trendline that shows the corporate share of PAC contributions having grown by 13 percent over the last ten years, while labor's has declined by 26 percent.

A profile of individual contributors to campaigns shows a similar bias. Those in the profile's highest income groups represented 11.3 percent of the national population, but 60.2 percent of all contributors; those in the lowest categories, 48 percent of the population, but only 15.2 percent of all contributors (Jacobson 1980, p. 65). And these figures "do not reflect the *amount* of money each income group gives; if those figures were available, they would unquestionably show even greater strength among the affluent, whose contributions are much larger than those of the middle class and poor" (Edsall 1984, p. 98).

Of course, the class bias of campaign finance is nothing new, as we have already seen (for a history of *Who Shakes the Money Tree*, see Thayer 1973). But money, and the bias it represents, have gone from important to vital in our time, when campaigns are pressed by the expensive weaponry of mass mail, polling, and television, not by an army of party workers. The astronomical increases in campaign spending over the last 30 years tell that story: between 1900 and 1950, the amount spent on congressional campaigns remained about the same in constant dollars. "Since 1974, House campaign expenditures have grown by an average of about 17 percent (in constant dollars)" every two years (Jacobson 1985, p. 162). The kind of "free speech" that can sway an electorate grows more expensive every day.

The first effect of class bias in campaign finance is not, as one might expect, on which voices *prevail* at election time but on the primordial question of which voices are *heard*: "money probably has its greatest impact . . . in the shadowland of our politics where it is decided who will be a candidate for a party's nomination" (Heard 1962, p. 34; see also Alexander 1976, p. 44). Dissenters from the status quo are unlikely to be able to raise even the entry fees for a viable candidacy, and to drop out before the race begins (Domhoff 1978, p. 144). The second effect of a privately financed election system is a windfall for the more conservative of the parties and for conservative candidates. In the 1981–82 election cycle, the Republican Party raised about five times as much money as the Democrats. Many scholars continue to attribute this disparity to the Republicans' earlier entry into computerized mail solicitation (Jacobson 1985, p. 151). But that theory has grown thin. The Democrats have now been using direct mail since 1980, and the gap between the parties is, if anything, widening (Jacobson 1985, p. 158). Curiously, scholars and journalists have resisted an obvious explanation: the income profile of money contributors looks a lot like the profile of Republican party identifiers; it also looks like the Democratic Party profile—turned upside down (Edsall 1984, p. 70). This Republican advantage, together with an edge in independent spending by PACs, meant that $10 million more was spent for Ronald Reagan than for Jimmy Carter in 1980 (Alexander 1984, p. 20).

Such superior spending on behalf of conservatives is not without its effects on the public mind. A New York *Times* computer analysis of spending and voting in the 1982 election suggests that the Republican

Party's "fundraising advantages played a critical role in preserving Republican seats." Leaders of the Democratic and Republican National Committees agreed that "the money advantage alone gave them 10 or 12 seats" (Clymer 1982, p. 1).

Nor has the bias of finance been without effect on the hearts and minds of politicians. "The acquisition of campaign funds has become an obsession on the part of nearly every candidate for federal office. The obsession leads the candidates to solicit and accept money from those most able to provide it, and to adjust their behavior in office to the need for money" (Drew 1983, p. 1). This is easiest to document when it translates into policy votes. For example, Kirk Brown's excellent study of congressional votes on two interest group sponsored bills controls for the influence of party and ideology on the votes and then concludes "that the [American Medical Association's and National Auto Dealer's Association's] campaign contributions of over $1.5 million to House members during the 1982 election provided the margin of victory" (1983, p. 49).

But money has changed more than particular policy votes. It has helped produce what is no less than a sea change in elite attitudes. The affluence of money givers and voters has helped make the Republican Party an increasingly cohesive voice for capitalist individualism (Edsall 1984, ch. 2). Republican congressional unity in support of the Reagan program has been "unusually high by historic standards" (Reichley 1985a, p. 197). Unfortunately, the influence of affluence has made the Democrats a more incoherent and, when push comes to shove, craven party than ever. In 1980, the Democratic National Committee created a "Democratic Business Council," which, according to DNC literature, provides the party's leadership with "business expertise" on "current and proposed legislation." The DNC also established its "Lexington Club" for patrons who donate $25,000 or more a year to the party. One of its express aims is to recruit businessmen to run as Democratic candidates. Meanwhile Representative Tony Coelho, chairman of the Democratic Congressional Campaign Committee, began working hard "to convince the business community that Democrats understand its needs and are thus deserving of business PAC support." And business interests have seen the wisdom of supporting at least incumbent Democrats. In recent elections the average Democratic House candidate has received as much money from corporate, trade, and professional PACs as from labor PACs—in sharp contrast to the early 1970s, when organized labor provided more than three times as much Democratic PAC money as business-oriented groups (Jacobson 1985, p. 167). Coincidentally, in 1981, congressional Democrats' formal response to Reagan's plan to repeal the New Deal and the Great Society began by praising the "bold new plan." "There is much in the President's program that most of us can enthusiastically embrace ... [including] refurbishing the nation's defenses, encouraging private investment to modernize America's industrial machinery, [and] lifting the burden of unnecessary government regulation" (in Tolchin 1981, p. 1). This Democratic "alternative" then went on to propose doing exactly what the Reagan budget proposed, with a pinch of moderation: it called for reductions of only 12 percent in social services spending instead of the 25 percent reduction Reagan wanted; and for an increase in defense spending of only $20 billion, instead of the $24 billion increase Reagan proposed.[21] But even the party leadership's nonalternative was not conservative enough to satisfy many members of the Democratic rank and file in Congress, who defected in droves to support, and carry the day for, the Reagan budget.

Later that year, Democrats engaged in a "bidding war" with Republicans, a contest to see which party could cut business taxes most. The "bidding," of course, was for PAC support (Drew 1983, p. 38). In 1982, the House Democratic Caucus published an "agenda for the future" that "strongly reflects the ... Democrats' interest in the [high-technology] industry as a source of funds." As one of the authors describes its proposals, it is "an attempt to say that Democrats are interested in growth—in the private sector and business growing and prospering" (Drew 1983, pp. 39, 50).

In 1984, the Democratic presidential candidate campaigned on a party platform described by the New York *Times* as "considerably more conservative" than its recent predecessors (Weaver 1984, p. 1). In his nomination acceptance speech, Walter Mondale invited listeners to "look at our platform. There are no defense cuts that weaken our security, no business taxes that weaken our economy, no laundry lists that raid our treasury," such as the national health insurance or jobs programs that had graced earlier Democratic platforms, but were gone by 1984 (New York *Times* 1984, p. 12).

Warming up for the 1988 presidential contest, the two front-running Democratic aspirants have pointedly dissociated themselves from New Deal liberalism. It has "run out of ideas," says Gary Hart (in Ladd 1982, p. 112). Mario Cuomo talks of how he laughed when a commentator associated him with that shopworn philosophy, and adds, "What are you when you reduce public employees ... when you come out for a tax cut ... when you spend more on the defense budget, which we call corrections, than any governor in history?" (quoted in Barnes 1985, p. 18).

The Democrats afflicted by this virulent contagion from the Right, as well as the commentators who approve of their affliction, argue that they caught it from "the people." They are wrong. The "conservative trend" in U.S. public opinion is a myth, concludes a recent comprehensive survey of poll data. Remarkably, as even Democratic politicians recanted, the public resisted. "There is little direct evidence that mass public sentiment has turned against the domestic programs of the New Deal, or even the most important components of the Great Society.... On the contrary, poll after poll demonstrates that the basic structure of public opinion in the United States has remained relatively stable in recent years" (Ferguson and Rogers 1986, p. 44).

Earlier, this chapter characterized that basic structure as liberal in the concrete, conservative in the abstract. We have argued that Americans were taught to think in that "schizophrenic" way by the double-binding rhetoric of post-New Deal Democracy: a limited collectivism was practiced, while capitalist individualism was preached. But even that limited collectivism is increasingly absent from the preachments and practices of Democrats in the 1980s. Can public opinion be far behind? Can it long withstand the new common sense?

Lobbying the People

Of course, monied interests have not been content to cultivate public opinion through the trickle-down of politicians' discourse alone. They have also worked the grass roots directly.

In 1978 a congressional committee estimated that corporations were spending $1 billion a year on political advertising—selling, not a product, but a point of view. The message of this advertising is, of course, that what's good for corporate America is good for America: "the most consistent theme... has been a sustained attack on the use of government money and regulation to solve social problems" (Edsall 1984, p. 117). Mobil Oil Corporation, for example, now spends about $30 million a year on "public affairs." One of the things its money buys is a regularly appearing column on the editorial pages of the New York *Times*, the Washington *Post*, the Chicago *Tribune*, *Time* magazine, and six other leading national news publications (Berry 1984, p. 140). While these "op eds" are aimed at opinion leaders, "Observations," another Mobil-produced column, is aimed at a popular audience. It reaches 80 million adult readers in Sunday newspaper supplements every other week. The Mobil vice-president in charge of lobbying the public points proudly to surveys showing that people exposed to the column "have a greater affinity for the free-market economy... than those with similar... characteristics who are not exposed" (Berkman and Kitch 1986, p. 283). Mobil also produces television commercials, often dressed to look like news programs and aired during local newscasts, as well as half-hour "documentaries" featuring "journalists" interviewing Mobil executives and other experts who favor Mobil's policies. Local stations can air these programs *in toto* or break them into interview segments for use in newscasts. The company also wages "media blitzes." Recently, 21 of its executives were dispatched to 21 target cities, where they appeared on more than 100 talk shows, news broadcasts, and radio call-in programs, as well as meeting with local editors (Berkman and Kitch 1986, pp. 283–90).

And Mobil is not an exception; it is just part of the large corporate movement to rewrite the rule. For example, "with an annual budget of only $2 million" the corporate-funded Advertising Council places about $500 million worth of free "public service announcements" on radio, television, newspapers, magazines, and buses each year (Domhoff 1978, p. 184). Sometimes these messages are naked ideology: "Today the research efforts of U.S. industry are actually lagging because of costly government regulations and discouraging taxation," warns one (cited in Berkman and Kitch 1986, p. 241). Usually, they are more subtle—and sinister—defining, for example, pollution as a function of the lassitude of litterbugs, not of corporations (Berkman and Kitch 1986, p. 292). And Madison Avenue isn't the only road to the public mind. The U.S. Chamber of Commerce, perhaps the most powerful lobby in the country, is now a "communications conglomerate," in the words of its president. Its "subsidiaries" include a monthly magazine and a weekly newspaper, each with a circulation of about 1 million; a television program of non-freewheeling "discussion and debate," carried by 150 TV stations; and a similar radio show carried by 400 stations (Loomis 1983, p. 182).

Then there is the schoolhouse road. "The public affairs departments of large corporations produce a great deal of educational material (pamphlets, film strips, and comic books), which they give away to school systems for use in the classroom. The purpose is to instill—critics say to propagandize—in students appreciation for business contributions to the well-being of America" (Berry 1984, p. 141).

The potential of corporate political advertising is written on the wall by a recent study of referendum campaigns. On an average, business outspent the public-interest groups that opposed them in these campaigns by a ratio of 27 to 1. Of the 14 campaigns studied, business prevailed in all but 3 (Lydenberg 1981).

Perhaps an even darker portent has been business' ability to help direct the unformed discontents of so much of rootless, religious America. The money that launched such flagships of the New Right as the Committee for the Survival of a Free Congress, the American Legislative Exchange Council, and the Liberty Lobby was plutocrat money (Bollier 1982, pp. 15–38; Crawford 1980, ch. 1). The CSFC, for example, has invested its talents wisely, building an "outstanding" nationwide network of grassroots precinct organizations for conservative congressional candidates (Crawford 1980, pp. 15–16).

Since their founding in the late 1970s, these and other New Right organizations have nursed the "social issues" grievances of white, fundamentalist America, but added an odd balm to the treatment: heavy doses of capitalist individualism. They have produced "an emerging political force in U.S. politics" (quoted in Reichley 1985b, p. 324).

Finally, money even bought the opinion beyond price—scholarly opinion. Corporations did it by endowing "think tanks," thus providing the time, research resources, and collegial setting in which conservative scholars and their words could flourish. For example, the conservative Heritage Foundation, endowed by such corporate arch-champions of free enterprise as Joseph Coors, Richard Mellon Scaife, and William Simon saw its budget grow from about $1 million in 1976 to over $7 million by 1981. Similar growth, sources of support, and ideologies can be found in the Hoover Institution, the American Enterprise Institute, the National Bureau of Economic Research, a large number of smaller academies, a host of endowed university chairs, and a plethora of conservative scholarly journals (Edsall 1984, pp. 117–20). The most thoughtful study of the "neo-conservatism" springing from the brow of this corporate support describes the process this way:

Talent is always a scarce resource, and neoconservatives have discovered an old-fashioned means to deal with scarcity—money. Nelson Rockefeller's late Commission on Critical Choices offered [two neoconservative scholars] $100,000 to obtain on short order fifteen essays analyzing "the ideas and values of human nature inherent in U.S. institutions. . . ." As one scholar, accustomed to receiving fees of $75 to $300 from liberal journals . . . remarked of this windfall, "It certainly clears one's calendar and concentrates the mind" (Steinfels 1979, p. 13).

From these opinion leaders in academia, journalists, politicians, and eventually the public have learned "the" conservative alternative to the liberal economic and foreign policies that seemed, by the late 1970s, to be manifest failures.[22] Of course, there was another alternative—the one on the Left—but it was less heavily endowed, and so less widely disseminated.

CONCLUSION?

Today, the plutocracy's 200-year war on political parties is all but won. The people's only organizing engine is all but wrecked; the heart, the promise of democracy, all but broken. In its stead, churning ahead with terrible efficiency, the engines of hegemony carry us ever farther from what we might have been.

NOTES

1. The terms "brokerage" and "programmatic" party are from Epstein (1967, ch. 10).

2. "High" is in the eye of the beholder. The statistical likelihood, from frontier days to the present, has been that "the race will be to the well born" (Pessen 1969, p. 349). And Sombart's observation that the U.S. working class was weighted down with "apple pie and roast beef" was made at a time when 11 of 12 million Americans had annual incomes below $1,200. Among these families, the average annual income was $380, well below the "accepted poverty line." About half of all U.S. families had no real property (Trachtenberg 1982, p. 99).

3. Although it can certainly be argued that racial and ethnic divisions were often fostered by party elites, as well as by businessmen (see below, on the creation of the "system of 1896"); that the early extension of the franchise was a "passive revolution" carried out by political elites with the express purpose of mollifying working class discontent (Ginsberg 1982); and that the partisan rhetoric of an affluent, classless society far surpassed the often squalid reality. Others have argued that, however they came about, these phenomena are simply not adequate to account for the absence of a working class party (Katznelson 1981, ch. 1; Lipset 1984).

4. For a description of this process of recurrent "realignment," see Burnham (1970).

5. There were, of course, additional reasons for Bryan's defeat. For example, 1896 may have been merely a continuation of the trend set in 1893–94 when voters began to move away from the Democratic "party of depression" (Burnham 1982, p. 49). On the other hand, the kind of realignment that occurred in 1896 suggests that most voters were well aware that this new Democracy of Bryan was not the Democracy of Cleveland. It is also possible that Bryan, as an Anglo-Saxon, Protestant, dry, rural Westerner, was the wrong candidate for the Eastern polyglot working class (Burnham 1982, p. 50). Hollingsworth, for one, doubts this had much effect. It was the Republicans, not Bryan, who continued to play the "nativist card," and Bryan did better among immigrants than among any other urban group (Hollingsworth 1963, p. 98). Finally, it is certainly true that Bryan spent too little time among and said too little of interest to urban laborers (Burnham 1982, p. 49). At the same time, it should be pointed out that, for their own reasons, Democratic machine lieutenants in Eastern cities did try to win support for Bryan among workers. So long as Bryan headed the party, these often-Irish lieutenants would remain generals, replacing the Brahmin Anglo-Saxons who had renounced the party after the "blatherskite's" nomination (Hollingsworth 1963, pp. 99–100).

6. For a longer discussion of the uses of nativism in establishing hegemony, see Chapter 7.

7. Because it is hard for issues to survive without party competition, it is also hard to sort out the independent effects of these two variables. But what evidence there is hints that the death of important issues was by no means a spurious factor. In Ohio, for example, competition did not decline steeply as it did in other Northern states, but turnout did (Burnham 1982, p. 38).

8. In other industrialized Western nations, where socialist parties speak clearly to the needs of working class and poor people, turnout at elections is frequently 30–40 percent higher than in the United States.

9. For a fuller account of American racism and nativism, see Chapter 7.

10. Another popular game is the "threat and reassurance" game, which helps

us externalize anxieties. See Edelman 1971, pp. 77–78; Elder and Cobb 1983, p. 67). Its bogey, in the postwar era, has been the "communist menace," the "Evil Empire," the "bear in the woods."

11. Politicians and pollsters have argued that building a campaign around the cues provided by public opinion polls is the democratic way. That might be true if this "public opinion" had been formed after a careful presentation, by the parties, of political alternatives. But of course no such presentation is made, partly because the polls advise against it. The result is the "public opinion" of Plato's cave dwellers. On issues and ideologies, it is ill informed, inconsistent, evanescent (Erikson, Luttbeg, and Tedin 1980, ch. 2). Instead, it mistakes the "candidate images" projected on the cave wall for the substance of the campaign. Creating such a "public opinion," "following" it, and calling that democracy is an irony of Orwellian proportion.

12. The authors' more widely cited finding is that many political commercials do "contain substantial information" (Patterson and McClure 1976, p. 102). Two caveats are in order here. First, their survey was of the 1972 presidential campaign, an unusually programmatic one by recent standards (Page 1978, p. 103). But more importantly, the finding that some commercials articulated candidates' issue positions was based on an extravagantly generous definition of "issue stand." For example, The Nixon campaign most frequently communicated four issue stands:

—Richard Nixon favored honoring our commitments to other nations.
—Richard Nixon had done an effective job of handling China.
—Richard Nixon had done an effective job of handling Russia.
—Richard Nixon did not favor spending less money on the military
  (Patterson and McClure 1980, p. 328).

But surely an "issue stand" is something about which not everyone agrees, and which advocates or opposes a policy. By these criteria, the first three statements listed above fail to be "issue stands."

13. Since 1980, the Democrats, still tampering with failure, have retrenched slightly from primaries, and selected more delegates in open caucuses, *ex officio*, and by state committee. In 1984, 55 percent of all delegates were chosen in primaries (Wekkin 1984, pp. 186–87).

14. It is possible that the party might have become more programmatic if nominations had been left in the hands of party-organization activists. They have always been more aware of party ideology than the rank and file (Jackson, Brown, and Bositis 1982). And recently, one of their incentives for nominating broker-age-style candidates has eroded: continued encroachment on state and local patronage by civil service systems has meant the gradual replacement of party "professionals" with "amateurs" more interested in purity and less interested in victory (Hirschfield, Swanson, and Blank 1962; Wilson 1962; Owen and Margolis 1983, pp. 19–20).

15. Page argues that the clarity of McGovern, while an improvement over the norm, has been overrated (1978, pp. 55–56). Nonetheless, issue voting and ideological consistency did increase significantly in both the Goldwater and McGovern years (Nie, Verba, and Petrocik 1979, p. 375).

16. Recently, pollsters have noted a small "uptick" in a few trust measures

asking specifically about "the government in Washington." In part, this reflects the appreciation of the alienated Right that Ronald Reagan has finally taken a stand, and done something about, their agenda (Miller 1983, p. 19). The alienated Left, of course, awaits its voice.

17. Edsall points out that these figures, based on census data, "probably understate the voting disparity between rich and poor, because the nonvoting poor tend to claim more often that they have voted than do nonvoters from other income groups" (1984, pp. 181–82).

18. Apologists for this Victorian "democracy" point out that, in some elections at least, non-voters' preferences as between the two available candidates did not differ substantially from those of voters, and would not have changed election outcomes (Wolfinger and Rosenstone 1980). But this is precisely why many nonvoters drop out: the failure of the "available candidates" to speak clearly to the needs of working and lower class people leaves this group no choice that would differ from that of middle class voters. A recent study concludes that the "lack of a clear choice" between candidates and the lack of any candidate close to one's own position are strongly related to non-voting, even as a host of factors usually used to explain non-voting are controlled. The author attributes this feeling of being unrepresented to our single-member district, plurality rule election system that discourages non-centrist third parties and makes the "third choice" non-voting. He points out that a similar pattern of non-voting among the working class obtains in Canada—except where the socialist third party is a voting option (Zipp 1985). A further argument is that policy preferences of non-voters do not differ much from those of voters. How could they, when neither party has yet articulated policy possibilities that differ much from those of the other? Until a working class alternative is formulated, support for it among non-voters will have to remain "latent" (Schlozman and Verba 1979, p. 209).

19. Zeigler and van Dalen (1976, p. 95) show that interest groups are weak where parties are coherent, and strong where they are not.

20. In 1980, corporate political action committees made up 35 percent of all interest group contributions; trade and professional associations, 29 percent; and predominantly conservative "independent" PACs, 12 percent. Together, they made up 76 percent of all interest group contributions. In addition to these direct contributions to campaigns, which are limited in size by federal election law, independent PACs also mount their own campaigns, usually on behalf of conservative candidates and against liberals. These expenditures are not limited by law.

21. The Democratic conservatism of the 1980s is often attributed to Ronald Reagan's having produced a "mandate" for such policies. In fact, it preceded Ronald Reagan. For example, Jimmy Carter, who often referred to himself as a "farmer, a businessman, and a scientist" spent his last year in office increasing defense spending while cutting social services spending.

22. Of course, the relationship of scholars, dollars, and the policy formation process is older than neo-conservatism. Such important "policy-planning and consensus-seeking organizations of the power elite" as the Council on Foreign Relations and the Committee for Economic Development were created decades ago. But they represented an individualism leavened by Progressive and New Deal ingredients. " 'Nonpartisan' and 'objective' are the passwords" (Domhoff

1978, p. 62). The new objects of corporate largesse represent a more unadorned conservatism. One of them has recently published a manual to help corporate donors "determine what a potential grant recipient represents politically." The manual, praised by corporate executives as aiding "the cause of good government in a free society," "succinctly criticizes ideological waffling" (Ethics and Public Policy Center catalog 1986, p. 29).

REFERENCES

Alexander, Herbert. 1984. "Making Sense about Dollars in the 1980 Presidential Campaigns." In *Money and Politics in the United States*, edited by Michael J. Malbin, pp. 11–37. Chatham, N.J.: Chatham House.

———. 1976. *Financing Politics*. Washington, D.C.: Congressional Quarterly Press.

Alford, Robert R., and Eugene C. Lee. 1968. "Voting Turnout in American Cities." *American Political Science Review* 62:796–813.

Barnes, Fred. 1985. "Meet Mario the Moderate." *New Republic*, April 8, pp. 17–20.

Beard, Charles. 1962. *The Supreme Court and the Constitution*. Englewood Cliffs, N.J.: Prentice-Hall.

Bentley, Arthur. 1949. *The Process of Government*. Evanston, Ill.: Principia Press.

Berkman, Ronald, and Laura W. Kitch. 1986. *Politics in the Media Age*. New York: McGraw-Hill.

Berry, Jeffrey M. 1984. *The Interest Group Society*. Boston: Little, Brown.

Bluestone, Barry. 1984. "Hidden Traps on the Road to Economic Recovery." *Scholastic Update*, December 14, pp. 10–11.

Bollier, David. 1982. *Liberty and Justice for Some*. New York: Frederick Ungar.

Brown, Kirk F. 1983. "Campaign Contributions and Congressional Voting." Paper presented at the annual meeting of the American Political Science Association, Chicago.

Burnham, Walter Dean. 1982. *The Current Crisis in American Politics*. New York: Oxford University Press.

———. 1970. *Critical Elections*. New York: W. W. Norton.

Campbell, Angus, Gerald Gurin, and Warren E. Miller. 1954. *The Voter Decides*. Evanston, Ill.: Row, Peterson.

Chubb, John E., and Paul E. Peterson. 1985. "Realignment and Institutionalization." In *The New Direction in American Politics*, edited by John E. Chubb and Paul E. Peterson, pp. 1–33. Washington, D.C.: Brookings.

Clymer, Adam. 1982. "Campaign Funds Called a Key to House Races." New York *Times*, November 5, p. 1.

Crawford, Alan. 1980. *Thunder on the Right*. New York: Pantheon Books.

Dahl, Robert. 1956. *A Preface to Democratic Theory*. Chicago: University of Chicago Press.

Dennis, Jack. 1980. "Changing Public Support for the American Party System." In *Paths to Political Reform*, edited by William J. Crotty, pp. 35–66. Lexington, Mass.: D. C. Heath.

Dionne, E. J. 1980. "Definitions of Character Found Elusive to Voters." New York *Times*, October 31, p. 18.

Domhoff, G. William. 1978. *The Powers That Be*. New York: Random House.

Drew, Elizabeth. 1983. *Politics and Money*. New York: Macmillan.

Ebner, Michael H., and Eugene M. Tobin. 1977. "The Age of Urban Reform." In *The Age of Urban Reform*, edited by Michael H. Ebner and Eugene M. Tobin, pp. 3–12. Port Washington, N.Y.: Kennikat Press.

Edelman, Murray. 1971. *Politics as Symbolic Action*. Chicago: Markham.

Edsall, Thomas Byrne. 1984. *The New Politics of Inequality*. New York: W. W. Norton.

Elder, Charles D., and Roger W. Cobb. 1983. *The Political Uses of Symbols*. New York: Longman.

Epstein, Leon D. 1967. *Political Parties in Western Democracies*. New York: Praeger.

Erikson, Robert S., Norman R. Luttbeg, and Kent L. Tedin. 1980. *American Public Opinion*. 2nd ed. New York: John Wiley and Sons.

Exoo, Calvin F. 1983. "Ethnic Culture and Political Language in Two American Cities." *The Journal of Ethnic Studies* 11:79–105.

Feldman, Stanley. 1982. "Economic Self Interest and Political Behavior." *American Journal of Political Science* 26: 446–66.

Ferguson, Thomas, and Joel Rogers. 1986. "The Myth of America's Turn to the Right." *The Atlantic Monthly*, May, pp. 43–53.

Formisano, Ronald P. 1983. *The Transformation of Political Culture*. New York: Oxford University Press.

Free, Lloyd A., and Hadley Cantril. 1968. *The Political Beliefs of Americans*. New York: Simon and Schuster.

Ginsberg, Benjamin. 1982. *The Consequences of Consent*. New York: Random House.

Goodwyn, Lawrence. 1976. *Democratic Promise*. New York: Oxford University Press.

Grodzins, Morton. 1960. "American Political Parties and the American System." *Western Political Quarterly* XIII: 974–98.

Harrington, Michael. 1984. "Comment on Pluralism and Political Parties." In *Failure of a Dream*, rev. ed., edited by John H. M. Laslett and Seymour Martin Lipset, pp. 523–29. Berkeley: University of California Press.

Hawley, Willis. 1973. *Nonpartisan Elections and the Case for Party Politics*. New York: Wiley.

Hays, Samuel P. 1964. "The Politics of Reform in Municipal Government in the Progressive Era." *Pacific Northwest Quarterly* 55:157–69.

Heard, Alexander. 1962. *The Costs of Democracy*. Garden City, N.Y.: Doubleday.

Hill, David B., and Norman R. Luttbeg. 1983. *Trends in American Electoral Behavior*. Itasca, Ill.: F. E. Peacock.

Hirschfield, Robert S., Bert E. Swanson, and Blanche D. Blank. 1962. "A Profile of Political Activists in Manhattan." *Western Political Quarterly* 15: 489–506.

Hollingsworth, J. Rogers. 1963. *The Whirligig of Politics*. Chicago: University of Chicago Press.

Jackson, John S., Barbara L. Brown, and David Bositis. 1982. "Herbert McClosky and Friends Revisited: 1980 Democratic and Republican Party Elites Compared to the Mass Public." *American Politics Quarterly* 10: 158–80.

Jacobson, Gary C. 1985. "The Republican Advantage in Campaign Finance." In *The New Direction in American Politics*, edited by John E. Chubb and Paul E. Peterson, pp. 143–74. Washington, D.C.: Brookings.

————. 1983. *The Politics of Congressional Elections*. Boston: Little, Brown.

————. 1980. *Money in Congressional Elections*. New Haven: Yale University Press.

Jencks, Christopher, et al. 1979. *Who Gets Ahead?* New York: Basic Books.

Joslyn, Richard A. 1980. "The Content of Political Spot Ads." *Journalism Quarterly* 57: 92–98.

Judd, Dennis R. 1979. *The Politics of American Cities*. Boston: Little, Brown.

Katznelson, Ira. 1981. *City Trenches*. New York: Pantheon Books.

Key, V. O. 1956. *American State Politics*. New York: Alfred A. Knopf.

————. 1949. *Southern Politics in State and Nation*. New York: Alfred A. Knopf.

Kiewiet, D. Roderick, and Douglas Rivers. 1985. "The Economic Basis of Reagan's Appeal." In *The New Direction in American Politics*, edited by John E. Chubb and Paul E. Peterson, pp. 69–90. Washington, D.C.: Brookings.

Kleppner, Paul. 1982. *Who Voted?* New York: Praeger.

Kleppner, Paul, Walter Dean Burham, Ronald P. Formisano, Samuel P. Hays, Richard Jensen, and William G. Shade. 1981. *The Evolution of American Electoral Systems*. Westport, Conn.: Greenwood Press.

Ladd, Everett Carll. 1982. *Where Have All the Voters Gone?* New York: W. W. Norton.

Leinenweber, Charles. 1984. "Socialism and Ethnicity." In *Failure of a Dream*, rev. ed., edited by John H. M. Laslett and Seymour Martin Lipset, pp. 244–68. Berkeley: University of California Press.

Lemann, Nicholas. 1985. "Implications: What Americans Wanted." In *The Elections of 1984*, edited by Michael Nelson, pp. 259–76. Washington, D.C.: CQ Press.

Lindsay, Vachel. 1954. "Bryan, Bryan, Bryan, Bryan." In *A Pocket Book of Modern Verse*, edited by Oscar Williams, pp. 265–72. New York: Washington Square Press.

Lipset, Seymour Martin, and William Schneider. 1983a. *The Confidence Gap*. New York: The Free Press.

————. 1983b. "Confidence in Confidence Measures." *Public Opinion*, August,/September, pp. 42–44.

Loomis, Burdett A. 1983. "A New Era: Groups and the Grass Roots." In *Interest Group Politics*, edited by Alan J. Cigler and Burdett A. Loomis, pp. 169–90. Washington, D.C.: CQ Press.

Lowi, Theodore J. 1985. "An Aligning Election, A Presidential Plebiscite." In *The Elections of 1984*, edited by Michael Nelson, pp. 277–302. Washington, D.C.: CQ Press.

————. 1979. "Party, Policy, and Constitution in America." In *The American Party Systems*, 2nd ed., edited by William N. Chambers and Walter D. Burnham, pp. 238–76. New York: Oxford University Press.

Lydenberg, Steven D. 1981. *Bankrolling Ballots Update 1980*. New York: The Council on Economic Priorities.

McClosky, Herbert, Paul J. Hoffman, and Rosemary O'Hara. 1960. "Issue Conflict and Consensus among Party Leaders and Followers." *American Political Science Review* 54: 406–27.

McCormick, Richard P. 1975. "Political Development and the Second Party System." In *The American Party Systems*, 2nd ed., edited by William N. Chambers and Walter D. Burnham, pp. 90–117. New York: Oxford University Press.

Madison, James. 1964. "Federalist Number 51." In *The Federalist Papers*, by James Madison, Alexander Hamilton, and John Jay. Edited by Andrew Hacker, pp. 121–25. New York: Simon and Schuster.

Margolis, Michael. 1977. "From Confusion to Confusion: Issues and the American Voter, 1955–1972." *American Political Science Review* 71:31–43.

Miller, Arthur, 1983. "Is Confidence Rebounding?" *Public Opinion*, June/July, pp. 16–20.

Miller, Arthur H., Warren W. Miller, Alden S. Raine, and Thad A. Brown. 1976. "A Majority Party in Disarray: Policy Polarization in the 1972 Election." *American Political Science Review* 70:753–78.

Miller, William. 1968. *A New History of the United States*. Rev. ed. New York: Dell.

New York *Times*. 1984. "Text of Mondale Acceptance Speech." July 20, p. 12.

Nie, Norman H., Sidney Verba, and John R. Petrocik. 1979. *The Changing American Voter*, enlarged ed. Cambridge, Mass.: Harvard University Press.

Olson, Mancur. 1971. *The Logic of Collective Action*. Cambridge, Mass.: Harvard University Press.

Owen, Raymond E., and Michael Margolis. 1983. "From Organization to Personalism: The Demise of the Local Political Party." Paper presented at the annual meeting of the Northeastern Political Science Association, Philadelphia.

Page, Benjamin I. 1978. *Choices and Echoes in Presidential Elections*. Chicago: University of Chicago Press.

Patterson, Thomas E., and Robert D. McClure. 1980. "Television and Voters' Issue Awareness." In *The Party Symbol*, edited by William Crotty, pp. 324–34. San Francisco: W. H. Freeman.

———. 1976. *The Unseeing Eye*. New York: Putnam.

Pessen, Edward. 1969. *Jacksonian America*. Homewood, Ill.: Dorsey Press.

Pitkin, Hanna F. 1972. *Wittgenstein and Justice*. Berkeley: University of California Press.

Polsby, Nelson W. 1983. *Consequences of Party Reform*. New York: Oxford University Press.

Pomper, Gerald 1972. "From Confusion to Clarity: Issues and the American Voter." *American Political Science Review* 66: 389–400.

Popkin, Samuel, John W. Gorman, Charles Phillips, Jeffrey A. Smith. 1976. "Comment: What Have You Done for Me Lately? Toward an Investment Theory of Voting." *American Political Science Review* 70:779–805.

Rae, Douglas W. 1967. *The Political Consequences of Electoral Laws*. New Haven: Yale University Press.

Raines, Howell. 1984. "Reagan Appears to Succeed by Avoiding Specific Issues." New York *Times*, September 23, p. 1.

Ranney, Austin. 1983. "Nonvoting Is Not a Social Disease." *Public Opinion*, October/November, pp. 16–20.

———. 1976. "Parties in State Politics." In *Politics in the American States*, 3rd ed., edited by Herbert Jacob and Kenneth N. Vines, pp. 51–92. Boston: Little, Brown.

Reichley, A. James. 1985a. "The Rise of National Parties." In *The New Direction in American Politics*, edited by John E. Chubb and Paul E. Peterson, pp. 175–202. Washington, D.C.: Brookings.

———. 1985b. *Religion in American Public Life*. Washington, D.C.: Brookings.

Royko, Mike. 1971. *Boss*. New York: Signet.

Rubin, Richard L. 1981. *Press, Party, and Presidency*. New York: W. W. Norton.

Sabato, Larry J. 1981. *The Rise of Political Consultants*. New York: Basic Books.

Schattschneider, E. E. 1960. *The Semi-Sovereign People*. New York: Holt, Rinehart, and Winston.

Schlozman, Kay Lehman, and Sidney Verba. 1979. *Injury to Insult*. Cambridge, Mass.: Harvard University Press.

Shienbaum, Kim Ezra. 1984. *Beyond the Electoral Connection*. Philadelphia: University of Pennsylvania Press.

Smith, M. Brewster, Jerome Bruner, and Ralph White. 1964. *Opinions and Personality*. New York: Wiley.

Sombart, Werner. 1984. "American Capitalism's Economic Rewards." In *Failure of a Dream*, rev. ed., edited by John H. M. Laslett and Seymour Martin Lipset, pp. 452–67. Berkeley: University of California Press.

Sorauf, Frank J. 1984. *Party Politics in America*. Boston: Little, Brown.

Steinfels, Peter. 1979. *The Neoconservatives*. New York: Simon and Schuster.

Thayer, George. 1973. *Who Shakes the Money Tree?* New York: Simon and Schuster.

Thelen, David P. 1972. "Progressivism as a Radical Movement." In *Main Problems in American History*, vol. 2, edited by Howard H. Quint et al., Homewood, Ill.: Dorsey Press.

Thernstrom, Stephan. 1984. "Socialism and Social Mobility." In *Failure of a Dream*, rev. ed., edited by John H. M. Laslett and Seymour Martin Lipset, pp. 408–26. Berkeley: University of California Press.

Thomas, Norman. 1984. "Pluralism and Political Parties." In *Failure of a Dream*, rev. ed., edited by John H. M. Laslett and Seymour Martin Lipset, pp. 516–22. Berkeley: University of California Press.

Thompson, E. P. 1966. *The Making of the English Working Class*. New York: Vintage Books.

Time. 1978. "The Swarming Lobbyists." August 7, pp. 14–22.

Tolchin, Martin. 1981. "Democrats to Seek Significant Changes in Tax Cut Proposal." New York *Times*, February 21, p. 1.

Trachtenberg, Alan. 1982. *The Incorporation of America*. New York: Hill and Wang.

Truman, David B. 1958. *The Governmental Process*. New York: Alfred A. Knopf.

Verba, Sidney, and Norman H. Nie. 1972. *Participation in America*. New York: Harper and Row.

Weaver, Warren. 1984. "Democratic Panel Finishes Platform for Fall Campaign." New York *Times*, June 24, p. 1.

Weinstein, James. 1968. *The Corporate Ideal in the Liberal State*. Boston: Beacon Press.

Wekkin, Gary D. 1984. *Democrat versus Democrat*. Columbia: University of Missouri Press.

White, John K., and Dwight Morris. 1984. "Shattered Images: Political Parties in the 1984 Election." *Public Opinion*, December/January, pp. 44–48.

Wilentz, Sean. 1983. "Artisan Republican Festivals and the Rise of Class Conflict in New York City, 1788–1837." In *Working Class America*, edited by Michael H. Frisch and Daniel J. Walkowitz. Urbana: University of Illinois Press.

Wilson, James Q. 1962. *The Amateur Democrat*. Chicago: University of Chicago Press.

Wolfinger, Raymond, and Steven Rosenstone. 1980. *Who Votes?* New Haven: Yale University Press.

Woodward, C. Vann. 1955. *The Strange Career of Jim Crow*. New York: Oxford University Press.

Zeigler, L. Harmon, and Hendrik van Dalen. 1976. "Interest Groups in State Politics." In *Politics in the American States*, 3rd ed., edited by Herbert Jacob and Kenneth N. Vines, pp. 93–138. Boston: Little, Brown.

Zipp, John F. 1985. "Perceived Representativeness and Voting: An Assessment of the Impact of Choices vs. Echoes." *American Political Science Review* 79:50–61.

3

The Bias of the News

Calvin F. Exoo

The basis of our government being the opinion of the people, the
very first object should be to keep that right, and were it left to me
to decide whether we should have a government without newspapers,
or newspapers without a government, I should not hesitate a moment
to prefer the latter.

Thomas Jefferson

To be able to see every side of every question;
To be on every side, to be everything, to be nothing long;
To pervert truth, to ride it for a purpose...
To sell papers...

Edgar Lee Masters, "Editor Whedon"

Press watchers have not been much kinder to his profession than Editor
Whedon was. The news, they have agreed, is neatly tailored to the commercial and ideological interests of media magnates. The news is ill suited
to its public trust-keeping the flame of popular control alive with information. We shall begin by breaking this indictment down into a bill of
particulars, and then ask how such a thing could happen. How did the
watchdog of the people become the lapdog of the plutocrats?

THE USUAL DEFINITION OF BIAS

Conventional wisdom has it that the news media are often guilty of partisan bias-favoritism toward one or the other of the mainstream

parties or ideologies–Democrats, Republicans, liberals, or conservatives. We might also call this kind of bias "anti-normative," because it violates the norm that the news should be "objective"–evenhanded in the treatment of such parties and points of view. Conventional wisdom also tells us that partisan bias usually points to the Left, favoring liberal spokesmen and values. As is often the case with the "common sense,"[1] these particular sagacities are much too conventional and not very wise.

Evidence suggests that when partisan bias does exist, it is usually conservative.[2] For example, Bagdikian reviewed 84 studies that had found partisan bias in newspapers. In 88 percent of those cases, the bias was "pro-Republican and pro-conservative" (1972). Repeated surveys of newspaper endorsements have found them overwhelmingly favorable to conservative candidates. For example, in 1984, 394 newspapers endorsed Ronald Reagan's candidacy; 76 endorsed Mondale's (Thimmesch 1984). And Bagdikian's review indicates that such editorial page colorations often spill over into the news columns. Based on studies linking endorsements to voting behavior, a third analysis concludes, "It would seem that the normal Republican trend of the press is worth at least a couple of percentage points to the Republican party nationwide. Humphrey might have defeated Nixon in 1968 for example, with a more equitable division of newspaper endorsements between the two major party candidates.... For lower offices... one might expect that a newspaper would be more, not less, influential" (Erikson, Luttbeg, and Tedin 1980, p.136).

But the important truth about partisan bias is not that it is usually conservative, but that it is a red herring: it misleads us away from the real, pervasive bias of the media. The preoccupation of citizens and scholars with partisan bias has focused the curative powers of the people and the profession on the head cold of the media, while below, in its bones, a cancer consumes it.

The best studies of such large, prestigious media as the television networks, the wire services, and major newspapers find them more or less evenhanded in their treatment of Democrats, Republicans, liberals, and conservatives (Hofstetter 1976; Robinson 1983; Ranney and Robinson 1985). That is not surprising. Such organizations are, after all, bearers of a standard of objectivity to which all journalists aspire. It is also unsurprising that surveys such as Bagdikian's, which include small and medium-sized newspapers, should find partisan bias. For the small paper, there is no great prestige to protect; there are no Pulitzers likely to be won, and the hand of owners who are not steeped in the norm of objectivity will lie heavier on the production of the news. But even here, on the small paper, the force of journalists' values contravenes partisan bias. Because of them, "no executive is willing to risk embarrassment by being accused of open commands to slant a story" (Breed 1955, p.327).

So partisan bias occurs in the interstices between the "normal," the approved. And evidence suggests that those interstices have grown smaller over time. For example, between the 1930s and the 1960s, the rate at which newspapers changed their Washington correspondents' stories for political reasons declined (Bagdikian 1973).

Much more serious than partisan bias, because it is uncountered and therefore pervasive, is the structural bias of the news. Structural bias is that which occurs as a result of the approved routines of newsmen and news organizations, as a result of their system for selecting some kinds of information as news and rejecting other kinds as "not news." Of course newsmen have such a system. After all, there is a whole wild world of facts out there, an infinitude of information, and the journalists' lariat (the "newshole") is too small to capture it all.

So the complaint of this chapter is not that the news media have a news selection system and a resulting structural bias. That is inevitable. The complaint is that the media's bias is hegemonic: it is monolithic and plutocratic. The news outlets that offer alternative realities are so few and so obscure[3] that few Americans ever blinked when Walter Cronkite presumed to say night after night, "And that's the way it is." What is worse, this monolith, this *kratos*[4] was not built by or for the *demos*, the common people, but by and for the *oligos*, the few. This structural bias is the one that will concern us; it is the one in the marrow of the news. The next section will describe it: what does it include, what does it exclude, and why?

WHAT IS NEWS? THE STRUCTURAL BIAS OF THE MEDIA

The News Is Trivial

Somehow, the media manage, day in and day out, to refine a rich lode of sociopolitical information into a high grade of trivia. This process begins with the selection of "stories." A group of newspaper and television editors, asked to describe their criteria for choosing what's news, listed:

1. Proximity: or, as Abbie Hoffman once put it, "The headline in the *Daily News* today reads BRUNETTE STABBED TO DEATH. Underneath, in lower case letters 6000 Killed in Iranian Earthquake... I wonder what color hair they had" (quoted in Tuchman 1978, p.v).

2. Sensationalism: "violence, conflict, disaster... scandal... the kinds of things that excite audiences."

3. Familiarity: "News is attractive if it involves familiar situations... or pertains to well-known people."

4. Timeliness and Novelty: "News must be something that has just occurred and is out of the ordinary" (Graber 1980, pp.63–65).

Notice that "socially significant" is not one of the shibboleths capable of getting a story past the gatekeepers. Despite Jefferson's fond hope, a story's ability to empower ordinary citizens by teaching them how politics works and how it affects them does not make it "newsworthy."

The fruit of these criteria are the crime, accident, and human interest stories that often preempt less sensational political stories, even though the latter have more to do with "who gets what" in the lives of news consumers. Of course, crime and human interest events have their own important social stories to tell: violent crime is most often forged in the inhuman crucible of lower class life; white-collar crime is winked at by the penal system, and so forth. But these are unspectacular stories, and so they are largely untold. Meanwhile, the sensational events produced by these social forces parade across the front page, unconnected to their causes, leaving us with the ignorant impression that they occur randomly, or purely as the result of personal pathology. This pattern is most extreme on local television news shows, whose "eyewitness" cameras subsist on "action," on spectacle. But the more prestigious network news is not above the temptation to favor exciting pictures over important issues. An NBC cameraman who had covered Vietnam put it plainly: "What the producers want on film is as much blood and violence as we can find. That's the name of the game, and every cameraman knows it" (quoted in Epstein 1973, p.163). And neither is the problem limited to television. For example, during a recent four-week period, 48 percent of metro-page stories in the widely respected Chicago *Tribune* were crime, accident, or "human interest" stories. Further subtracting the portion of the two-page metropolitan section that goes to advertising left about two stories per issue devoted to local politics (Exoo 1984).

Even when important issues are covered, the criterion that insists the news be new has often meant a limited shelf life for even the most urgent ongoing issues. Lipsky and Olson show that news stories about ghetto rioting were fewer and less alarmed in the late 1960s then they had been earlier, giving Americans the impression that the incidents themselves had declined. In fact, the amount of property damage done in ghetto uprisings was three times as great in 1968 as it had been in 1964 (Lipsky and Olson 1976; Epstein 1973, pp.23–24). In the same way did "battlefield" stories about Vietnam come to the end of their "newsworthiness" at ABC News when, in March 1969, the executive producer of that network wrote to his correspondents, "The time has come to shift some of our focus from the battlefield ... to themes and stories under the general heading: We Are On Our Way Out of Vietnam" (quoted in Epstein 1973, p.17). Apparently, the novelty of this theme was more compelling than the truth, which was that in March of 1969, we were not on our way out of Vietnam.[5]

When important stories do manage to find their way into the news, they are often trivialized by being "personalized" and "dramatized" (terms from Bennett 1983, ch.1). For example, during elections, policy issues become sideshows to such center-stage melodramas as the "horse race" of preference polls, the "parcheesi" of campaign strategy, and the "hoopla" of parades and motorcades. Patterson reports that almost 60 percent of network, newspaper, and newsmagazine reports of the 1976 election viewed it as a "game." Less than 20 percent of coverage was concerned with issues and policies (Patterson 1980, p.24; Weaver et al. 1981, p.38).

Even such election-issue reporting as the media does is personalized, dramatized, and of dubious value. "Issues" the press happens to like are often emphasized over issues of interest to candidates and voters (Patterson 1980, p.36; Weaver et al. 1981, p.142). The archetype of these media issues is the gaffe. In 1976 Jimmy Carter said he lusted after women, and this indecorous truism somehow became news. Gerald Ford painted himself into a verbal corner about Eastern Europe, a place neither candidate could or would do much about anyway, and his misstep found the headlines. As Patterson's data makes clear, this lavish attention to the etiquette of the electoral affair comes at the expense of serious attention to what the candidates will do to us or for us in our very lives: more than 50 percent of these media "issues" were heavily reported in 1976; only 15 percent of the policy issues were given heavy coverage (1980 p.36). Non-electoral political conflict is also personalized for melodramatic effect. The soap operas of Reagan vs. O'Neill, Watt vs. the world, or the perennial "squabbling among the president's advisors" are serialized *ad nauseam*, preempting discussions of the issues at hand, the larger forces arrayed on both sides, or the way institutional constraints often make these titanic struggles a meaningless sound and fury.

In addition to dramatization and personalization, the news trivializes social problems by "fragmenting" them (Bennett 1983, ch.1). Press coverage severs events from their connection with other political events, with theory, and with history. They are signalized, not explained. As a result, they seem to come at us as discrete, random occurrences. Insofar as events are attributed to any causes at all, they are again personalized— left on the doorstep of individuals, not institutions. Attention is turned from deep to surface explanations. For example, the premise of most stories about unemployment in the United States is an event (usually, the release of the latest unemployment figures by the Bureau of Labor Statistics). Recently, journalists have categorized these figures as "alarming-worsening" (over 10 percent) or "improving-encouraging" (below 10 percent and lower than last month's figure). This event is then personalized by relating it to the policies of the incumbent administration. (Critics are quoted as saying high rates prove Reaganomics is failing or White House officials are quoted as saying declining rates prove Reaganomics is working.) These reports never mention the fact that the United States has been much more "tolerant" of unemployment than most other industrialized Western nations have been, or the fact that public policy toward unemployment has changed little from one administration to the next since the 1930s. Such historical and comparative observations might in turn lead to broader theories explaining U.S. unemployment policy in terms of a historical antipathy to government intervention; or in terms of the political strength of American entrepreneurs, who may find a relatively high unemployment rate to be in their interests; or the political weakness of the American working class, unorganized as it is by a *bona fide* working class party; or in terms of the theory of perfect competition and the "invisible hand." Each of these explanations ties unemployment "events" to each other, but also to history, theory, and to other political events, leaving the reader with a sophisticated explanation or set of competing explanations of politics. But they are never offered by the media, and readers are left with the primitive impression that political events are either imposed on us randomly, as if by the gods, or else are influenced mainly by the epic struggles of those Homeric figures, our presidents and congressional leaders.

Warren Breed and Herbert Gans have separately done "reverse content analyses" of the news, chronicling what's not there. Conspicuously absent were precisely those problems and concepts social scientists have often deemed fundamental to understanding America, for example, the concepts of class and power structure, and their uneasy truce with democratic values. One reason for their absence is surely that they *are* chronic, complex problems, tangled thickets, not neatly diced events (Gans 1979, p.23; Breed 1958).

How does trivializing the news give the *kratos* to the *oligos*? By anesthetizing the *demos* to the central questions of politics: who does, who should, get what, and how? A people that thinks of politics as parades and personality clashes has no sense that there are "real heads broken in the fustian and the rattle" (quotation from Vachel Lindsay 1954, p.215). Oblivious to the war, ordinary Americans have lost it before it begins, by default. Through the Morphean chemistry of the news, politics itself has become an opiate of the people.

The News Is Establishmentarian

The structural bias of the news buttresses the status quo indirectly, by diverting attention to trivialities and away from questions pregnant with the power to change. But the news also directly supports the establishment, by espousing its values and allowing its satraps to define our problems and monopolize our options. Herbert Gans argues that the "enduring values of the news" include:

1. Ethnocentrism: Reporting and editorials in the wake of the Nixon resignation, for example, were unabashed odes to the American system, to "the structure unshaken, the genius of American democracy renascent" (New York *Times* editorial, quoted in Paletz and Entman 1981, p. 164).

2. Altruistic Democracy: This is "an emphasis on . . . the official norms of the American polity . . . derived largely from the Constitution." But this emphasis is a selective one, concerned most with such system-supportive themes as the duties (and sometimes failures) of political leaders (to be selfless, meritocratic) and of citizens (to "participate in democracy"—that is, endorse the system by voting). "Violations of the civil liberties of radicals and . . . criminals are less newsworthy . . . [as are] economic obstacles to democracy."

3. Responsible Capitalism: This is "an optimistic faith that . . . businessmen . . . will compete with each other in order to create increased prosperity for all, but that they will refrain from unreasonable profits and gross exploitation of workers or customers." American news is, of course, "consistently critical" of socialist economies, including such Western-democratic incarnations as Sweden and France. A recent *Time* cover story exults, "Free enterprise . . . is the spirit of the age. Spurred by the economic successes of the U.S., . . . countries everywhere are taking the fetters off individual initiative and cutting back the welfare state." Stopping along the way for a special-section slap at "Europe's Fading Reds," eight pages of breathless testimony from conservative economists gushingly concludes: "The most productive figure in history is the individual trying to improve his status. . . . Countries that want to develop . . . or stay abreast . . . are finding themselves drawn to free enterprise, which lets people loose so that they can lose their economic shackles" (Greenwald 1986, p. 39).

4. Small Town Pastoralism: This "may in the end be a surrogate for a more general value: an underlying respect for tradition of any kind, . . . valued because it is . . . orderly, and order is a major enduring news value."

5. Individualism: "It is no accident that many of the characters in Kuralt's pastoral features are 'rugged individualists.' . . . [The news assumes that] capitalism enhances this value; socialism erodes it."

6. Moderatism: That "which violates the law, the dominant mores, and enduring values is suspect. . . . Thus, groups which exhibit what is seen as extreme behavior are criticized . . . through pejorative adjectives or satirical tone."

7. The Desirability of Social Order: This "decries" violent or potentially violent threats to the authority of public officials."

8. The Need for Leaders to Maintain Order: Leaders are "people who, because of their political or managerial skills, or personal attributes which inspire others . . . move into positions of authority . . . and the foremost leader in America is the president, who is viewed as the ultimate protector of order" (Gans 1979, pp. 42–63).

But why were these values not discussed under the heading "partisan bias"? Are they not the familiar plaint of the Left that the media is conservative? No, these values are not conservative. They are, like the values of the American establishment, centrist (see Chapter 1, p. 10; Weinstein 1968, ch. 1; Dye and Zeigler 1978, pp. 111–13). "Extremists" of the Right are neglected and derided along with those of the Left (Shoemaker 1984). Capitalism is approved, but not unfettered capitalism, only "responsible capitalism" (an oxymoron?). Thus, both the Left *and* the Right are correct when they complain that media bias excludes them. They are wrong only in supposing that what excludes them is a prejudice for the other side; in fact, the media's is a strong prejudice for the center.

Nevertheless, is not a centrist bias an ideological preference, a partisan bias? While you or I might think so, neither the producers nor the consumers of the news would agree. These values are, in fact, so "established," so long unquestioned as to seem unquestionable. To reporters and readers, they are no longer values, they are just "good common sense," and as such do not reflect partisan bias. Jack Newfield, himself a journalist, has presented a strikingly similar list, and says of it, "I can't think of any...correspondent who doesn't share these values. And at the same time, who doesn't insist he is totally objective" (1974, p. 56). As we shall see, several structural imperatives of news production converge to dictate that the news should be exactly this way: common sensible.

So far, support for the establishment has been seen as more or less explicit. But more often, this support is implicit, in the woof and warp of press practice. As a matter of course, for example, third parties and candidates are ignored by the news (Weaver et al. 1981, p. 83; Paletz and Entman 1981, p. 164; Robinson 1983, p. 58). So the countervailing, creative thinking of the Citizens, Libertarian, and other "minor parties" has amounted to so much crying in the wilderness, which doesn't carry far these days unless there is a mini-cam around. Apparently, a political idea is not a thing worthy of coverage unless it is attached to a candidate who is, or is fast becoming, a winner. In other words, it is the voter's job to choose which ideas shall be popular, although he has not heard most of them because they are not popular. Electoral Catch-22.

Groups or movements with radical views are also customarily left out when the media talk about policy problems and solutions outside election time. In seven large, high-quality newspapers over a recent 12-month period, only ten articles appeared that mentioned the U.S. Communist Party (Shoemaker 1984, p. 68). On those rare occasions when radical groups are covered, they might wish they hadn't been. Coverage fixes on the medium, excluding the message of radical groups. The frightening spectacle of the demonstration, the march, the riot is vividly recounted; the reasons for them are not. The sorry irony is that radical groups often adopt such spectacular tactics as a last-resort means of being heard. Once they adopt them, they are less likely than ever to be fairly heard, as news coverage depicts them as dangerous to the social fabric, and as unable to win support through the "normal," "democratic" process (Gitlin 1980).

While the media force radicals to the fringe of the crowd, spokesmen for the establishment are ensconced at the microphone. One large study of the Washington *Post* and the New York *Times* showed that over 60 percent of their front-page stories came from events such as press conferences, press releases, background briefings, and so forth, which are staged and managed by elites, usually senior government officials. Needless to say, these officials are usually cast as heroes in their own productions (Sigal 1973, pp. 115, 121). Although another 25 percent of the sampled stories were attributed to reporters' "enterprise," over 90 percent of those came from interviews, again usually with high-level government officials. None of the 1,146 stories sampled came from research done using books, journals, or statistical data. Other sources of the news besides high-level government officials also tend to be oracles of the establishment: spokesmen for corporations, for large interest groups, and from mainstream (not radical) academia (Paletz and Entman 1981, p. 193).

The result of this monopoly over the marketplace of ideas is predictable, since "few elites disagree about the essential desirability of the system they control" (Paletz and Entman 1981, p. 23). Gans notes that those "enduring values of the news" described above "coincide almost completely" with the rhetoric of "those public officials who are the journalists' major sources." Gans argues that these "oughts" enter the news "most pervasively" through official definitions of what is. So, when elites saw the Vietnam War as a "conflict between America and its allies, and a Communist enemy," the news did too. The news might, for a change from time to time, have viewed the war as a struggle against the vestiges of the old colonialism, with the United States entering as a bully of the new colonialism, unwilling to cede Asian markets or raw materials even to the principle of self-determination. But instead, the media referred so regularly to the North Vietnamese and the National Liberation Front as "the enemy," one might have thought "they were the enemy of the news media" (Gans 1979, p. 201; see also Hoch 1974, ch. 6). More recently, the media has followed the lead of authoritative sources to a constricted definition of "terrorism." The dictionary describes that word's meaning as "the political use of intimidation." But the media and its sources have reserved the term for the small-scale desperation of relatively powerless, often anti-U.S. groups like Palestinians. Meanwhile the "wholesale terrorism" of governments that use the torture and murder of untried civilians as instruments of public policy falls under the tepid appellation "possible violations of human rights." Not just coincidentally, most wholesale terrorists are allies of the United States government (Chomsky and Herman 1979, ch. 3).

At the local level, reliance on elites to define problems might help to explain the results of Breed's "reverse content analysis." Again, he found that those issues that independent sociologists said were most afflicting the communities they studied were not to be found in the communities' newspapers. Earlier, I suggested one reason for their absence might be their complexity. Another, which Breed suggests, is the fact that these issues were "system threatening," and thus not likely to be acknowledged by those at the source of the river of news (1958, pp. 205–06).

At this point, two objections urge themselves. First, my argument that the establishment monopolizes the news seems to forget the pride newsmen take in telling "both sides of the story." The phrase itself gives away the feet-of-clay assumption underpinning this practice: it presumes that, usually, there are only two important sides to a story (Exoo 1984, p. 14). Thus, the "dialectic" of the news consists of counterpoising elites whose disagreements over means are bounded by a gentlemen's agreement on the ends. When, for example, Reagan and congressional liberals clash over foreign policy, the idea that "Marxist-Leninist" revolutions ought to be discouraged is never in question. Disagreement is restricted to the question of how to discourage them. While that is not a trivial disagreement, neither is it fundamental, nor does it begin to suggest the range of intellectually respectable views on the subject.[6]

At this point journalists might fairly rejoin that foreign Marxist-Leninist leaders are often quoted (Sigal 1973, p. 121). Of course, their wells are poisoned by their very introduction as the "head of the Marxist-Leninist government of Nicaragua" and by the fact that no Americans appearing on the news share their perspective.

Recently ABC News exceeded the limits of "both sides" protocol by giving a spokesman for the Soviet Union several minutes of air time to respond to a Reagan foreign policy address. Then, chastened by strident criticism from fellow journalists and administration officials, the network apologized for providing the time and for not placing the Soviet's remarks "in context." As Benjamin Bradlee, a dean of U.S. journalism huffily explained, "There are two sides in a democratic society. Communism is not a third side."

What is more, the *way* in which the news counterpoises Democrats vs. Republicans, mainstream liberals vs. conservatives, and established interest group vs. established interest group further reinforces the status quo. Edward Jay Epstein, who spent six months observing the "dialectical" procedure at NBC News, describes it as one "in which the correspondent, after reporting the news happening, juxtaposes a contrasting viewpoint and concludes his synthesis by suggesting that the truth lies somewhere in between" (1973, p. 67). Such a centrist synthesis is *de rigueur*, even if the correspondent thinks the facts put the truth on the Left or the Right. For example, in the original version of an hour-long NBC documentary on gun control, former correspondent Robert MacNeil concluded that "it was necessary to restrict the ownership of firearms, and that Congress had not passed such a bill because of the pressures put on it by the 'well-financed' lobby led by the National Rifle Association." The network "softened" the documentary and replaced his conclusion with one (read by MacNeil himself) that "ran directly contrary to what he apparently believed to be the true findings of the investigation—that the legislation was . . . forestalled by the gun lobby, not by 'reasonable men' disagreeing on the 'form' of the law" (Epstein 1973, p. 69).[7] What could be nicer for the various estates than to have the truth automatically located at the epicenter of their interests?

A second objection to the establishmentarianism thesis points to that intrepid figure, the investigative journalist. But the structural bias of the news has leashed this "watchdog of the public interest." Even in investigative journalism, where problems barge into the public consciousness without an introduction from elites, press coverage turns attention from deep to surface explanations, often by personalizing the story: the authorities are to blame; the regime is not questioned. Reporting of the Watergate, Lance, Meese, and Ferraro affairs bruised the heads of the principals involved, but only the heel of the political economy, which, it has been ably argued, nurtures such scandals (Altheide and Snow 1979; Orr 1980; Tuchman 1978, p. 87).

HOW THE NEWS AFFECTS THE PUBLIC

Does the media affect attitudes? Early socialization and voting studies didn't think so. When voting studies found that people's voting intentions changed little over the course of heavily publicized and reported campaigns, they concluded that the media lacked impact (Lazarsfeld, Berelson, and Gaudet 1944; Campbell et al. 1960). When socialization researchers asked children where they learned about politics, they were much more likely to mention parents or teachers than the media.

Recently, the academic common sense about the media has changed. Over the past 25 years, television has become ubiquitous, and time spent with the mass media has jumped by 40 percent. "On an average day, 80 percent of all Americans are reached by television and newspapers. On a typical evening, the television audience is close to 100 million people, nearly half the entire population." Today, the average U.S. grade-school child spends 27 hours a week in front of the television set—more time than in school (Graber 1980, pp. 120, 122). At the same time, the methodology of socialization research has been refined, measuring the sources of direct influence through more precise questions (Coldevin 1972) and beginning to measure the enormous indirect influence the media have on children, by way of parents, teachers, and peers (Hollander 1971; Phelan 1977). Reassessing the older studies, Neil Hollander has dubbed the media, "the new 'parent' " (1971).

At the same time, voting studies have begun to wonder whether it makes sense to define media influence in terms of changes in the party or candidate preferences of voters, given that the media's "horse race" coverage of the campaign does not provoke evaluations of candidates by voters (Patterson 1980, p. 89), and given that the media rarely show a candidate preference when they do discuss the substance of the campaign (Lemert 1981, p. 60). In light of this pattern, researchers have begun to ask whether there are tracings on the public mind of the bias the media *does* pervasively evince—structural bias.

How does the news affect attitudes? Earlier, this chapter asserted that trivialized news makes for a politically anesthetized public. Evidence for that assertion abounds. For example, Patterson found that voters' perceptions of candidates during the 1976 election campaign mirrored the media's odd priorities:

Impressions [of the candidates] . . . tended to be stylistic, associated with the candidates' mannerisms and campaign performance. These included thoughts about the candidates' personalities, campaign success and style, and personal backgrounds. People were much less likely to form political impressions, those concerning the candidates' . . . leadership abilities, political backgrounds, and issue positions. . . . No exact coefficient can be attached to the relationship, but there was a remarkable parallel between the themes of . . . news coverage and the impressions people developed (1980, p. 134).

The same was true of voters' perceptions of "what was important" during that campaign. "Election news emphasized the game rather than matters of policy and leadership, and it was the game that dominated people's thoughts. The correlation between journalistic emphasis and public preoccupation was in fact very high, more than +.85 at every point once the campaign was under way" (Patterson 1980, p. 98; for similar findings, see Weaver et al. 1981, p. 39; Graber 1980, p. 184).

The "garbage in-garbage out" relationship between the news and the citizen also applies to politics outside the electoral arena. Doris Graber argues that human beings assimilate information by fitting it into a preexisting "schema"—a cognitive structure consisting of organized knowledge about situations and individuals that has been abstracted from prior experiences. It is used for processing new information and retrieving stored information (1984, p. 23). Functions of schemata include determining "what information will be noticed . . . and stored" and making "it possible for people to go beyond the immediate information presented to them and fill in missing information. This permits making sense from abbreviated communications" (p. 24). Unfortunately, the "socialization of Americans . . . leaves a number of gaps in the schema structure. These gaps then make it difficult to focus public attention on some important problems." For example, there is a "nearly total lack" of understanding about how public institutions work and a "sparsity" of knowledge about public policies (p. 208). The schemata that do exist bespeak a set of shared stereotypes, often of the civics-class storybook variety, which in turn "means that public political thinking tends to lack flexibility" (p. 207).

The media share responsibility for this sad state in several ways. First, fragmented, trivialized news must bear some blame for the gaps between schemata and the froth within them, because the "media play a significant part in early as well as later phases of socialization" (Graber 1984, p. 206).

Second, the fact of fragmented news combines with the fact that schematic deficiencies are most egregious among low status Americans to mean that they are least able to perform the functions of schemata, to "go beyond the immediate information presented to them and fill in missing information," to make sense out of the "abbreviated communications" of the media. The result is "the knowledge gap," a situation where, as mass media information increases, the high-status information-rich get richer and the poor stay poor (Donohue, Tichenor, and Olien 1975; Graber 1984, p. 210).

This "relative deprivation of knowledge" leads to "relative deprivation of power." For example, because "lower status groups do not know as much at the end of a campaign about the issues and the candidates, they are less able to vote in their own interests and more able to be manipulated by political advertisements" (Moore 1982, p. 9). As surely as knowledge is power, so the nescience wrought by the news among low status Americans is powerlessness.

And third, perhaps obviously, the media's monolithic "status quo bias," the "deference" paid to the American system has certainly contributed to Americans' uncritical "commonality in thinking" (Graber 1984, p. 206).

But perhaps the media's most important effect has to do with the lethal mixture of cynicism and naiveté in American public opinion. We noted earlier the tendency of investigative journalism to scapegoat authorities for problems, exculpating the system.[8] That journalistic voice is eerily echoed in the long-standing tendency of Americans to think politicians are "bumbling or uncaring or corrupt," but to continue to endorse basic institutions (Graber 1984, pp. 207–08; Lipset and Schneider 1983, pp. 384–92). Because "the news media have never given powerless Americans the necessary information to link the ubiquitous rotten apples to the structure of the barrel," discontentments have become frustration or resignation instead of demands for useful change (Paletz and Entman 1981, p. 167).

This then is the news—trivial, anesthetic, establishmentarian; a reverse Robin Hood, robbing power from the poor to give to the rich. How has this come about? How has Jefferson's dream become Editor Whedon's nightmare?

THE SOURCES OF BIAS

Governmental Pressures

The most visible governmental influence on the news is the Federal Communications Commission, the federal agency charged with regulating the broadcast industry on behalf of "the public interest." In accord with that mandate, the FCC issued the Fairness Doctrine in 1949, requiring that when a controversial issue is discussed on television or radio, the airing station must present contrasting viewpoints.

While this regulation has made local television news less partisan than local newspapers, it has not variegated the marketplace of ideas. This is mainly because the Commission has allowed television news producers to decide what constitutes a "fair reply." Their decision has involved the constant incantation of the "both sides" litany discussed above: establishment liberal spokesman is counterpoised with establishment conservative spokesman, followed by correspondent concluding that the truth lies somewhere in between. This ritual has indeed warded off the FCC, even though it completely excludes the "contrasting viewpoint" of radicals: no broadcaster's license has ever been revoked for violation of the Fairness Doctrine. In fact, the FCC has actively encouraged these exclusive definitions of "fairness" and of "contrasting viewpoints." "It is not," says the FCC Fairness Primer, "the Commission's intent to make time available to Communists or to the Communist viewpoints" (quoted in Epstein 1973, p. 64).

A less visible and more sinister source of government pressure comes from the use of official power to pry favorable coverage out of the news media. For example, in 1969, when the news media covered the tide of protest against Richard Nixon's escalation of the air war in Vietnam, the president turned his formidable displeasure on the press. In the fall of 1969, Vice-President Spiro Agnew toured the nation, blistering the "liberal bias" of the "effete snobs" who controlled the press. These "nattering nabobs of negativism" were, according to Agnew, using their news coverage of the anti-war demonstrations to purvey their own similar position to the public (Bennett 1980, p. 319). Agnew implied that the networks had violated the FCC's fairness requirement and thus should be investigated by that commission, whose members are selected by presidential appointment. Eventually, the FCC did investigate charges of "news staging" by the networks. Administration pressure continued with the 1972 filing of an anti-trust suit against the three major networks by the Justice Department. Although the Justice Department denied that the suits were politically motivated, broadcasters believed other administration spokesmen, who implied that they were.

During the period, news coverage of protest activities declined significantly. In their stead, the networks began to cover a series of support rallies, prayer days, and patriotic demonstrations organized around the country by the White House (Bennett 1980, pp. 318–19). More recently, a New York *Times* staffer reported a massacre implicating the U.S.-backed government of El Salvador. Although his story was independently corroborated, the reporter was removed from his position after harsh criticism of it by a high-ranking Reagan-administration official. (Intriguingly, this same official was involved in the attempted cover-up of a similar, Vietnamese massacre, in 1973). Shortly thereafter, the *Times* hired a new Central American reporter, described as "the best friend the [Reagan-backed] Nicaraguan contras had in American journalism" (Hamill 1985, p. 20).

But a caveat is in order. While these cases *illustrate* the problem, they may also overstate it. The notion that the press is and should remain "independent" is cherished by press and public alike. It seems to have been a sufficient garlic wreath against all but the most lupine public officials. Thus, although Gans found that journalists believed "themselves to be under frequent pressure," his interviews also suggested that "successful pressure leading to censorship or self-censorship, is rare" (1979, p. 252).

On the other hand, similar reasoning might bring us to an opposite conclusion—that governmental pressure is a *larger* problem than it appears to be. Precisely because independence is a cardinal rule for journalists, surrendering to pressure is a cardinal sin, and the sinner is loath to confess it (Gans 1979, p. 251). It is conceivable that the governmental abuses that have surfaced are only the tip of an iceberg all the more deadly for being mainly submerged.

Pressure from Advertisers

Advertising is the *sine qua non* of American news. Between 60 and 80 percent of newspaper revenue comes from advertising (Udell 1978, pp. 26, 69; Hoch 1974, p. 169). Virtually all revenue of over-the-air commercial television comes from advertising.

Now this dependence on advertising should not be taken, by itself, to mean control by advertisers of editorial policy. Again, the norm of independence mitigates advertiser influence. And, one scholar has argued, the monopoly most newspapers have in their markets gives them the power to enforce that norm (Hulteng 1979, p. 9). Indeed, most business and financial editors insist that they would rebuff editorial suggestions from advertisers (cited in Hoch 1974, p. 164).

On the other hand, 22.6 percent of respondents to the same survey reported that they would "puff up or alter or downgrade" business stories at the direction of their advertisers. And again, we might suspect that this figure is depressed somewhat by the reluctance of editors to confess to this professional sin.

The *frequency* of successful influence by advertisers is one of those questions that is bound to hide from social science. At the same time, there is another obvious point to be made about advertiser influence on the news: it does happen. It happens more often in competitive than in non-competitive markets, more often on small than on larger papers (Gans 1979, p. 257), involving large more often than small advertisers. But it does happen. For example:

1. The president of the Grocery Manufacturers of America crowed of winning editorial support against the late Senator Philip Hart's truth-in-packaging legislation, giving illustrations from eight magazines of his successful message that "the day was here when their editorial department and business department might better understand their interdependency... as they affect... the advertisers—their bread and butter." Although Senator Hart sent background material to 21 magazines, none covered his efforts. Instead, *Look* managed to find room for an article entitled, "Let's Keep Politics Out of the Pantry," concocted by a food industry spokesman (Hoch 1974, p. 162).

2. A former president of CBS News has revealed that the tobacco industry and its ancillaries pressured the network to downplay early news reports of the link between cigarette smoking and lung cancer. For example, Alcoa Aluminum (which supplied aluminum foil for cigarette packages) "dropped its sponsorship of a CBS news and documentary program after the program ran a number of stories that offended Alcoa's customers. The program was gradually shifted from a weekly to a monthly format" (Bennett 1980, p. 316).

3. When Chicago-based Sears-Roebuck was charged by the Federal Trade Commission with widespread advertising deception, the story was big news around the country, but was not news in Sears' hometown. Some of the Chicago media did not cover the story at all; others buried it in back pages with fleet mentionings. It is interesting to note that, apparently, Sears did not need to threaten the media to obtain this reticence. This case, like many others under the heading of "pressure," seems to have been a classic "non-decision": fearing *potential* conse-

quences, the "non-decider" simply fails to do what he normally would (see Bachrach and Baratz 1970 for an extended discussion of non-decisions; see Hoch 1974, p. 168 for other examples of non-decisions by the news media).

4. Television documentaries typically have low audience ratings and so are hard to sell to advertisers. In fact, they probably wouldn't exist at all if television didn't need a relatively cheap way of satisfying FCC requirements for programming "in the public interest," and of staying on the air during times when the network has resigned itself to a small share of the audience. But low ratings mean that demure advertisers must be wooed, sometimes too ardently, at the cost of editorial virtue. It is not unusual for sponsors "looking ... for identification with a particular news message" to choose the subjects of documentaries, as well as to keep "in close touch" during production, at times examining scripts and rough cuts, and even altering program content. Even when the sponsor does not choose the subject of the documentary, 'A process of self-censorship is at work,' since the news executives and documentary producers generally assume that the sponsor prefers 'soft subjects' ... [to] 'hard,' or controversial programs" (Epstein 1973, p. 128; for additional instances of advertiser influence, see Barnouw 1978).

Media Owners and Managers

Is it only coincidence that trivial, establishmentarian news dovetails perfectly with the vested interests of the media's owners and managers? Social science is again hard pressed to answer that question, partly because owner pressure, like advertiser or official pressure, is a journalistic taboo. Although this has made the frequency of this kind of influence hard to establish, the *fact* of it is not. Like advertiser pressure, it happens (see Hoch 1974, p.145 for examples). On the other hand, the conclusion of several studies has been that, especially in large "quality" organizations, executive officers intervene only rarely in editorial decisions (Gans 1979, p.84; Wolf 1972; Exoo 1984).

But the most sensitive observers of this question have shown us how management *influence* can be a heavy hand even while *intervention* remains a delicate touch. Influence begins with the hiring of editors. "I'm the chief executive. I set policy and I'm not going to surround myself with people who disagree with me," says Otis Chandler of the Los Angeles *Times* (quoted in Paletz and Entman 1981, p.15). From there, influence is an almost unconscious process of acculturation, as editors learn their limits with the publisher through the sonar of trial and error (Bennett 1980, p.238), as reporters see what is elided from or rewritten in their columns (Tuchman 1972, p.662), and, especially, as all of them read what is and is not done in their own newspapers (Breed 1955).

Although the "policy" thus imposed is sometimes a partisan or Left/Right bias, that happens less often today than formerly and happens more often to small newspapers than to large news organizations. Today, in the large "quality" newsroom the message of this subtle system of control is all the more powerful because it is coated with the soothing language of journalistic norms. As we shall see, those norms have come, partly through this process of top-down teaching, to enjoin the triviality and establishmentarianism chronicled above. In the end, media owners and managers do not often forcibly inject their interests into the news for a very good and simple reason: they don't have to.

"Authoritative" Sources

Leon Sigal's exhaustive study of news production at the Washington *Post* and the New York *Times* concludes: "News is . . . less a sampling of what is happening in the world than a selection of what officials think– or want the press to report–is happening" (1973, p.188). Why is that? As we shall see below, the term "news business" is not a metaphor. Between the lines of every day's news is a profit/loss ledger. This means that every editor's life is a struggle against the commercial elements: space, time, and cost. Daily the newsman must:

1. Fill a "newshole" large enough to carry a heavy load of advertising lineage.
2. Do this with a staff that will not weigh too much on the debit side of the ledger.
3. Do it under deadline.

The result of these imperatives is that management now measures newspaper performance in such terms as "man-hours per news column" and "man-hours per page" (Udell 1978, p.86). The editor under these guns, "knowing that he lacks the manpower even to cover all of Washington, let alone the country . . . tries to . . . cover the key beats," that is, the highest echelons of officialdom (Sigal 1973, pp.10–11). But perhaps "cover" is too generous a word for what reporters can do while chased by that Fury, the deadline. Even on the highly regarded Chicago *Tribune*, most reporters must file at least a story per shift. A busy day on the beat might call for two or three stories. That pace leaves enough time to attend an event, buttonhole two or three "experts" who can be relied on to yield pithy, if predictable, quotations, and file the story. On less well-endowed newspapers, the pace–and the coverage—are worse (Exoo 1984, p.11; Sigal 1973, p.52).

Television news faces these elements, and one more: the additional cost of a film crew severely limits the number of such crews deployed, and so the number of stories that can be covered. The result is: "Camera crews must be assigned to scheduled events that will almost certainly materialize on schedule.... Assignment editors therefore tended to give preference to happenings planned in advance for the press" (Epstein 1973, p.146).

Costs also limit the research facilities available to journalists. Amazingly, the CBS Evening News had a research staff of one at the time Epstein did his study of the networks. And in the crucial half hour before air time, its research library was closed (Epstein 1973, p.140). Likewise, the national desk of the Washington *Post*, at the time of Sigal's study, had "little research help" (1973, p.11).

Where the fifth estate lacks such resources as time and staff to routinely do extensive research, the other estates, those "covered" by the press, have been happy to fill the breach. In fact, government and corporations have responded to the need of the press for an agenda and for information by creating a full-blown industry. Press agents have been in business since the nineteenth century, but, wrote Edward Bernays, father of the public relations industry, "It was the astounding success of propaganda during the [First World] War which opened the eyes of the intelligent few in all departments of life to the possibilities of regimenting the public mind" (quoted in Schudson 1978, p.14). Another industry founder, Ivy Lee, described for his employer, John D. Rockefeller, how the business worked in the case of publicizing a Rockefeller gift to a university:

In view of the fact that this was not really news, and that the newspaper gave so much attention to it, it would seem that this was wholly due to the manner in which the material was "dressed up" for newspaper consumption. It seems to suggest very considerable possibilities along this line (in Schudson 1978, p.138).

By the mid–1920s, it was estimated that more than half the stories appearing in the New York *Times* originated in the work of press agents. In 1930, political scientist Peter Odegard wrote, "Many reporters today are little more than intellectual mendicants who go from one publicity agent or press bureau to another seeking 'handouts' " (quoted in Schudson 1978, p. 144).

Today, the public relations army is more formidable than ever. Estimates are that from 30–50 percent of the now-huge White House staff is involved with media relations. The Defense Department alone spends billions of dollars annually on public relations (Bennett 1983, p. 41). Its press agents now outnumber Pentagon reporters by a ratio of about 4 to 1 (Sigal 1973, p. 54). Is it any wonder that over 60 percent of front-page stories in the Washington *Post* and New York *Times* are "inspired" by establishment proceedings, press releases, press conferences, and "non-spontaneous events" (Sigal 1973, p. 121)?

This last category remains one of the most ingenious products of the public relations machine—the "pseudo-event," a happening staged by elites to attract the media spotlight and bathe themselves in the warm glow of favorable publicity (Boorstin 1961). It is designed to fit like a glove the media's need for predictable, quickly coverable, dramatic events. For example, in 1969 Richard Nixon moved to stem the adverse publicity flowing from a massive oil spill off the coast of Santa Barbara. After announcing that the situation was under control, Nixon conducted an "inspection tour" of a clean Santa Barbara beach. The news media covered the pseudo-event as news, and did not expose the event's illusory quality: the fact that this stretch of beach had been cleaned especially for this event, while miles of beach on either side "remained hopelessly blackened" (Molotch and Lester 1974).

The press did not expose this Nixon shadow show for the same reason it rarely reveals how one-sided and self-serving are its sources: to do so would be to "dismantle the news net" (Tuchman 1978, p. 87)—to expose the porousness of that net, calling into question the validity of the news itself, and to untie reporters' relationships with elite sources, those ties that bind the news net together and make what's known as newsgathering possible (Sigal 1973, p. 55).

The Commercial Imperative

Much of the bankruptcy in the marketplace of ideas can be traced to a thriving business in the other marketplace. Or, as Lincoln Steffens put it, "Politics is business. That's what's wrong with it. That's what's the matter with everything," and he included journalism on his list (1957, p. 4).

The categorical commercial imperative is, of course, profit (Paletz and Entman 1981, p. 10; Epstein 1981, p. 127; Exoo 1984). In the news business, size of profit is a function of the size and demographic profile of the audience—those readers or viewers who in turn attract advertisers. The foremost marketing job of the established media is not to attract an audience, but to keep the large, profit-producing one they already have. This is most true of television, whose managers conceive of audience as a river that will continue to flow along one channel unless it is somehow diverted. Thus, a "significant portion" of the audience for a network's evening news show is inherited from the local news broadcast that precedes it (Epstein 1973, pp. 93–94).[9]

The analog to "audience flow" in newsprint is the medium's subscribing audience. They constitute more than three-fourths of a newspaper's readership. What is more, they are more affluent than the single-copy reader. This makes them a more desirable audience for advertisers, and thus a more profitable audience for newspapers (Bogart 1981, pp. 46–

47). The considerable brand loyalty of the newspaper subscriber means that, just as the television station inherits viewers from the previous time slot, so the newspaper "inherits" its subscribers from year to year, unless the river of readership is diverted (Engwall 1981, p. 70).

So the bottom-line question becomes: how to maintain audience flow? Not, the answer begins, by improving editorial content. For example, investing in research or investigative staff will not pay for itself in increased audience. The television viewer, like the newspaper or newsmagazine subscriber, does not see (and so doesn't miss) what news is not there, what news the competition might be offering (Sigal 1973, pp. 10, 72; Epstein 1973, pp. 94–97).

Instead, from the Mount Sinai of audience maintenance come these twin commandments: Do not bore your audience. Do not offend them. Either sin risks changing the course of the river and tempting the wrath of the profit margin (Bennett 1980, p. 307; Graber 1980, p. 62).

How does the news choose to avoid "boring" its audience? Market researchers in this area, called "news doctors," have prescribed a diet very like the sugary pap described earlier under the heading "trivialized news": "A new face here, a new set there, here a format, there a helicopter, more crime, less city hall, more local color, more pictures, fewer talking heads, shorter stories, more weather, [more] society and women's sections... [in short] the deemphasis of politics in favor of human interest irrelevancies" (Bennett 1983, pp. 72–73; See also, Shapiro 1976; Bordewich 1977).

How does the news avoid "offending" its audience? By choosing sources, stories, facts, and themes that do not threaten established cultural values. This includes the kind of sources and themes described in Chapter 1 as "the American unison" and described earlier in this chapter under the heading "establishmentarian news." It excludes almost everything else (Paletz and Entman 1981, p. 252; Graber 1980, p. 79). "Do we question the system?" mused a Chicago *Tribune* editor, "Of course not. If we did, we wouldn't be representative—or read" (Exoo 1984). There, in one basket, are the chicken and the egg. But which is which? Are the dearth and narrowness of ideological debate in such institutions as the press (the schools, the parties) the effect—or the cause—of the American consensus. Isn't "being representative" another Catch–22? The popular mind will decide which groups and ideas make the news, but the popular mind knows nothing of a wide range of alternative groups and ideas, because they haven't made the news.

The centrist bias produced by audience imperatives is exacerbated by the primordial role of the wire services. Small research staffs have forced television networks to rely heavily on the wire services for story ideas and story lines. Seventy percent of the reporting assignments handed out at NBC, for example, came from "the wires" (Epstein 1973, pp. 141–

43). Non-national newspapers, of course, take all their national and international news from the wire services. The audience imperative of these wire services is to please the universe of potential subscribers, huge and diverse in the political leanings of its editors and audiences. Thus, these prime movers of the news are even less likely than other media to engage in interpretive reporting, much less to adopt a controversial story line (Semple 1974, p. 89; Rubin 1981, p. 63).

Television networks are also especially chary of controversy. They are like wire services in the sense that they "wholesale" their wares to "retailers"—in this case television stations that "affiliate" with one or the other of the networks. Of course, it is important for network programming to be to affiliates' liking. The larger the number of affiliates a network has, the larger will be its audience share, and the more it can charge advertisers. What is more, an affiliate has the right, under FCC regulations, to refuse to broadcast any program offered by its network that is not to the station's liking. Such refusal of "clearance" causes ratings and profits to drop. What kind of programming has affiliate appeal? As described by one network vice-president, "Affiliates tend to be owned by people in another business—newspapers, automobile dealers, Coke distributors—and run by salesmen or former announcers. Their politics is Republican, their ideals are pragmatic and their preoccupation with return on invested capital and the safety of their [FCC–granted] license to broadcast is total" (quoted in Epstein 1973, p. 56). Translation: networks that wish to win new affiliates, keep current ones, and avoid clearance problems would do well to engage in what one network news producer called his "self censorship" (Epstein 1973, p. 57) of programming that might threaten the "common sense."

The Role of Journalists' Norms

So far, this discussion of the sources of bias has been typical of social science, where too often relationships between human beings "assume the fantastic shape of relations between things," as Marx put it. Journalists are not "things" moved about, insensate and indifferent, by "social forces," like the pressures listed above. Journalists are men and women who can fight back, surrender, or make a truce. In fact, what journalists have done is to forge a philosophy of news and a corresponding casuistry of norms that:

1. Help newsmen to resist the pressures toward anti-normative bias (from the commercial or partisan interests of advertisers, government officials, and media owners). Journalists themselves insist that the main influence on their work is "newsworthiness," that is, journalistic standards, not the interests of

editors or advertisers (Flegel and Chaffee 1971), and, as we have seen, scholars who have watched journalists work have not seen much such "improper" influence (Gans 1979, pp. 84, 252).

2. Dignify the news, and so let newsmen live at peace with the stronger pressures (the commercial imperative and the need to rely on establishment sources as authoritative). In fact, as we shall see, journalists' norms have joined these pressures to produce the structural biases described earlier.

The cornerstone of these journalistic values is, of course, the norm of objectivity. Present in rough form as early as the earliest modern news (Schudson 1978, p. 21), the norm was refined in the early decades of this century into a bulwark for an emerging "profession" besieged by charges of crassness and bias. Although the combined critiques of the lost generation (Schudson 1978, ch. 4), and the new journalism (Flippen 1974, ch. 1) have blurred the meaning of objectivity at its edges,[10] the core of the concept remains pristinely clean and fervently believed by journalists. The job of the newsman, it professes, is to depict the world's important events, accurately and disinterestedly (Johnstone, Slawski and Bowman 1976, ch. 7).

The problem is: how to choose unbiased facts when there are none. Given the infinitude of interesting facts, stories, leads, angles, and sources; and given that liberals, conservatives, and radicals of the Right or Left will always disagree over which of these facts, and so forth, are "important" and "newsworthy," the question becomes: how to avoid bias when bias is inevitable? Journalists have responded to this paradox with a set of "rituals"—elaborate contortions designed to placate the implacable demand for objectivity "almost the way a Mediterranean peasant might wear a clove of garlic around his neck to ward off evil spirits" (Tuchman 1972, p. 660; Gans 1979, pp. 275–76).

This response to one paradox has created another: the norm of objectivity, in the professed service of freeing the people, has in fact helped shackle them to a cave-wall shadow show. Included in the objectivity liturgy is the ritualized telling of "both sides" of a story, using "authoritative" sources, that is, those "in a position to know more than other people" (Tuchman 1972, pp. 665–72). Thus, journalists' norms help the FCC give us the form of a debate. At the same time, they join time/cost constraints to give us establishment Tweedledums and Tweedledees as the substance of that debate.

Another norm designed to ward off charges of bias is that facts and stories should comport with "common sense" (Tuchman 1972, pp. 674–75). This "common sense" is much like the one Gramsci described as the assumptions of the hegemonic culture—assumptions so widely held and rarely questioned as to seem less like value choices than like *a priori* judgments. So this "common sense" norm joins with the stultified agenda of elites and the commercial commandment against offending audience to write the status quo in stone. For example, the truth about massacres and bombings of civilians by U.S. forces in Vietnam went unreported by the establishment press for years, although firsthand reports of these incidents had appeared often in the radical press and even in the mainstream foreign press. Reason: the stories were not "consensible," sounding more like "communist propaganda" than like the American G.I. "everyone knows" (Sigal 1973, pp. 40–41).

This need to partake of the common sense has produced one of the most bizarre behavior patterns outside of zoology: pack journalism. It affects mainly reporters who cover the same beat for rival media. These reporters read one another's work religiously and huddle together at every opportunity to decide what the day's "story" is, what is the lead, what are the facts, and so on (Crouse 1973). This herd instinct may be one more reason for the lack of variety at the media bazaar. A recent study found that 71 percent of the stories aired on national television news in a particular week were carried by all three networks (Bogart 1981, p. 176).

The need for consensibility also makes journalists especially susceptible to what I will call the "conservative fallacy" of any ongoing institution. This is the unremarkable human tendency to accept, for the most part unquestioningly, "the way things are usually done," and to emulate it. Thus, academics teach in the way they were taught, and reporters write in a way they have learned by reading their predecessors. The faith and sins of the fathers are visited upon the children. For example, when journalists are asked to reflect on the trivialization charge, "their responses suggest that their benchmark for answering the question, 'How much crime is too much?' or 'How deep should analysis go?' is not some external standard such as 'numerical predominance of crime over political stories is too much.' . . . Instead, the benchmark is 'How well are we doing compared with other news media?' " (Exoo 1984, pp. 9–10). If our coverage is not more trivial than theirs, then we are meeting the standard set by the journalistic common sense. United we fall.

A third rain dance for objectivity is "documentary reporting." Telling only those stories that reporters either witness firsthand or hear from reliable sources is supposed to ensure that the news is "the facts," not embellishment or advocacy (Bennett 1983, p. 86). But again, the question is: which facts? The documentary norm means that the media's need is not only for facts that are dramatic and quickly coverable, but also predictable, so that they will be visible to the reporter or to his reliable sources. Thus, this norm helps deliver journalists straight into the hands of press secretaries and pseudo-event stage managers, whose statements and happenings are timed precisely to be predictable and visible to reporters.

As we have seen, journalists' norms often fail to contravene pressures toward the structural bias of the news. In fact, Lance Bennett has argued that the covalence of norms and pressures is no accident (1983, pp. 78–81). These norms were really rationalizations *ex post facto* the commercial construction of the news. While I would not disagree that commerce has shaped American news and thereby American culture, I would add that the relationship has not been completely one-sided: American culture has had an Achilles heel that helped make what we now know as the news both commercially and normatively appealing.

This point is most compellingly made by a look at history, without which the road we have so long since taken seems the only way; the themes and enthymemes of contemporary journalism seem unquestionably sensible. We begin our look at abandoned paths and roads not taken in 1833, the year the New York *Sun* signaled the dawn of modern news.

A BRIEF HISTORY OF THE NEWS

Newspapers in existence before 1833 were aimed at either political or mercantile elites. This was partly because of the clumsiness of printing technology, which made the newspapers too expensive for plebian consumption. The "news" of the mercantile paper was mainly marine news—the comings, goings, and cargoes of ships in the local harbor. The political papers were indentured to the parties that subsidized them. These parties seem to have been possessed of the naive notion that the way to win an election was by force of argument, and so their newspapers consisted mainly of political commentary and editorials. Originally these were full of erudition, full of allusions to history, philosophy, and Greek mythology, but they descended into personalities as Andrew Jackson showed how an *ad hominem* press could be used as a way of tying grass-roots notables into the nexus of a national party (Rubin 1981, ch. 1).

But even by the 1830s, capitalism had already carved a niche for a *mass* medium. The factory and shop-made goods that had exploded into the economy in the previous two decades needed to be marketed, sold—advertised. At the same time, improvements in printing technology, transportation, and literacy levels were making it possible to produce and distribute an advertising medium to a wide audience. The New York *Sun*'s achievement was to see this niche, and the shape of the medium that would fill it. The *Sun* was hawked by newsboys in the street for a penny a piece. In its advertising, raucous claims for patent medicines and lotteries replaced the staid notices of legal transactions or public sales found in the elite press. But the change reaching farthest—all the way into the VDTs of today's New York *Times*—occurred in the unabashedly commercial[11] news columns of the penny papers. There, "selling the people replaced telling the people" (Rubin 1981, p.82); news replaced views (Schiller 1981, pp.3–7). Human interest stories and melodramatic descriptions of "events" replaced the argument and analysis of the elite press.

Although the norm of objectivity was not born until the 1920s, it too was conceived in the penny press. Its editors proudly trumpeted their "unbound independence" from the patronage-wielding parties, and competed to give "the earliest, the fullest, and most correct intelligence on every local incident" (New York *Transcript*, quoted in Schudson 1978, p.23). Actually, this "independence from politics" was mainly indifference to it. In its stead, stories of rapes, robberies, suicides, abandoned children left in baskets, and the brawling of drunken sailors were the common and salacious fare of most penny papers.

The sea-changing success of the penny press was immediately apparent. Within a few months, the New York *Sun* had the largest circulation of any paper in New York City. Within two years, 2 other papers had aped its way. Together, the 3 had a combined circulation twice that of all 11 dailies publishing before the advent of the *Sun* (Schudson 1978, p.18).

The next chapter in the commercial construction of the news was written by the Associated Press. In 1848, a number of newspapers pooled some of their reporters and unfurled the banner of the AP, to provide economical coverage of far-flung events to all of them and to hundreds of other newspaper subscribers over the newly available telegraph wires. In its coverage, the AP eliminated two vestiges of earlier news whose end had begun in the penny papers: partisanship, which would have limited sales to subscribers of varying partisan stripe; and political analysis, which could not be economically transmitted over the wires. These were replaced by the documenting of events whose facts could not be controverted and could be cheaply transmitted on one end of the wire, easily "reconstructed and embellished" on the other (Bennett 1983, p.79).

With the rise, in the 1880s, of department stores and national brand names, advertising became an industry. In turn, so did the monitoring of newspaper circulation. The entrepreneurs who seized this day were the likes of William Randolph Hearst and Joseph Pulitzer, whose "yellow journalism" told in bold face what working class news had become—an extravagant use of illustrations; lurid, multi-column headlines; seductive portraits of the lives of the rich and famous; "women's" pages displaying the allure of being a fashionable consumer; and, especially, sensational, often-prevaricated "news" of crimes, accidents, scandals, and bizarre or sentimental "human interest." This formula mesmerized New York's working multitudes, especially that anxious, hopeful 40 percent of the population of foreign birth, to whom Pulitzer's pages were the perfect screen for receiving their projected fears and desires. The New York

World went from a circulation of 15,000 in 1883, when Pulitzer bought it, to over 250,000 in 1886. His winning formula is one on which today's tabloids, with their own enormous working class readership, have been unable and unwilling to improve (Hoch 1974, p.195; Curran, Douglas, and Whannel 1980, p.293).

But the bottom line of the news business is not only audience size, it is also audience demographics. In 1896, Adolph Ochs began to realize the commercial potential of a relatively small but affluent audience when he purchased the New York *Times*. The *Times* pointedly contrasted the coverage of the yellow "freak journals" with its own, which "will not soil the breakfast cloth," is "all the news that's fit to print," but "not a school for scandal" (Schudson 1978, pp.106–20). At the same time, Ochs was shrewd enough to intuit what pollsters later proved: that social and political analysis may bore or offend even educated readers, and that even educated readers are attracted to "human interest" stories (Curran, Douglas, and Whannel 1980). But he began a stress on "decency," and he filled the unspoken demand of classes that saw themselves as "independent and participant" for "accurate, impartial" political information. The resulting fusion was a newspaper that rendered important events in trivialized, establishmentarian terms. It captured the heart of the up-scale classes, and ever since, the *Times* has been one of the national leaders in advertising lineage, and has operated in the red only once since 1895, during the strike of 1962 (Sigal 1973, p.10).

But Ochs' coup was not only commercial. It conquered the culture as well. At the same time that he sold his newspaper to affluent New Yorkers, he sold his idea of a newspaper to journalists everywhere. Repeated surveys have shown that, above all other newspapers, journalists read, respect, and try to emulate the New York *Times* (for example, Johnstone, Slawski, and Bowman 1976, p.88).

Following the New York *Times* model, most newspapers reduced their partisanship during the 1920s and 30s, but then saw less reason to report politics at all, and coverage of it declined (Rubin 1981, p.114). This tendency has been exacerbated since that time, as market researchers have honed their polling skills and revealed that human interest stories have "universal appeal," transcending age, class, and gender (Curran, Douglas, and Whannel 1980, p.294). In the wake of these findings, even the New York *Times* has increasingly succumbed, not just to trivializing important subjects, but to ignoring them. Its 1976 format change reduced coverage of local and national news by 11 and 30 percent, while the number of society and women's pages nearly doubled (Shapiro 1976). At the same time, half of all newspapers of over 100,000 readers and 42 percent of those with 50,000 to 100,000 added "life-style" sections in a single two-year period, 1977–79 (Bogart 1981, pp.150–51). Leo Bogart, who for over 20 years has conducted polls of readers for the

American Newspaper Publishers Association calls these innovations "a marketing *tour de force*" (1981, p.151).

This history of the news can be viewed as a series of commercial innovations, which, when successful, were copied. At the same time, most of these innovations were described in their time as the truth that would make us free. To the extent that that was a significant part of their appeal,[12] the fault lies not in our commercial stars but in ourselves. What was it about American culture that allowed it to mistake meaningless facticity for the bulwark of democracy?

By the 1830s, the Enlightenment had converted the Western world to its faith in science: the idea that the disinterested pursuit of knowledge would make a better world in the social and political, as well as in the material and technological realms. To the public mind,[13] the methodology of this great enterprise involved only the undaunting job of accumulating facts (Schiller 1981, p.83).

This new faith that the objective pursuit of the facts would lead to the "correct political solution" found an especially receptive body of believers in the United States. Unmarked as they were by the fault lines of feudalism, Americans had always agreed that there is one common weal, one *res publica*. Even by the time modern news came squalling into the world, working class Americans continued to hold the truth of individualism self-evident. Although, by the 1830s, their dream of upward mobility to master-craftsman status was increasingly beleaguered and defensive as mass production consigned more and more of them to a permanent status of wage earners, American workers continually reaffirmed the right of individual property, "as that which binds together these United States" (quotation from *The Mechanics Press*, in Schiller 1981, p.28). Unlike their English counterparts (Thompson 1966, pp.788–806), they did not see themselves as a class with interests opposed to those who owned the factories where they worked.

In parts of class-conscious Europe, the view of the news is that from that infinitude of facts out there, competing political philosophies can and should draw together competing political realities, each of which comports with verifiable fact but differs from the others over values (Wiro 1982). In the United States, there were no competing political philosophies. This consensus made possible Americans' simple faith in the definite article of the news: *the* facts, *the* reality could and should be objectively reported. "It Shines for All," boasted the logo of the New York *Sun*. Our "only guide," said James G. Bennett, the great apologist of the penny press, is "good, sound, practical common sense" in the "great cause" of "truth, public faith, and science, against falsehood, fraud, and ignorance" (Schiller 1981, pp. 48, 80). Ye shall know the facts, and the facts shall make you free. Nearly a century later, American journalism had not come much further, even in the writing of the great prophet of the now-canonized professional code of objectivity, Walter Lippman. He called the "ideal of objective testimony...cardinal" and described it as the "habit of disinterested realism of the scientist" (from Schudson 1978, p.155). But beneath the flourishing rhetoric lay the withered truth: the news had become the "disinterested" account of trivia, the "objective testimony" of elites.

EPILOGUE

Pick up a paper. Turn on the news. What does it say?

Fire claimed the life of a west-side woman today...on charges of murdering her infant son,...as the number of Americans living in poverty declined for the third consecutive month....An exuberant President Reagan...was sub-machine-gunned to death during a traffic dispute as his family watched,...while Dole, who has often joked with reporters about the rivalry in recent weeks... was listed in critical condition at St. Luke's hospital in Birmingham,...where thousands of demonstrators roamed the streets, clashing with riot police, smashing store windows and looting shops...of the communist-backed rebel forces, ...many of whom appear to have suffered assaults at the hands...of a race too close to call. Reliable sources indicate that...despite the nationwide manhunt for...a "monstrous act of vicious cowardice,..." there was no apparent motive.

With coffee and toast, we take them in, the banalities of horror. They do not bore us. They do not offend us. They do not enlighten us. And we are here, "as on a darkling plain," surrounded by the incandescent, inconstant light of the news, flashing now upon a murder, now upon a war, now upon a hackneyed explanation, illuminating nothing. Sometimes what we seem to see for a split second is terrifying. Often it is a show, fun to watch, like fireworks. Usually it is reassuring in its sameness. Never does it light the deep dark of our ignorance. News flashes. Signal flares for an army of the night.

NOTES

1. Gramsci's term for the conventional wisdom.
2. For a contrary opinion, see Efron (1971). The liberal bias argument has been roundly and effectively criticized elsewhere on methodological grounds— see Hofstetter (1976) and Frank (1975). Also cited in support of the liberal bias argument is the fact that many reporters, especially those working for large, prestigious news organizations describe themselves as "liberals" (Lichter and Rothman 1982). But these are precisely the organizations where personal viewpoint is most likely to be preempted by the norm of objectivity (Epstein 1973, p. 207; Robinson 1983). Besides, Gans and Epstein have separately concluded that scratching the surface of the newsman's "liberalism" shows him to be centrist and apolitical (Epstein 1973, pp. 211-15; Gans 1979, pp. 211–12), an impression

affirmed by a more recent survey of news media personnel. This one compared their attitudes to those of a spectrum of "opinion leaders" and found their attitudes more liberal than those of businessmen and farmers, but less liberal than those of Democrats, labor leaders—and the public at large (Verba and Orren 1985, p. 79). For an extended critique of the Lichter-Rothman thesis, see Gans (1985).

3. For a look at what else there is besides "all the news that's fit to print," compare coverage of a current event in *Time* or *Newsweek* to coverage in *The Guardian* or *In These Times*.

4. Influence, sway, rulership.

5. The announcement of this theme also has much to do with the ability of political elites to define the truth for the media. More of that below.

6. Readers may be so used to this anti-socialism being unquestioned in the news that it now seems unquestionable. Those who think so should consult Wilber (1969) or Heilbroner (1963).

7. For the newspaper equivalent to television's dialectic, called "writing it down the middle," see Sigal, 1973, p. 68.

8. A related phenomenon involves the predominance of "bad news" over "good," including negative reporting of presidential candidates (Robinson 1981). Conservatives have argued that this produces an anti-system bias. Evidence suggests that citizen mistrust has followed the media's pointing finger—to authorities, not to the system (Lipset and Schneider 1983).

9. The fact that local news is often the source of the river of audience flow puts enormous pressure on local news to try to attract, not just maintain an audience. This pressure has helped make local news especially susceptible to the influence of "news doctors"—market researchers whose dubious nostrums are described below.

10. Disagreement among newsmen centers around the question of whether they should confine themselves to "reporting the facts" or go on to explain those facts. Despite hyperbole about this latter idea "exploding the concept of the news," "interpretive reporting" remains a rather staid concept, based on the objectivity ideal. Interpretation itself, it is believed, can and should be "objective," telling "both sides" of the story (Markel 1974).

11. For example, "James Gordon Bennett linked the content of his New York *Herald* quite openly to his ultimate goal—business success" (Schiller 1981, p. 47).

12. That extent is difficult to determine, but we do have some fragmentary evidence. One of the main reasons Americans give for reading newspapers has to do with the duty to be informed (Bogart 1981, ch. 5).

13. And, to some extent, even to the predominantly Baconian scientists of the day (Schiller 1981, p. 84).

REFERENCES

Altheide, David L., and Robert P. Snow. 1979. *Media Logic*. Beverly Hills: Sage.

Bachrach, Peter, and Morton S. Baratz. 1970. *Power and Poverty*. New York: Oxford University Press.

Bagdikian, Ben H. 1973. "The Fruits of Agnewism." *Columbia Journalism Review*, January/February, pp.9–23.

———. 1972. "The Politics of American Newspapers." *Columbia Journalism Review*, March/April, pp.8–13.

Barnouw, Erik. 1978. *The Sponsor*. New York: Oxford University Press.

Bennett, W. Lance. 1983. *News: The Politics of Illusion*. New York: Longman.

———. 1980. *Public Opinion in American Politics*. New York: Harcourt, Brace, Jovanovich.

Bogart, Leo. 1981. *Press and Public: Who Reads What, When, Where, and Why in American Newspapers*. Hillsdale, N.J.: Lawrence Earlbaum Associates.

Boorstin, Daniel. 1961. *The Image: A Guide to Psuedo-Events in America*. New York: Atheneum.

Bordewich, Fergus M. 1977. "Supermarketing the News." *Columbia Journalism Review*, September/October, pp.23–36.

Breed, Warren. 1980. *The Newspaperman, News, and Society*. New York: Arno Press.

———. 1958. "Mass Communication and Sociocultural Integration." *Social Forces* 37:109–16.

———. 1955. "Social Control in the Newsroom: A Functional Analysis." *Social Forces* 33:326–35.

Campbell, Angus, Philip E. Converse, Warren E. Miller, and Donald Stokes. 1960. *The American Voter*. New York: Wiley.

Chomsky, Noam, and Edward S. Herman. 1979. *The Political Economy of Human Rights*. Vol. 1. Boston: South End Press.

Cirino, Robert. 1971. *Don't Blame the People*. New York: Vintage Books.

Cohen, Bernard C. 1963. *The Press, the Public, and Foreign Policy*. Princeton, N.J.: Princeton University Press.

Coldevin, Gary O. 1972. "Internationalism and Mass Communications." *Journalism Quarterly* 49:365–8.

Crouse, Timothy. 1973. *The Boys on the Bus*. New York: Random House.

Curran, James, Angus Douglas, and Gary Whannel. 1980. "The Political Economy of the Human Interest Story." In *Newspapers and Democracy*, edited by Anthony Smith. Cambridge, Mass.: MIT Press.

Donohue, G.A., P.J. Tichenor, and C.N. Olien. 1975. "Mass Media and the Knowledge Gap: A Hypothesis Reconsidered." *Communication Research* 2:3–23.

Dye, Thomas R., and L. Harmon Zeigler. 1978. *The Irony of Democracy*. North Scituate, Mass.: Duxbury Press.

Efron, Edith. 1971. *The News Twisters*. Los Angeles: Nash Publishers.

Engwall, Lars. 1981. *Newspapers as Organizations*. Westmead, Eng.: Gower.

Epstein, Edward Jay. 1981. "The Selection of Reality." In *What's News?* edited by Elie Abel. San Francisco: Institute for Contemporary Studies.

———. 1973. *News from Nowhere*. New York: Vintage Books.

Erikson, Robert S., Norman R. Luttbeg, and Kent L. Tedin. 1980. *American Public Opinion*. New York: John Wiley and Sons.

Exoo, Calvin F. 1984. "Journalists' Perspectives on the Critique of Political Journalism." Paper presented at the annual meeting of the Northeast Political Science Association.

Flegel, Ruth C., and Steven H. Chaffee. 1971. "Influences of Editors, Readers, and Personal Opinions on Reporters." *Journalism Quarterly* 48:645–51.

Flippen, Charles C., ed. 1974. *Liberating the Media.* Washington, D.C.: Acropolis Books.

Frank, Robert S. 1975. "The IAS Case against CBS." *Journal of Communication* 25:186–89.

Gans, Herbert J. 1985. "Are U.S. Journalists Dangerously Liberal?" *Columbia Journalism Review,* November/December, pp.29n33.

———. 1979. *Deciding What's News.* New York: Pantheon Books.

Gitlin, Todd. 1980. *The Whole World Is Watching.* Berkeley: University of California Press.

Graber, Doris J. 1984. *Processing the News.* New York: Longman.

———. 1980. *Mass Media and American Politics.* Washington, D.C.: Congressional Quarterly Press.

Greenwald, John. 1986. "A New Age of Capitalism." *Time,* July 28, 1986, pp.28–39.

Hamill, Pete. 1985. "Fear and Favor at the New York *Times,*" *The Village Voice* 30:17–24.

Heilbroner, Robert L. 1963. *The Great Ascent.* New York: Harper and Row.

Hoch, Paul. 1974. *The Newspaper Game.* London: Calder and Boyars.

Hofstetter, C. Richard. 1976. *Bias in the News.* Columbus: Ohio State University Press.

Hollander, Neil. 1971. "Adolescents and the War: The Sources of Socialization." *Journalism Quarterly* 48:472–79.

Hulteng, John L. 1979. *The News Media.* Englewood Cliffs, N.J.: Prentice-Hall.

Johnstone, John W.C., Edward Slawski, and William W. Bowman. 1976. *The News People.* Urbana: University of Illinois Press.

Kraus, Sidney, and Dennis Davis. 1976. *The Effects of Mass Communication on Political Behavior.* University Park: The Pennsylvania State University Press.

Ladd, Everett Carll, and Seymour Martin Lipset. 1980. "Anatomy of a Decade." *Public Opinion* 3:2–4.

Lazarsfeld, Paul, Bernard Berelson, and Hazel Gaudet. 1944. *The People's Choice.* New York: Columbia University Press.

Lemert, James B. 1981. *Does Mass Communication Change Public Opinion after All?* Chicago: Nelson-Hall.

Lichter, Robert, and Stanley Rothman. 1982. "Media and Business Elites." *Public Opinion,* December/January, pp.42–46.

Lindsay, Vachel. 1954. "Bryan, Bryan, Bryan, Bryan." In *A Pocket Book of Modern Verse,* edited by Oscar Williams. New York: Washington Square Press.

Lipset, Seymour M., and William Schneider. 1983. *The Confidence Gap.* New York: The Free Press.

Lipsky, Michael, and David J. Olson. 1976. "The Processing of Racial Crisis in America." *Politics and Society* 6:79–103.

Markel, Lester. 1974. "Objective Journalism." In *Liberating the Media,* edited by Charles C. Flippen. Washington, D.C.: Acropolis Books.

Molotch, Harvey, and Marilyn Lester. 1974. "Accidents, Scandals, and Routines: Resources for Insurgent Methodology." In *The TV Establishment,* edited by Gaye Tuchman. Englewood Cliffs, N.J.: Prentice-Hall.

Moore, David. 1982. "Political Campaigns and the Knowledge Gap Hypothesis."

Paper presented at the annual meeting of the Northeast Political Science Association.

Newfield, Jack. 1974. "Journalism: Old, New and Corporate." In *The Reporter as Artist: A Look at the New Journalism*, edited by Ronald Weber. New York: Hastings House.

Orr, C. Jack. 1980. "Reporters Confront the President: Sustaining a Counterpoised Situation." *Quarterly Journal of Speech* 66:17–32.

Paletz, David L., and Robert M. Entman. 1981. *Media-Power-Politics*. New York: The Free Press.

Patterson, Thomas E. 1980. *The Mass Media Election*. New York: Praeger.

Phelan, John M. 1977. *Mediaworld*. New York: Seabury Press.

Ranney, Austin, and Michael J. Robinson. 1985. *The Mass Media in Campaign '84*. Washington, D.C.: American Enterprise Institute.

Robinson, John P. 1974. "The Press as Kingmaker: What Surveys Show from the Last Five Campaigns." *Journalism Quarterly* 51:587–94, 606.

Robinson, Michael J. 1983. "Just How Liberal Is the News?" *Public Opinion*, February/March, pp.55–60.

———. 1981. "A Statesman Is a Dead Politician: Candidate Images on Network News." In *What's News*, edited by Elie Abel. San Francisco: Institute for Contemporary Studies.

Robinson, Michael J., and Margaret A. Sheehan. 1983. *Over the Wire and on TV*. New York: Russell Sage Foundation.

Rubin, Richard L. 1981. *Press, Party, and Presidency*. New York: W.W. Norton.

Schiller, Dan. 1981. *Objectivity and the News*. Philadelphia: University of Pennsylvania Press.

Schudson, Michael. 1978. *Discovering the News*. New York: Basic Books.

Semple, Robert. 1974. "The Necessity of Conventional Journalism: A Blend of the Old and the New." In *Liberating the Media*, edited by Charles C. Flippen. Washington, D.C.: Acropolis Books.

Shapiro, Fred C. 1976. "Shrinking the News." *Columbia Journalism Review*, November/December, pp.23–27.

Shoemaker, Pamela J. 1984. "Media Treatment of Deviant Political Groups." *Journalism Quarterly* 61:66–75, 82.

Sigal, Leon V. 1973. *Reporters and Officials*. Lexington, Mass.: D.C. Heath.

Steffens, Lincoln. 1957. *The Shame of the Cities*. New York: Hill and Wang.

Thimmesch, Nick. 1984. "The Editorial Endorsement Game." *Public Opinion*, October/November, pp.10–14.

Thompson, E.P. *The Making of the English Working Class*. New York: Vintage Books.

Tuchman, Gaye. 1978. *Making News*. New York: The Free Press.

———. 1972. "Objectivity as Strategic Ritual: An Examination of Newsmen's Notions of Objectivity." *American Journal of Sociology* 77:660–79.

Udell, Jon G. 1978. *The Economics of the American Newspaper*. New York: Hastings House.

Verba, Sidney, and Gary R. Orren. 1985. *Equality in America*. Cambridge, Mass.: Harvard University Press.

Weaver, David H., Doris A. Graber, Maxwell E. McCombs, and Chaim H. Eyal. 1981. *Media Agenda-Setting in a Presidential Election*. New York: Praeger.

Weinstein, James. 1968. *The Corporate Ideal in the Liberal State*. Boston: Beacon Press.

Wilber, Charles. 1969. *The Soviet Model and Underdeveloped Countries*. Chapel Hill: University of North Carolina Press.

Wiro, Osmo. 1982. "Government and Media in Scandinavia." In *Government and the Media—Comparative Dimensions*, edited by Dan Nimmo and Michael W. Mansfield. Waco, Tex.: Baylor University Press.

Wolf, Frank. 1972. *Television Programming for News and Public Affairs*. New York: Praeger.

4

The Great American Dream Machine

Douglas Kellner

During the first two decades of the twentieth century, leisure in the United States became increasingly dominated by forms of entertainment manufactured by corporations, which were simultaneously interested in maximizing profit and selling "the American Way of Life" (Goldman and Wilson 1977). The culture industries sold dreams, thrills and mass-produced fantasies that helped socialize individuals into American values, institutions, and forms of behavior (Adorno and Horkheimer 1972). New media like film, radio, and television successively appeared on the American scene and captivated large audiences and portions of leisure time. They celebrated the pleasures of the consumer society and commodity consumption; romantic love and family life; institutions like the military, police, legal system, and state; and values of individualism, consumer capitalism, and American-style representative democracy. Popular culture in the United States helped determine proper style and social behavior, gender role construction and behavior for "men" and "women," and the sort of dreams and fantasies that reproduced the values and ideologies of the socioeconomic and political system.

As the twentieth century developed, more and more leisure time was spent in the consumption of popular culture entertainment, and even the forms of news and information became dominated by the narrative forms of entertainment as mass communications and culture became increasingly important social forces (Kellner 1980).

We shall investigate in this chapter the origins, development, and forms of the consumer and media society that we live in today, and the ways that popular entertainment contributes to political socialization by helping to produce individuals to fit into and adapt to the existing social order. We shall see that seemingly harmless and "fun" products like the movies, popular music, advertising, and TV serve to transmit dominant myths, ideologies, and values of U.S. society, and thus serve to influence how we see, experience, understand, and act in our social lives. We will begin with some reflections on the movies, since the film industry was one of the first and most important of the entertainment machines to appear in American life.

HOLLYWOOD AND THE AMERICAN DREAM

Film soon became the most popular and influential form of mass culture in the United States (Sklar 1975; Jowett 1976). Film was probably the first mass-produced cultural form of the twentieth century, which introduced a new technology and mode of entertainment that soon after its introduction changed patterns of leisure activity and began to play an important role within social life.

Early films were the inventions of technicians and entrepreneurs like the Lumières and Méliès in France, and the Edison Corporation in the United States. The first films ranged from the documentaries and quasi-documentary realist fictions produced by the Lumières and Edison to fantasy fictions of Méliès. The genres that would characterize Hollywood film soon began to appear with Westerns like *The Great Train Robbery* (1903), the melodramatic social dramas of D.W. Griffith, costume and historical dramas like *Ben Hur* (the first of several versions appeared in 1899), horror films, and comedies by Mack Sennett, Charlie Chaplin, Buster Keaton, and others.

The demand for films was great and the early film studios began repeating and reproducing the formulas and types of film that were most popular. Consequently, Hollywood films were divided into the most popular types of genres like the western, melodrama, gangster film, horror films, and, with the coming of sound, the musical (Schatz 1981).

Film rapidly became the dominant form of popular culture in the United States. Indeed, for the first half of the twentieth century—from 1896 to the 1950s—movies were the most popular and influential medium of culture in the United States. The number of theaters grew from about 10,000 storefront nickelodeons with daily attendance of 4 to 5 million in 1910 to around 28,000 movie theaters by 1928 (May 1983). In the 1920s the average audience was between 25 and 30 million customers a week (May 1983) while by the 1930s from 85 to 110 million people paid to go to the movies each week (Dieterle 1941). Consequently, films became a major force of socialization providing role models, instruction in dress and fashion, in courtship and love, and in marriage and career.

Early films, however, were produced largely for working class, immigrant and urban audiences, and some critics of the movies thought that they had negative or subversive effects (Jowett 1976). For example, the comedies of Charlie Chaplin made fun of authority figures, and romantic dramas were attacked by the Legion of Decency for promoting promiscuity. And crime dramas were frequently attacked for promoting juvenile delinquency and crime. On the other hand, films were believed to help "Americanize" immigrants, to teach their audiences how to be good Americans, and to provide escape from the cares of everyday life (Ewen and Ewen 1982).

Whereas films from around 1903–15 sometimes presented poverty and social struggle from progressive perspectives sympathetic to the poor and oppressed, beginning in the 1920s many films began focusing on the rich and can be read as advertisements for the consumer society (May 1983). Cecil B. deMille's comedies and dramas of modern marriage, for example, can be seen as marriage and fashion models, and the romantic films of the 1920s can be read as "manuals of desire, wishes, dreams" (Ewen and Ewen 1982, p.102).

Yet conservatives continued to worry about subversive effects of the movies, and due to pressure from civic groups and the threat of government regulation, a set of censorship boards were set up with the cooperation of the film industry, which eventually established a Production Code (Jowett 1976). Explicit limits were set on the length of allowable kisses (with mouth shut, of course), no nudity or explicit sexuality was allowed, such things as prostitution and drugs could not be portrayed, criminals had to be punished, and religion and the church could not be criticized (the code is reproduced in Jowett 1976). The Production Code lasted from the 1930s to the 1960s (although it was challenged in the 1950s) and set firm ideological parameters to Hollywood films.

But the crucial determinant of the ideological functions of Hollywood film had to do with control of film production by major studios and the emergence of the studio system from around 1917 through the 1960s (Bordwell, Staiger, and Thompson 1985). Hollywood film production became dominated early on by giant studios, which monopolized the patents necessary for film production and projection, and which primarily produced films for profit.

Since the studios repeatedly reproduced the types of film that they thought were the most popular, Hollywood cinema became primarily a *genre cinema* in which popular formulas are repeated in cycles or genres (that is, types) of film—westerns, gangsters, melodramas, horror films, and so on. The most popular genres of film deal with the central conflicts, problems, and concerns of a society. The western, for example, deals with conflicts between civilization and threats to civilization, whereas the gangster film deals with threats to law, order, and social stability within an already established urban society. Melodramas, social comedies, and musicals deal with conflicts and problems within domestic concerns like family and romance, whereas war films and adventure genres generally deal with conflicts in the public sphere outside domestic circles.

Genres become established when visual, stylistic, and thematic concerns become formalized into an immediately recognizable system of conventions. The western, for example, developed into a generic form featuring conflicts between cowboy heroes and villains in the familiar setting of the West. The plot contained gunfights, chase scenes, and eventual defeat of forces of disorder; the visual imagery utilized alternating desert and small town or homestead scenes, horses, saloons, and sets of bad guys posed against the "good" townspeople, homesteaders, and cowboy hero.

Genres were a preferred type of film for the Hollywood studio system since they were popular, conventional, and easy to reproduce. The studios were set up like factories with big barns, rows of barracks, stock sets, and so forth, in a production process that thrives on formulas and conventions. Thus following the economic imperatives of the capitalist system to produce products as quickly and cheaply as possible to maximize production and profits, the Hollywood cinema became a genre cinema (Schatz 1981).

In order to resonate to audience fears, fantasies, and experiences, the Hollywood genres had to deal with the central conflicts and problems in U.S. society, and had to offer soothing resolutions, assuring its audiences that all problems could be solved within existing institutions. Western films, for example, assured its audiences that "civilization" could be maintained in the face of threats from criminals, "foreigners," and villains of various sorts, and celebrated individualism, white male authority figures, and violence as a legitimate way of resolving conflicts. In the westerns' mythological vision of American history, it was glossed over that the villains in many westerns (that is, "Indians," Mexicans, and so forth) were the land's original inhabitants who had had their property stolen by the white settlers, presented as being forces of civilization. Instead, the central problem of the western was the "taming" of the West, the triumph of "civilization" in the "wilderness," the triumph of "Good" over "Evil" (see Wright 1977; Jewett and Lawrence 1977).

Gangster films appealed to people's fear of crime and fascination with criminals; on the whole, they inculcated the message that "crime does not pay" and showed police and the legal system able to contain crime and to deal with criminals (Warshow 1970). But gangster films also explored cultural contradictions and conflicts in values central to U.S. society. Gangsters are, in fact, prototypal capitalists who will do anything to get money; they do what capitalists do in their ordinary business activity (that is, anything to make a buck). Gangster films thus explore the tensions within American life between making money and morality, between self-interest and legality, and between private and public interests. The gangsters are fantasy characters who act out secret audience desires to get ahead no matter what, although it is still not clear if their repeated punishment (mandated by the Production Code) actually helped prevent crime through dramatizing what would happen if one broke the rules of the game and stepped outside the law, or promoted crime through making the gangsters—often played by popular figures like James Cagney or Humphrey Bogart—the most dynamic, attractive, and vital figures.

Melodramas, social comedies, and musicals in turn legitimated male-dominated romance, marriage, and family, and moral rectitude as the proper road to happiness and well-being. Musicals followed formulas of boy meets girl, boy loses girl, and boy gets girl to celebrate the desirability of male-dominated romance. Melodramas dramatized what would happen to wayward women or willful men who failed to conform to dominant gender roles. They celebrated hardworking mothers who sacrificed their own happiness for their children, thus projecting the proper role for women (for example, *Imitation of Life*; *Stella Dallas*; *Mildred Pierce*; and others), and intimated that life's greatest happiness derived from marriage and family. And social comedies, too, celebrated marriage and family as the proper goals for men and women (Cavell 1982). Indeed, David Bordwell claims that in his random selection of 100 "typical" Hollywood movies, 95 made romance at least one important line of action while, in 85, heterosexual romantic love was *the* major focus (Bordwell, Staiger, and Thompson 1985, p.16).

In any case, Hollywood genre films tended to promote the American Dream and to provide vehicles for dominant myths and ideologies. The genres taught that money and success were important values; that heterosexual romance, marriage, and family were the proper social forms; that the State, police, and legal system were legitimate sources of power and authority; that violence was justified to destroy any threats to the system; and that American values and institutions were basically sound, benevolent, and beneficial.

In this way, Hollywood film, supported by other forms of popular culture, established a certain *hegemony*, or cultural dominance of certain institutions and values to the exclusion of others. As Raymond Williams argues:

I would say that in any society, in any particular period, there is a central system of practices, meanings and values, which we can properly call dominant and effective.... In any case what I have in mind is the central, effective and dominant system of meanings and values, which are not merely abstract but which are organized and lived. That is why hegemony is not to be understood at the level of mere opinion or mere manipulation. It is a whole body of practices and expectations; our assignments of energy, our ordinary understanding of the nature of man and of his world. It is a set of meanings and values which as they are experienced as practices appear as reciprocally confirming (Williams 1973, pp.8–9).

Hollywood film is thus implicitly "political" in the way it tends to support dominant American values and institutions. The more explicitly political functions of Hollywood cinema generally emerge in times of social crisis. During both World War I and World War II, war films and other genres advocated patriotism and presented the "enemy" in stereotypical terms. During the Cold War anti-communist period, Hollywood produced a genre cycle of anti-communist films that depicted the threat to democracy and the American Way of Life in the "communist conspiracy" (Shain 1974). Whereas, during World War II, Russians were presented positively as our allies against fascism, from the late 1940s on through *Rambo* they are generally presented as the incarnation of evil (there will be more discussion of the resurgence of anti-communism in popular culture in a later section of this chapter).

After a particularly conservative period during the 1950s, in the 1960s there was an emergence of both more radical and socially critical films, although there was a reaction against 1960s' and 70s' radicalism in the films of the 1980s. Generally speaking, however, Hollywood films have presented dominant dreams and fantasies and have celebrated the American Way of Life. The institution of theater going contributes to the cultural power of the films. When the lights are turned out, the spectator relaxes and is invited to identify with larger than life characters and compelling images and situations. The darkened theater encourages fantasy and a dream-like state of consciousness whereby one's conscious defenses are down and one may unconsciously assimilate the values and attitudes being portrayed on the silver screen.

Hollywood films thus assumed significant cultural power and helped promote the values, life-styles, and institutions central to U.S. society. Films therefore became a central focus of leisure activity, an important vehicle of socialization, and an integral part of the consumer society that became the defining feature of U.S. society in the twentieth century.

ADVERTISING AND THE RISE OF THE CONSUMER SOCIETY

Today we are surrounded by mass media and the messages and images of the consumer society. We wake up and turn on the radio, television, or a record player. We go to school or work and observe the clothing styles of those around us; we talk about and perhaps admire people's possessions; we enjoy household gadgets and products, and are bombarded on all sides with advertising messages to buy, consume, and possess the wonders of the commodity society.

When, where, and how did the consumer society arise and why did it become such a central force in our lives? Does consumption make us happier, freer, and better off than we were in a less consumer-oriented environment? How are our attitudes, behavior, and values shaped by advertising and all the institutions of the consumer society? What role does advertising and consumerism play in legitimating the socioeconomic system in the United States and in making us compliant players in the American game of competition, success, and material consumption? And how can we become more rational consumers and free ourselves from media manipulation and advertising indoctrination?

Probably few of us raise these questions. Most of us have grown up in a society inundated by magazines, television, and radio with their ubiquitous ads. Most of us go to shopping malls or stores and are confronted with slickly packaged goods and a wealth of services—all for the right price, of course. We are used to everything from sexual to medical services having a price tag and are told that there is no free lunch: everything in the society is a commodity and we are led to believe that consumer capitalism is the best socioeconomic system in the world. Is this so? And how did consumer capitalism come to play such an important role in our lives?

As Elizabeth and Stuart Ewen tell us in their important history of the consumer society, consumerism and Americanism were promoted by mass images beginning in the nineteenth century when newspapers began selling advertising and when corporations attempted to impress their brand name and product's image on the consumer (Ewen and Ewen 1982). The Ewens tell the story of how a young Czech girl, Anna Kuthan, was fascinated by the labels on bales of cotton and the products she handled as a servant girl in Vienna; these "channels of desire" promised a new world of commodity paradise, of happiness through consumption. She eventually immigrated to the United States and the reality was a life of hard work and suffering compensated by a few brand name products that she had always dreamed of. Was she, in fact, better off leaving her home and traditions to toil in a New York ghetto? Was the possibility of enabling her children to own a house in the suburbs worth her own life of toil? Is consumption the way to happiness?

The consumer society evolved into the dominant form of American society after World War II. It had its origins in the big department stores (Macy's, Gimbel's, Marshall Field's) and the mail order houses (Sears', Ward's) that began in the nineteenth century (Ewen and Ewen 1982).

It was promoted by the advertising agencies and corporate campaigns of the 1920s but was postponed first by the Great Depression of the 1930s, which dramatized the failures of capitalism to provide a rational society without State intervention (Ewen 1976), and then by World War II, which dramatized the darker side of twentieth-century drives for power and profits. After World War II, returning servicemen came home with large amounts of back pay and the corporations tooled up to make the consumer society a reality. New goods, services, shopping centers, and marketing techniques appeared, and the move toward the suburbs and rise of television helped promote the consumer society (Jezer 1982).

From the 1950s to the present might be seen in retrospect as the Age of Consumption. But how do advertising and consumption socialize us into being compliant participants in the American Dream? First of all, what is significant about advertising is not the fact that it's selling this or that toothpaste, shampoo, or car, but that it's selling consumerism as a way of life and is promoting the belief that happiness is to be found through consumption. Advertising implies that a solution to every problem can be found through the commodity purchased, and thus offers commodity solutions to all the problems of life. You're not getting enough dates? Buy the proper mouthwash, deodorant, perfume, or after-shave lotion and all will be well. You're not successful sexually? Buy a new car, better clothes, more up-scale alcohol and toys and you'll score. This sounds crude but it is the clear message of most fashion ads and a large percentage of magazine ads, which use sexual desires and insecurity to sell their products—and sometimes include blatantly subliminal sexual imagery as well (Key 1972).

Advertising also promises commodity solutions to health problems. You're not feeling well? Just take Geritol for tired blood; XY and Z for headaches; A or B for heartburn or indigestion; or eat Wheaties, the breakfast of champions, or Total or K, and you'll supposedly be bursting with vim, vigor, and vitality.

Advertising also plays on fears that one is either not attractive enough or is not properly playing one's role in life. Do you want to be a good housewife and mother? Buy X soap to eliminate ring-around-the-collar; brand P frozen pizza to bring your family to quasi-orgasmic ecstasies; and Q bathroom deodorant and sweetener to give your toilet more appetizing smells and colors. Want to have a happy family life? Go to MacDonald's, pig out on Big Macs, and enjoy the pleasures promised to all good Americans (and to be sure to have plenty of stomach remedies at home to deal with the aftermaths of junk food orgies).

Do you want to have fun, enjoy community, and social acceptance? Join the Pepsi generation; or be a Pepper; or drink Coke or the Uncola, 7-Up (and be sure to have a good dentist for when your teeth start rotting). And girls, do you want to be a Total Woman? Easy, just buy a 24-hour perfume so you can work your ass off at the office or school; come home and fix dinner and clean up the house, and still be sexy and sweet smelling for hubby or boyfriend. And do you want to be really respected and desired, boys? Just get a new luxury car, read *Playboy* or *Esquire* to see what you need for your pad, and just wait for the bunnies to come running over (and hope that they don't bring any sexual diseases with them).

The point that I am trying to make is that ads offer commodity solutions to all problems, and present consumption as the route to happiness. Therefore, advertising not only sells products but tries to sell consumerism as a way of life, the American Way of Life. It provides role models showing us how to be a proper man or woman, and sells specific values like romance and sexuality as crucial values of fundamental importance. In turn, it uses desires for sex and romance to sell specific products.

Advertising also sells institutions like the family, and American values like individuality, gratification through consumption, and the joys of ownership. As Robert Goldman has argued, certain ads promote an idealized version of American history and the institutions and values of corporate capitalism as they try to huckster their products (Goldman 1984). For instance, McDonald's ads frequently contain images of small town America, family life, middle class affluence, and integrated Americana, which surround the images of the Big Macs and Macmuffins that they are trying to get you to buy.

Other ads promote American ideology by equating consumerism with "Freedom of Choice" (that is, between their light and regular beer) or tell you to be an "individual" by buying this or that product, or dousing yourself in this or that perfume or after-shave lotion. And note that "individualism" here is defined in terms of possession, consumption, and style—as opposed to thought, action, dissent, rational behavior and autonomy, which were previous definitions of individualism promoted by the Founding Fathers and nineteenth century individualists like Thoreau, Emerson, or Whitman.

Advertising and consumerism are thus of crucial social importance for producing the needs, values, and behavior that have become a cultural dominant in the contemporary United States. Advertising is consequently a crucial part of the ideological apparatus of consumer capitalism. Consumerism is thus an all-important instrument of social control and a means by which individuals are integrated into society. Today in the United States, individuals are manipulated and indoctrinated by consumerism into social conformity and into accepting the American Way of Life as the only way of life.

But what's wrong with all of this and what can be done about it? First of all, the rise of the consumer society has meant the homogenization of America and has contributed to the incredible power enjoyed by corporations that have come to control all facets of life in the United States. Marty Jezer points out, in his history of life in the United States after World War II, that as recently as 1950 there were about 450 breweries selling their own local brands of beer and there were hundreds of brands of soft drinks, as well, locally produced by small businesses. But with the development of corporate capitalism, these smaller companies were driven out of business and, by 1970, the number of breweries was down to 70, with the 10 largest corporations controlling 70 percent of the market (Jezer 1982, pp.135–38). The result was the homogenization of America.

Indeed, corporate control of the economy has made the United States look alike all over: drive down Anystreet U.S.A. and you will see generic America in the form of filling stations selling the same brands of gas everywhere, fast-food chains selling the same junk food, video stores renting the same (quite small) selection of films, and chains of other products selling the same goods everywhere. How has this come about and what have we lost?

Through quasi-monopolies, advertising, price-fixing, mergers, and other corporate developments, giant corporations have come to dominate the economy and society in the United States. Thus commodity production and distribution have become standardized, homogenized, and centrally controlled—all of the standard accusations against socialism! There are less products produced locally, less crafts and artisan production, and thus less variety and diversity of goods. Moreover, the consumer must pay for the entire corporate infrastructure and advertising, marketing, packaging, and so forth. Any corporation advertising products on television or other advertising media passes down costs to the consumer. All packaging and marketing expenses are part of what we pay for brand name goods. Thus in effect we are subsidizing entire industries and agencies, which are trying to manipulate, indoctrinate, and exploit us.

But what can we do? First, we should become rational consumers and see that anything advertised on television is probably overpriced, since astronomical advertising expenses have been factored into the price. Generally, generic products can be had of the same or better quality and at a lower price. Moreover, when it comes to food, corporate food has been sprayed with pesticides, preserved with chemicals, and treated with synthetics that are often harmful to one's health; and, of course, the very term "junk food" suggests that it's lacking in nutrition. Many other products are overpriced and are shoddily constructed. "Planned obsolescence," for example, has been one of the scandals of the U.S. automobile industry and one of the reasons this industry is no longer competitive on the world market: as early as the 1950s, Vance Packard argued that U.S. automobiles were produced to self-destruct after a short time to force consumers to buy new models (Packard 1960).

I do not want, however, to polemicize here against consumption and commodities per se. Consumption can be a legitimate pleasure and commodities can be of use and value to us. One does not have to buy junk food, worthless nostrums, overpriced cars, or shoddy goods. If one looks, one can always find alternatives. But I am suggesting that one should be very careful in buying any products produced by giant corporations, which are likely to be overpriced, injurious to health, shoddily constructed, and likely to self-destruct. Moreover, one may be buying simply because of manipulation by advertising to do so (Kellner 1983). To avoid such manipulation and exploitation: buy generic; buy from small businesses or local products, or crafts; or buy used products from friends or someone you trust. Most important: seek out alternative institutions like food co-ops, or more healthy products like fruit juices instead of soft drinks, the desire for which is no doubt the product of manipulation and bad habits. Moreover, one should learn to protect oneself against manipulation by advertising through becoming aware of how ads are constructed; of what techniques are being used; what devices are used to manipulate; and what general social messages are being sent.

Indeed, despite propaganda from corporations and advertising agencies, one should see advertising itself as a parasitical industry dedicated to manipulation and not to providing information, as advertisers claim. At least, this is true of most TV and magazine advertising. Indeed, while in 1950 6.5 billion dollars was squandered on advertising in the United States, by 1970 40 billion was spent, and by 1980 56 billion was wasted— far more money than was cumulatively spent on schooling! Advertising is a disgraceful waste of resources, talent, and time. A rational society would ban advertising completely or would simply use it for informational purposes.

However, in the United States, advertising is a prime manipulator of consumer demand and a source of political socialization and propaganda for the system, although it is not usually perceived as such. Moreover, advertising has come to dominate broadcasting and the media system in this country, to the detriment of us all. To pursue this argument and to reflect on the central roles of radio and television in our lives, let us now reflect on the history of broadcasting in the United States.

BROADCASTING AND THE MEDIA SOCIETY

Radio was a magical technical invention developed at the turn of the century to supplement the telegraph, by sending messages via voice over distances through magnetic waves. It was first developed for commercial and military applications (Czitrom 1982) but by the 1920s was becoming a major industry itself. Early ham radio operators sent out regular programs from technically crude "studios" and soon department stores and other institutions began sponsoring regular broadcasts of music, news, or sports events. Curiously enough, government officials like Herbert Hoover attempted to prevent commercials from cluttering up broadcasting. When he was secretary of commerce in 1922, Hoover stated that the radio issue was one of the few instances where the public was unanimously in favor of an extension of federal government powers, and both Hoover and President Calvin Coolidge were in favor of a public utility attitude toward broadcasting. Hoover argued that "Radio is not to be considered merely as a business carried on for private gain, for private advertisement, or for the entertainment of the curious. It is to be considered as a public trust, and to be considered primarily from the standpoint of the public interest" (Hoover in Center for the Study of Democratic Institutions 1959, p.10).

Early on, therefore, advertising was banned from radio or was strictly limited. Inevitably, however, radio was used for advertising and soon became dominated by corporations and the advertising industry. This process was facilitated by the development of the network system, whereby giant networks came to control broadcasting in the United States. By the early 1940s, the three networks that dominate television today—CBS, NBC, and ABC—were the major networks in the United States.

Indeed, by the 1930s, advertisers (the "sponsors") produced and controlled most of the entertainment broadcast over the radio, whereas the networks themselves limited production to music and educational programming. As Barnouw puts it: "In the sponsor-controlled hours, the sponsor was king. He decided on programming. If he decided to change programs, network assent was considered *pro forma*. The sponsor was assumed to hold a 'franchise' on his time period or periods. Many programs were advertising agency creations, designed to fulfill specific sponsor objectives. The director was likely to be an advertising agency staff employee. During dress rehearsal, an official of the sponsoring company was often on hand in the sponsor's booth, prepared to order last-minute changes" (Barnouw 1978, p.33).

Sponsors produced what they considered to be the most popular type of programming in order to maximize the audiences that would be exposed to their "messages." Thus radio followed the genre system of film and regularly broadcast episodic series, which fit into genres like soap operas, cowboy and gangster series (both *Gunsmoke* and *Dragnet*, for instance, were popular radio series before they moved over to television), comedy series like *Amos and Andy* or *Jack Benny*, music shows, and some talk and discussion programming. Consequently, rather mindless entertainment came to dominate the airwaves during the "golden age of radio."

Moreover, in part because of pressures from newspapers, there were severe restraints on news programming: by the 1930s, broadcasters agreed that no news item would exceed 30 seconds and that news bulletins would only provide material for two 5-minute news broadcasts a day. However, rising interest in the events in Europe during World War II eventually led to broadcasters increasing their news output (Charney 1948).

Radio broadcasting was thus dominated by entertainment and served to reproduce cultural hegemony by celebrating the same all-American values dominant in Hollywood films—family, romance, material success, individualism, patriotism, and so forth. Soap operas projected proper role models for men and women and dramatized the pain and suffering brought about through the violation of social norms (Herzog 1941). Extramarital sex, for instance, brough unwanted pregnancies and social ostracism, and every series had a villainess who attempted to disrupt happy marriages or romances. Westerns and gangster series idealized male authority figures and, like their cinematic counterparts, legitimated violence as a way to eliminate threats to the existing order. The radio also produced new superheroes like the Lone Ranger, Superman, Batman, and others, who represented archetypes of Good and defended American values against those who threatened existing law and order (Jewett and Lawrence 1977).

The hero myth, in fact, became a central part of American mythology. A standard scenario depicted an idyllic, Edenic situation suddenly threatened by intruders (for example, "Indians;" gangsters, monsters, and so on). The people are incapable of dealing with the threat and are forced to rely on superheroes who come from outside to deal with the problem. There is a confrontation between the hero and the villains, and the hero triumphs and returns the unstable situation to stability and order. This generic situation, which presents all social conflict and problems as a battle between Good and Evil, is a constant of American film, comic books, radio, and television (Jewett and Lawrence 1977) and is arguably a key to the conservative mind-set that sees the universe in such simplistic terms.

This mind-set informs, for example, the world-view of the first Hollywood President, Ronald Reagan, who seems to have assimilated the mythical view of the Hollywood films that he played in for several decades. This mind-set sees all conflict in terms of a titanic battle between Good and Evil; postulates Evil as absolutely bad, destructive and violent; and requires the total obliteration of Evil to ensure the triumph of Good. Thus Reagan and his conservative followers see the Soviet Union as the "Evil Empire," which incarnates absolute evil and must be opposed and destroyed. By implication, the Nicaraguan Sandinista government is violently opposed as part of the "Evil Empire" and murderous "contras" are supported in their chimerical efforts to overthrow the popularly supported Sandinista government in Nicaragua.

This conservative mind-set projects all evil onto its enemies and sees itself as wholly good. Such a world-view is totally inappropriate to the real world, however, where there is usually no clear-cut division between Good and Evil, and wherein most nations, individuals, and situations contain a complex mixture of good and bad. And in an era of nuclear weapons where hostility between the superpowers can lead to the total destruction of the earth and its inhabitants, such simplistic views are positively obscene. They contribute to the possibility of nuclear holocaust and preclude negotiations that recognize every country as a mixture of good and bad features. Whatever our differences, we must live and work together if we are to survive as a species.

Popular entertainment in the United States thus promotes myths and a mythical view of the world that can serve to legitimate one's own country, institutions, and way of life. "With God on Our Side" and "My Country, Right or Wrong" are political anthems supported by American popular entertainment, which does indeed present Us as the embodiment of virtue, truth, and freedom, and Them as the embodiment of evil, slavery, and lies.

Not all popular entertainment, however, is unidimensionally supportive of the existing system. As noted, some early films contained socially critical aspects, and there was some political discussion and debate on network radio during the 1930s (Barnouw 1978). In general, however, control of broadcasting was even tighter than control of the film industry—for broadcasting soon became dominated by giant corporations, who controlled the form and content of both radio and television in ways that usually supported their own interests.

In particular, the three oligopolistic networks homogenized programming so that the same types of programs, news, and ads were broadcast everywhere in the United States simultaneously. And up until the end of the 1950s, advertisers themselves produced most of radio and television entertainment and had total control over their content. This lasted until the TV quiz scandals in the 1950s, when television networks took over control of programming after it was disclosed that popular quiz programs were fixed to ensure the victory of more likable contestants (Barnouw 1975, 1978). Henceforth, the networks and production companies, mostly in Hollywood, would produce television shows; and the networks would take responsibility for their content with "standards and practices" offices.

Domination of the U.S. broadcasting system by the giant networks also precluded development of alternative broadcasting. Although the Federal Communications Act of 1934 mandated that the people own the airwaves and that broadcasting must serve the "public interest, convenience and necessity" (Kahn 1968), in fact, the commercial networks used broadcasting to advance their own commercial interests. The defeat of the Wagner-Hatfield Bill in 1935, offered as an amendment to the Federal Communications Act of 1934, eliminated an attempt to allot "to educational, religious, agricultural, labor, cooperative, and similar non-profit-making associations one-fourth of all the radio broadcasting facilities within their jurisdiction" (Barnouw 1975).

Government and industry frequently suppressed technologies of communication in the interests of their exploitation by hegemonic corporations, such as the postponed introduction of FM radio; thwarting what could have been, a dramatic expansion of the number of broadcasting outlets and leading to the suicide of its inventor, Edwin Armstrong (Mosco 1979). Then in the 1940s the government, under pressure from the networks, chose to develop a VHF rather than a UHF television system, which enabled the networks to dominate U.S. television—whereas, if the UHF system had been originally mandated, a much more diverse and pluralistic system could have evolved (Mosco 1979). The networks and government also delayed the introduction of cable television and are now hampering the development of satellite television by allowing HBO and other cable networks to scramble signals. Thus they preclude the development of a direct broadcast system from satellites to dish owners, and instead force consumers to pay for each channel, ensuring corporate control of the satellite system and maximizing exploitation of consumers.

Network television thus emerged in the late 1940s from within the same framework as radio. The radio networks continued to dominate television; and the top radio stars and programs migrated to the television industry (that is, Jack Benny, Red Skelton, Perry Como, Patti Page, *Gunsmoke, Dragnet, Amos and Andy,* and so on), which broadcast the same type of series formats already developed by radio and film (that is, soap operas, situation comedies, cop and crime dramas, quiz shows, suspense thrillers, and so forth). From the beginning, television in the United States has been controlled by corporate interests, which used it to broadcast programs that by and large served their interests. Although some socially critical news and documentaries have been broadcast by the networks, the broadcast industries tend to put their interest in maximizing profit above the public interest of providing stimulating and thought-provoking information and entertainment.

In short, the networks have subordinated news and information to the requirements of profitability. Business predominated over communication to such an extent that CBS President William Paley publicly regretted the day that CBS issued corporate stock and told Bill Moyers that CBS simply could not afford to produce quality documentary or discussion shows regularly because "the minute is worth too much now" (Paley, cited in Halberstam 1979, p.734).

Indeed, most critics of network television have argued that the drive for maximum ratings and profit is responsible for the "lowest common denominator" programming and the sacrifice of television's higher potential as a vehicle of communication and entertainment (Johnson 1970). Because broadcasting is controlled by giant corporations interested in maximizing profits and is paid for by advertisers interested in maximizing ratings, television in the United States has become a "vast wasteland" (Newton Minow), wherein year after year "prime time television" is dominated by similar types of cop shows, adventure shows, situation comedies, and, in the 1980s, prime time soaps like *Dallas* and *Dynasty*, which celebrate the values and affluent life-styles of the class that itself owns and controls television.

From the 1970s into the 1980s, less and less time has been devoted to documentaries; and news and discussion seem, during the Reagan era, to be more conformist and conservative than ever before. Little criticism emerged in the television networks, for instance, of the Reagan administration's invasion of Grenada or bombing of Libya, and there was almost no coverage of the many demonstrations against these actions. Indeed, the "popularity" (in terms of polls) of these aggressive military actions is probably to a large extent due to the ways that television news and entertainment have tended to reinforce the values and world-view of the Reagan administration (see the following section).

In these ways, corporate biases and near-monopolistic control over the broadcast media have produced a contradiction between the First Amendment right to free speech, and the democratic concept of a public sphere, contrasted to actual restrictions on public debate, alternative views, and critical discourse in the broadcast media (Schiller 1973; Kellner 1981). We have here a typical example of the contradiction between capitalism and democracy, which is central to the American experience. A democratic social order would engage in popular debate of the central issues in a society, would give all sides of an issue an opportunity to make a case, and would then decide the issue after sufficient debate through democratic participation. In an advanced industrial technological order, access to the means of public communication is necessary to ensure that adequate presentation of various points of view and debate can take place. However, in a capitalist society in which the means of communication are concentrated in powerful corporations, access is denied or limited in the case of minority, oppositional, or alternative views. Studies have shown that the opinion spectrum presented is severely limited and that many groups and individuals are denied access to broadcast media (Schiller 1973). Restriction of access to the media and limitations on public debate contradict the need for an informed public that can participate in democratic politics. The mass media sacrificing public communication for commerce plainly exhibits that private ownership contradicts broadcasting's avowed purpose of serving the "public interest, convenience and necessity."

There are then contradictions between the nature and purpose of commercial television and a democratic social order. Paul Klein claims that people choose "the least objectionable program" and that network television maximizes its audience by offering non-controversial programs to keep from offending people (Klein 1972). Other network observers claim that this leads to "lowest common denominator" programming, which, in seeking a mass audience, avoids culture or controversy that challenge or provoke the audience. In this view, television is perceived as a commercial medium that seeks to attract, entertain, and pacify its audience, while selling commercial goods and ideology. Consequently, those who call television a "democratic" or a "populist" art fail both to understand the nature of democracy and to see how television has been replacing democratic participation by providing political spectacles and by reducing elections to a manipulation of political images.

Furthermore, there are contradictions between democracy and advertising, the lifeblood that sustains the network operation. Advertising seeks to show that whatever problems people have can be resolved by something they can purchase. It contains images that celebrate the society as it is and that do not stir people to political action or social participation. It suggests that happiness and value are located in the private sphere, encouraging a privatized, consumer existence. Democracy, however, thrives on controversy and requires participation in social processes, presupposing that people are motivated enough to want to get involved in public life. Democracy requires a lively public sphere where there is discussion, debate, and participation in collective, public decision making.

By attracting the audience with the lure of "free entertainment," television produces immense profits and gains enormous sociocultural power over its audience. Eventually, however, the audience pays for its "free entertainment." The advertiser pays the television network for the time-spot purchased according to how many people are supposedly watching at a given time, and its advertising expenses are in turn passed down to the consumer. Thus even in the privacy of one's home, one is being exploited by corporate capital. Not only is leisure "colonized" (Aronowitz 1972); it is a form of unwaged labor in which networks derive profits from the aggregate size of audience-viewing, while advertisers not only increase aggregate consumer demand, but also force the audience to pay higher prices for its commodities as the cost of viewing "free" TV (Smythe 1977).

John Brenkman argues that the isolation imposed on the audience by the consumption of mass-media experience in the home breaks down other forms of association and substitutes vicarious consumption of media images for active, participatory, communal culture (Brenkman 1979). The separation of the consumers of mass culture from each other at once produces an alienation from active cultural production and collective social experience as well as a replacement of the public sphere (Habermas 1962) by cultural consumption. In this way, "leisure" activity reproduces types of alienation, fragmentation, and domination found in the labor process, for in both one is not an active participant in control of one's activity but repeats willy-nilly the same activity, day by day, week by week.

Indeed, the sheer amount of time spent viewing television in the United States is astonishing. In 1975, the average television was on 6.25 hours per day, or more than 43 hours per week; up to the present, viewing has increased steadily each year. Statistics show that "the average American child has spent more hours watching television by the time he enters kindergarten than he will have spent in college classrooms getting a bachelor's degree; the aggregate of waking time spent by all individuals in the United States at their various occupations is 2.8 billion hours per week, at watching television (the second largest time-consumer), 1.5 billion hours" (Network Project 1973). Are we becoming a nation of videots (Kosinsky 1982)?

Now at this point, one might suggest that public television (PBS) provides infinitely superior fare to network television and thus provides a meaningful alternative within the U.S. broadcasting situation. However, this is only true up to a point. Although PBS has some programming vastly superior to the networks, much of it is elitist and dull; and local PBS programming tends to be second-rate. And an inordinate amount of programming is imported from Britain rather than produced in the United States. Thus PBS programming tends to be aimed at an up-scale "cultural" audience rather than to the whole public. This is especially true during the Reagan administration, which has tended to defund television programming and independent film productions made by women, blacks and other people of color, Native Americans, and other minority cultures.

In principle, however, public television should be defended against commercial broadcasting; and there should be political agitation for the level of public television found in West Germany, Britain, France, Italy, and most European countries. The United States spends less public money per person on television than almost any country in the capitalist world and accordingly has one of the weakest systems of public broadcasting—a national disgrace that an enlightened public should struggle to improve.

Now, it is also true that cable and satellite broadcasting offers significant possibilities for alternative broadcasting. I fear, however, that the golden age of cable is already over: I am disturbed that unrestricted scrambling of satellite signals will destroy the promise of satellite television. In the early 1980s, CBS Cable offered an exciting experiment, producing innovative television that included the best European movies, documentaries, provocative talk shows, and intelligent cultural production. However, after losing $35 million its first year (a mere pittance in the CBS pot), it shut down operations. At the same time, *Tele-France* broadcast the best French film, television, and culture for several hours a 116y on the SPN network, in the original French with subtitles, but this excellent service also closed down after a year. Obviously, the commercial system could not support such services.

Since 1979 when home satellite dishes were introduced to the consumer market, individuals have been able to buy this technology and receive a wealth of sports, entertainment, movies, news, and everything from a variety of round-the-clock religious programming to late-night pornography. Superstations in New York, Chicago, Atlanta, New Jersey, Dallas, and San Diego provided viewers programming and news from these cities; and two satellites provided programming from Mexico and Canada. In addition, one could view live news feeds, could be entertained by off-color jokes during commercial breaks of some live network programming, and could pick up satellite conferences ranging from corporate meetings by the Coke folks trying to overcome the disaster of the unpopular "new Coke" to conferences of scientists concerned about the dangers of nuclear war. The Global Village had arrived. By 1986, more than 1.5 million Americans owned satellite dishes and were able to receive over 100 channels on about 16 active satellites, with new channels appearing almost every month.

But on January 15, 1986 (a day of infamy for the U.S. broadcasting system), HBO-Cinemax began full-time scrambling of the signals that they send from satellites and that the owners of home satellite dishes had been receiving free of cost. By the end of 1986 it is possible, and increasingly likely, that Showtime, the Disney channel, the Playboy channel, other movie channels, the Christian Broadcasting Network, and the Cable News Network will also scramble their signals. This development presents a dire threat, I believe, to the existence and vitality of one of the most exciting technologies in the history of broadcasting.

This wealth and proliferation of accessible programming was directly a function of satellite technology. Not cable, local media systems, or the networks, but satellite television has been the cutting edge that has produced the most stupendous choice of programs in the history of broadcasting. The HBO-Cinemax decision to scramble threatens these developments because it threatens to make programming inaccessible or unaffordable to the vast majority of viewers. To be sure, HBO-Cinemax is offering to sell a decoder machine for about $395 and currently wants to charge around $20 a month for each pay-movie service—about twice what cable charges. Some of the other satellite channels that plan to scramble their signals later this year will be using similar decoders, although other types of decoders are currently in use. The satellite future promises a confusing variety of devices needed to decode signals, and exorbitant prices that only a few can afford, as well as general confusion and dismay surrounding an activity that should be a source of pleasure, information, and entertainment.

Most importantly, scrambling threatens to destroy the satellite industry and to put a brake on one of the most exciting cultural developments in recent history. Consequently, as I write this article, *public access* television provides one of the few possibilities for alternative television, and the only possibility to enable television to serve the interests of popular democracy. In 1972, the Federal Communications Commission mandated that every cable system with more than 3,500 subscribers must provide a public access channel and that cable channels on the larger systems should be put aside for government, educational, and community services. These channels were to be made accessible to the public on a non-discriminatory, "first come-first served" basis. By 1979, however, the Supreme Court struck down this ruling on the grounds that the FCC had exceeded its authority (Kellner 1985). The decision did leave open the right of communities that franchise cable systems to demand public access, and of Congress to pass laws requiring cable systems to provide public access channels and facilities. This uncertain situation means that some of the crucial political debates and struggles of the coming years will revolve around communications policies. Public access television holds the promise of a more democratic television system, and its suppression or elimination could prevent a more progressive type of television and public communication on television from developing.

Presently, over 600 cable systems have public access television, which makes possible a truly democratic television, responsive to the needs of the community. Here in Austin, Texas, I have worked since 1978 with Frank Morrow and others to produce a weekly television program, *Alternative Views*, which has now produced over 300 programs on a variety of topics. Our first program, in 1978, provided previews of the forthcoming Nicaraguan and Iranian revolutions, weeks before these events were discovered by the networks, through interviews with people from these countries. We then did hour-long in-depth interviews with ex-CIA agent John Stockwell, who discussed how he was recruited into the CIA, his experiences in Vietnam and Africa, and how after having been in charge of the ill-fated Angola operation he decided to resign and to criticize CIA practices and policies. We also held a series of gripping interviews: with John Henry Faulk, a Texas folk humorist who had been blacklisted from the entertainment industry during the McCarthy period and who eventually won a lawsuit against blacklisting; with Senator Ralph Yarborough, who told how he worked to finally pass the National Education Act, which made student loans available as part of a national defense package, and who also had many fascinating stories of Texan and national politics; and with American Atheist founder Madalyn Murray O'Hair, who expounded her views on religion and told how she successfully produced lawsuits to eliminate prayer from schools, thus preserving the constitutional separation between church and state. We also had discussions with Nobel Prize winner George Wald; former Attorney General Ramsey Clark; anti-nuclear activist Helen Caldicott; and many other well-known intellectuals, activists, and social critics.

As our connections grew, we began receiving documentaries from various filmmakers and began to mix a documentary and talk-show format. As more cable systems emerged, we expanded our market and are now shown in Washington, New York, Boston, San Diego, Minneapolis, Pittsburgh, Atlanta, and many other cities across the United States. Given what Fred Exoo describes as "the bias of the news" (see Chapter 3), we found it necessary to go to alternative news sources, like the Left press or more specialized business presses, to get stories or information excluded from mainstream news sources. Consequently, we now utilize a newsmagazine format, where we include stories or information excluded from mainstream media, in-depth discussion, and, when possible, illustrative documentary material. The reception of our program shows that people are both willing and eager to pay attention to in-depth news coverage of complex issues and to hear alternative views from more progressive standpoints than one usually finds in the mainstream media. This is true, in part, because the struggles and movements of the 1960s opened space for alternative institutions and culture, which has not been closed despite the conservative hegemony of the New Right during the Reagan administration. I will therefore next turn to discussion of important developments in U.S. popular culture over the last two decades and shall also broaden the focus of discussion to include oppositional cultures opposed to the more conservative mainstream.

POPULAR CULTURE, IDEOLOGIES, AND SOCIAL MOVEMENTS: TWO TEST CASES

Mainstream film, broadcasting, and other forms of popular culture have tended to be conservative in the sense that they largely function to conserve existing institutions of U.S. society. They are "liberal," however, in the sense that they adapt to social change and absorb new values, ideas, styles, and so forth. In order to maintain their audiences, mass media must respond to the dominant conflicts, new ideas, social movements, and actual events happening in the culture. To be sure, they attempt to co-opt and defuse more radical ideas and movements that threaten the existing order, but nonetheless they must respond, in some way at least, to massive movements like those of the 1960s and successful movements like the New Right, which seized power with the election of Ronald Reagan. To conclude my study of the ways that popular entertainment functions to aid political socialization and to form dominant beliefs and values, I want to discuss how a variety of forms of popular culture responded to the most dramatic new social movements of the 1960s and 1970s—the New Left and the New Right.

1960s Social Movements and Popular Culture

Social movements of the 1960s such as the New Left, Black and Brown Power, feminism, the hippie counterculture, and many other related movements brought about some of the most dramatic cultural, social, and political changes of the century. The 1960s provided a sharp rupture with the conservative climate and herd conformity of the 1950s, and represents a distinct and new era in U.S. history: the 1960s had its own music, film, life-style, and subcultures (Aronowitz et al. 1984).

To be sure, anticipation of the cultural upheaval of the 1960s began appearing in the tepid 1950s. The explosive force and power of rock 'n' roll pointed to dissatisfaction with social conformity and bland middle class life-styles. The rhythms of rock exhibit a restless energy and Elvis' gyrating pelvis showed some of the things that young people wanted to do with this energy. Rock 'n' roll constituted outright rebellion against social conformity and the standards, music, and style of the older generation. Thus the emergence of rock music previewed the generational war that would erupt in the 1960s. Whereas previous popular music was sentimental, bland, predictable, and tame (listen to Perry Como or Patti Page), rock was rowdy, rebellious, noisy, and wild. Likewise, the beat generation of the late 1950s produced a poetry and literature that also rebelled against middle class norms and literary propriety. And film figures like Marlon Brando in *The Wild One* or James Dean also provided models of non-conformity and rebellion.

But with the eruption of the 1960s, music, film, and fashion all popularized the values and rebellions of the 1960s movements. Drugs, sex, and rock 'n' roll were celebrated in the music of the Beatles, the Rolling Stones, Bob Dylan, the Doors, Country Joe and the Fish, the Jefferson Airplane, and other 1960s political, psychedelic, folk, and rock groups. The Jefferson Airplane chanted "help the revolution" in their *Volunteers* album; Country Joe and the Fish warned youth against dying in Vietnam; and Bob Dylan sang of change, rebellion, and a new age in songs like "The Time's They Are a Changin'," "Blowin' in the Wind," and "It's All

Right Ma, I'm Only Bleeding." Look at the films *Monterey Pop* (1969), *Woodstock* (1970), or *Concert at Big Sur* (1971) for indications of the extent to which youth in the United States emerged in open opposition to the society of their boring parents.

Films too participated in the countercultural movement, and countercultural youth were often referred to as the "film generation" (Kellner and Ryan 1986). Movies like *Bonnie and Clyde* (1967) celebrated rebellion and non-conformity; *The Graduate* (1967) was the first film to successfully depict youth alienation and the need for change; and films like *The Trip, Easy Rider, Woodstock, Billy Jack*, and so on, featured the counterculture and instructed youth in the arts of turning on, skinny-dipping, hip style, and non-conformity. Other films projected the views of the civil rights movement (*Guess Who's Coming to Dinner* and most Sidney Poitier films; *Nothing But a Man*; and *The Liberation of L.B. Jones*). And some films contained symbolic or literal advocation of Black Power and even black revolution (*The Lost Man, Uptight, Sweet Sweetback's Baadasss Song, The Spook Who Sat by the Door*). The New Left and student movement appeared in *Getting Straight, The Strawberry Statement, The Revolutionary*; and films like *Zabriskie Point* explored both countercultural and student rebellion (Kellner and Ryan 1986).

Proto-feminism appeared in films that dealt with the exploitation or rebellion of women like *Diary of a Mad Housewife, Wanda, Klute* and other Jane Fonda films. (Jane eventually emerged as the archetypal liberated woman/political radical figure of her age, although she was also able to successfully adapt to the 1980s.) These films were opposed, to be sure, by films that presented hippies, student radicals, black revolutionaries, and so forth, in a negative light (any Clint Eastwood film of the era, or films like *Panic in Needle Park, Drive, He Said*, or *Joe*, which attacked the hippie culture or student radicals). Other films showed rebellious women put back in their proper place by male power (*Straw Dogs, The Exorcist*, and the stalk-and-slash films of the 1970s and 80s, beginning with *Halloween*). Indeed, popular culture in the United States, especially film, has been marked by intense conflicts between more conservative and more liberal and progressive views during the past decades (see Kellner and Ryan 1986).

Television, however, missed the 1960s and was an extremely conservative and irrelevant cultural form. The only TV series to explicitly feature 1960s radicalism were cop shows like *Dragnet* or *Mod Squad*, which presented radicalism as a form of criminality that needed to be submitted to the discipline of law and order. And *Star Trek*, considered to be a "liberal" series, contained allegorical attacks on 1960s radicalism, as in the episode that shows space children (that is, hippies) to be pathetic misfits, or the episode where the Enterprise crew gets zonked out on drug spores and is rendered ineffective. Only TV news, in its limited form, presented real images of the 1960s during the decade and this presentation too was largely negative (Gitlin 1980).

During the 1970s, however, television too was liberalized, first in short-lived early–70s social dramas like *The Bold Ones* series, then in *All in the Family* and other Norman Lear situation comedies, culminating in *Mary Hartman Mary Hartman*, the most offbeat show in television history, and finally in mini-series like *Roots, Holocaust, The Moneychangers,* and so forth. The mini-series sympathetically portrayed the oppressive plight of blacks and Jews and attacked racist, fascist, and capitalist oppressors—leading one critic to believe that television may indeed contain progressive potential (Kellner 1979).

But in the Age of Reagan, both film and television moved to the Right as the New Right gained cultural power and MTV attempted to contain the explosive energies of rock in slick videos and media images reminiscent of the style of advertising.

Popular Culture in the Age of Reagan

The 1960s and 1970s were a bad time for conservatives. The Right's darling Barry Goldwater suffered the most massive political defeat in history in the 1964 election against Lyndon Johnson, and the movements of the 1960s challenged everything that the Right believed in. But in the 1970s the Right counterattacked. They blamed liberals, Democrats, and radicals for the decline of the U.S. economy and political clout, for the growth of a cumbersome welfare state, and for the decay of morals and traditional values. Ultra-Right-wing groups like Jerry Falwell's "Moral Majority" and Richard Viguerie's New Right organization used direct mail campaign tactics to help elect Ronald Reagan and unseat prominent liberal Senators like George McGovern, Birch Bayh, and Frank Church in the 1980 election. The moment of the New Right arrived.

Network television wasted no time in responding to the new political hegemony of the Right. The season after Reagan won, new law-and-order crime drama series appeared like *Strike Force, McClain's Law, Today's FBI, Code Red,* and *Magnum, P.I.,* which featured strong male hero figures who represent conservative law-and-order values and who were played by longtime, patriarchal movie and TV stars like James Arness, Robert Stack, and Lorne Greene. These shows were supposed to tap into perceived needs in the audience for reassurance from strong male authority figures and a return to conservative values. In fact, most of these series flopped, whereas the one new "liberal" cop show, *Hill Street Blues,* was a major critical and audience success of the decade, suggesting that the public wasn't really buying all of Reagan's conservative agenda.

Other new 1981 shows, during the first prime time season of the

Reagan era, included *Dynasty, Falcon Crest, Flamingo Road,* and *King's Crossing,* which joined *Dallas* to celebrate wealth and power. The 1982 season saw the (mercifully brief) appearance of two neo-imperialist epics, *Tales of the Golden Monkey* and *Bring 'em Back Alive,* which were pastisches of Indiana Jones, Frank Buck, and the white man's burden in tales that depicted Third World villainy and white male heroism. In 1983 appeared two military soap operas, *For Love and Honor* and *Emerald Point, N.A.S..* The first featured the lives and loves of young recruits—male and female—who, fittingly, were advertised as "Fit to Fight—Anywhere, Anytime"; and both, like the movies *Private Benjamin* (also made into a TV series), *Stripes, An Officer and a Gentleman, The Great Santini, Tank,* and so on showed the military as a place where love, honor, and good times were to be had, thus providing free advertisements for the free-enterprise volunteer army that the Reagan administration was rebuilding.

Mini-series during the first years of the Reagan administration included *The Winds of War, The Blue and the Grey, The American Revolution,* and (in case these past wars and their glories got boring) *World War III.* Furthermore, network producers, forgetting that the media are supposed to be relatively autonomous in relation to the state and economic system, presented a slew of series that advanced Reagan's political agenda. His demand for a military buildup found support in the series *From Here to Eternity* (based on the popular novel and film *World War II*) and *Call to Glory,* which dealt with military life at the time of the Cuban missile crisis. Both shows humanized the military at a point when the military's image needed to be refurbished, and they dealt with eras when the U.S. military wasn't properly prepared (as in the Pearl Harbor debacle, which is the centerpiece of *From Here to Eternity*) or had its moment of glory (as in 1962 when U.S. military power forced Khrushchev to withdraw Soviet missiles from Cuba during the Cuban missile crisis, which was the ideological center of the *Call to Glory* series and the explicit topic of its two-hour pilot: an Air Force captain is recruited to take pictures of the preparations for Soviet missiles in Cuba as TV news unfolds the Cuban missile crisis). The cumulative message seems to be that, without a strong military, we might be subject to enemy attacks as at Pearl Harbor, but, with a strong military, we can dictate policies to the Soviets as in the Cuban missile crisis; therefore we need a strong military buildup.

Now I am not claiming that the networks planned and orchestrated this message. Rather they are business machines seeking to maximize profits through maximizing their audiences; this leads them to produce programs that they believe resonate to present trends and to audience desires, fears, and fantasies—thus, programs attractive to mass audiences. Obviously, the networks thought that Reagan and his policies were popular and attempted to capitalize (literally) on this supposed popularity by producing programs that tapped into the syndrome. Consequently, as Reagan built up and unleashed the CIA, series heroizing intelligence work appeared, such as *Masquerade* (1984), wherein ordinary Americans like Cybill Shepherd were enlisted as intelligence operatives (since the KGB allegedly knew who all the U.S. spies were and, therefore, new recruits were needed)—thus, the fantasy: you too can be a spy for the CIA and fight the nasty Reds. In another short-lived spy fantasy, *Cover-Up* (1984), a woman fashion photographer (accompanied by a "hunk" who is an ex-Special Forces agent), becomes a "long rider" (that is, an undercover troubleshooter) after her undercover agent husband is killed by a villainous French corporation that wants to steal U.S. technology (no doubt, to sell it to the Evil Empire).

Then there was, and still is, *MacGyver* (1985), presenting another ex-Special Forces agent as a "survival expert" who helps people get out of difficult jams, and *The Equalizer* (1985), about an ex-intelligence agent who helps people in distress (originality and *difference* are not the prime virtues of prime time television). Now, a series on the heroic exploits of the CIA has long been announced but, as far as I know, never appeared. As Reagan and his cronies contemplated and carried out military intervention in the Third World, series promoting macho interventionism or high-tech weaponry, like *The A-Team, Blue Thunder, Airwolf, Riptide, Knightriders*, and others, appeared. Two 1985 mini-series celebrated that lovable old fascist *Mussolini* and that farseeing tyrant *Peter the Great*; and Ronald Reagan's preferred class—the rich and powerful—were lionized in series too numerous to mention.

For the sake of the historical record, I cannot resist discussing two episodes of these Reaganist fantasies for their incredible and audacious revision of history and advancement of blatantly Right-wing ideology. Let us first examine a 1984 episode of the TV series *Blue Thunder*, a spin-off from a movie that featured a high-tech surveillance helicopter. The episode describes a trip to a Caribbean island where there is a U.S. medical school and a black population suffering under Marxist-Leninist dictatorship. In this rewriting of Grenada, a group of white U.S. mercenaries, funded and directed by the KGB, are planning to assassinate the black leader Maurice Priest (evidently, Bishop was demoted to Priest for the episode) so that a military coup led by Soviet-oriented Marxist-Leninists could take over. The Blue Thunder team connects with democratic resistance forces and prevents the Soviet coup from taking place. On the way out, the helicopter crew disobeys orders in order to blow up a Soviet-Cuban arms depot (a more glamorous target than the mental institution that the U.S. forces accidentally bombed during the actual Grenada invasion). Then, returning home, the crew hears the news version of what happened: a Soviet-Cuban clique took over the Priest government and the U.S. president has undertaken a heroic counter-action to liberate the island—an action facilitated, in this fantasy, by the Blue Thunder bombing of the arms depot.

More historical revisionism surfaces in a 1984 *Call to Glory* episode, when (after heroically documenting the existence of Soviet missile bases in Cuba during the Cuban missile crisis) an Air Force captain (Craig T. Williams) suddenly becomes a diplomat sent to Vietnam to investigate the Diem regime. The regime is shown to be extremely repressive and inept—thus, retrospectively, justifying CIA involvement in Diem's assassination, so that a more effective government could be formed (it wasn't). The Vietnamese are shown, for the most part, to be corrupt, repressive, or ineffectual—victims needing help from strong, well-meaning Americans like Craig T. Williams; and the American hero is shown to be totally decent, strong, and heroic. To be sure, there were questions raised in this episode as to what the United States was doing in Vietnam, in the first place; but the cumulative (narcissistic and chauvinistic) message was that Americans are basically good and decent people who sometimes make minor mistakes out of misguided idealism. That is a difficult position to sustain in the light of U.S. foreign policy in the last four decades, but it is precisely the Reaganite mythology used to elicit support of the contras and an aggressive anti-communist foreign policy—a policy that, in the Age of Star Wars, is becoming increasingly dangerous and pathological.

Now, as mentioned, I am not claiming that these TV series were necessarily part of a right-wing conspiracy nor that they are devastating indicators of a long-term turn to the Right in the United States, since most of the series failed or (like *The A-Team*) are not unambiguously Right-wing. However, most of the Right-wing films that appeared during the Age of Reagan *were* arguably produced by Right-wing production groups to advance a Right-wing agenda; moreover, many *were* extremely popular and clearly helped to legitimate New Right politics during the 1980s.

Indeed, as Michael Ryan and I argue in our book *Camera Politica*, Hollywood film during the late 1970s helped to provide a cultural basis for the triumph of the New Right. The most popular films advanced conservative values: for example, the *Rocky* films showed that, with hard work and enterprise, one could become a success—a message echoed in other popular working class films of the era like *Saturday Night Fever* and *Staying Alive* (in which John Travolta rises above working class squalor to become king of the 2001 Disco in Brooklyn and then a broadway star) and *Flashdance* (in which a hardworking young woman wins admission to ballet school and the hand of her wealthy boss).

After a wave of liberal and radical black films in the late 1960s and early 1970s, which transcoded civil rights and Black Power discourses (Sidney Poiter films for liberalism; and Black Power films like *Up Tight*,

Sweet Sweetback's Baadasss Song, and *The Spook Who Sat by the Door* for more radical perspectives), black films from the midn1970s to the present tend to be more moderate and depoliticized. Welfare for blacks was attacked in *Claudine* (1974), and a Bill Cosby-Sidney Poitier film urged blacks to get *A Piece of the Action.* Most 1980s films featuring blacks projected either Richard Pryor/Eddie Murphy integrationist fantasies or historical dramas that safely located racial oppression in the past (*The Soldier's Story, The Color Purple*).

Other films that advanced conservative values include the *Star Wars* films, which celebrate military virtue, male heroism, and a quasi-mystical force that aids the triumph of Good and the destruction of Evil in the universe. Not by accident, I suggest, did our Hollywood president choose the phrase "Evil Empire" to describe the Soviet Union; and, I argue the term "Star Wars" accurately describes Reagan's military space program. Moreover, the Empire did strike back at Grenada and the Malvinas (*Newsweek* actually used the title "The Empire Strikes Back" on its cover about the Malvinas/Falkland War), and, no doubt, the Republicans are hoping for the "Return of the Jedi" for the 1988 presidential election—Jack Kemp, perhaps.

Ryan and I detected the shift in Hollywood film culture to be around 1977n78, when a series of films appeared that we see as providing a cultural foundation for New Right political ideology and whose popularity pointed to a shift to the Right inU.S. culture. These films differ from the socially critical liberal and radical films of 1967–77 by offering an affirmative vision of either a past unsullied by social conflicts (for example, *Grease,* one of the most popular films of 1978, which returned to the 1950s) or a present transcending conflict (for example, the vision of religious redemption at the end of *Close Encounters of the Third Kind,* another 1978 blockbuster), or through redemption by superheroes projected in the *Star Wars* and *Superman* series and other hero films that were so popular in the late 1970s and early 1980s. We suggested that one of the reasons the Right succeeded where the Left failed was that the Right provided a positive vision of the future, whereas films and culture of the Left failed to provide attractive alternatives, appealing to a country beset by over a decade of intense social conflict and decline in military power and prestige, and wracked with economic crisis, as well.

The success of conservative films in the late 1970s and early 1980s is significant, for it marks a distinct shift in U.S. film and political culture. Our studies indicate that films from 1967–71 predominantly reflected the outlooks of liberals, radicals, and feminists and the discourses of new social movements in a period that we believe is one of the most creative periods in the history of Hollywood film. The period of 1971–77, approximately, is a period of contestation between Left-liberal radicalism and growing conservatism but the most significant films represent genre transformations and new socially critical genre cycles that cumulatively articulate a socially critical, pessimistic and negative ethos. We believe that these liberal films, such as the political and corporate conspiracy cycles, the Jane Fonda films, revisionist westerns, musicals and detective films, reveal why liberalism in the 1970s failed. Such liberal films (*Executive Action, The Parallax View, Three Days of the Condor, Twilight's Last Gleaming, Winter Kills,* and so on) vilify the State (in the hands of the Right) and thus promote anti-Statist attitudes, which the Right then successfully exploited. The problem is that liberals depend on a strong State to implement their welfare and regulatory programs.

Other films, like the more optimistic ones of the Jane Fonda variety, primarily depict individual solutions to social problems that demand collective, political solutions—and thus strengthen the individualism that is also a main pillar of Rightist ideology, which the Right successfully utilized in their appeal for unfettered entrepreneurism against State collectivism.

Some radical and liberal films (many of the political conspiracy films already mentioned; and *Chinatown, Network,* and so on) are so negative and pessimistic that they see no solutions to social problems and thus promote apathy and cynicism. Consequently, we feel that many liberal and even radical films ultimately played into the hands of the Right and promoted Reagan's agenda, and failed to offer any affirmative, positive, alternative vision—as did the more conservative films and Reagan's political rhetoric.

Moreover, during the 1980s, many Hollywood films aggressively took up Reagan's rightist ideology and political agenda. Reagan's fanatic anti-communism was transcoded and advanced in some of the most popular films of the era: the return-to-Vietnam series culminating in *Rambo*; communist invasion films like *Red Dawn* and *Invasion, U.S.A.*; and *Rocky IV*, which featured a communist villain in ads for the film announcing, "This Time, He's Fighting For All of Us." Other explicitly anti-communist films include *Octopussy, Firefox, White Nights, Moscow on the Hudson,* and numerous minor films by the Cannon-Globus-Golan group, which gained notoriety as a Right-wing production company with its series of ultra-Right, ultra-macho celluloid weapons (*Missing in Action* and other Chuck Norris meathead epics).

As an example of the aggressiveness of the Rightist militarist films in the Age of Reagan, let us reflect briefly on the thematics, success, and political use of *Rambo*—one of 1985's blockbuster hits and probably the most discussed film of recent years. *Rambo* is an obvious candidate because of its aggressive Right-wing ideology, its popularity, and the fact that Ronald Reagan himself stated, during a frustrating period of dealing with so-called terrorists, that he'd just seen *Rambo* and would know what to do next time. This was a shocking admission by Reagan, that he really believed violence was the best way to solve conflicts, and shows how the Hollywood president—and, unfortunately, large segments of the population—have assimilated a Manichean world-view from Hollywood movies, wherein Evil is so bad and We are so good that only violence will eliminate threats to our well-being—a mind-set that later, in 1986, encouraged the Reaganites to bomb Libya.

Now, *Rambo* is but one of a whole series of return-to-Vietnam films that began with the surprising success of *Uncommon Valor* in 1983 and of the two Chuck Norris *Missing in Action* films of 1984N85. All follow the same formula of representing the return to Vietnam of a team of former vets or of a superhuman, superhero vet like *Rambo* to rescue a group of U.S. soldiers "missing in action," who are still imprisoned by the malicious and evil Vietnamese and their Soviet allies.

Rambo synthesizes this return-to-Vietnam cycle with another cycle that shows returning vets transforming themselves from wounded and confused misfits to superwarriors (*Rolling Thunder, Firefox, First Blood*). All of these post-post-Vietnam syndrome films show the United States and the American warrior hero victorious this time. Thus, they cumulatively exhibit an inability to accept defeat and project symbolic compensation for loss, shame, guilt, and so forth, by depicting Us as Good and this time victorious and Them as Evil and this time receiving a well-deserved defeat. Cumulatively, the return-to-Vietnam films therefore exhibit a defensive and compensatory response to military defeat in Vietnam and, I argue, an inability to learn the lessons of the limitations of U.S. power and the complex mixture of good and bad involved in situations like Vietnam.

On the other hand, *Rambo* and the other Sylvester Sallone/Chuck Norris meathead films can be read as symptoms of the victimization of the working class. Both the Stallone and Norris figures are resentful, remarkably inarticulate, and undereducated—indicative of the many undereducated U.S. working class youth who are offered the military or violent self-display as primary ways of affirming themselves. Rambo's neurotic resentment is less his own fault than the fault of those who run the social system in such a way that it denies his class access to the institutions of articulate thought and mental health. Denied self-esteem through creative work, they seek surrogate worth in metaphoric substitutes like sports (Rocky) and nationalism (Rambo). It is symptomatic that Stallone plays both Rocky and Rambo at a time when economic recession is driving the Rockys of the world to join the military where they become Rambos for Reagan's interventionist foreign policies.

The Rocky-Rambo syndrome, however, puts on display the pathetic and pathological masculism that is at the bottom of conservative socialization and ideology. The only way that the Rockys and Rambos of the world can gain recognition and self-affirmation is violent and aggressive self-display. And Rambo's pathetic demand for love at the end of the film is an indication that the society is not providing adequate structures of mutual and communal support to sustain healthy interpersonal relationships and ego ideals for men in the culture. Unfortunately, the Stallone films intensify this pathology precisely in their celebration of violent masculism and militarist self-assertion.

What is perhaps most curious, however, is how *Rambo* appropriates countercultural motifs for the Right. Rambo has long hair, wears a headband, eats only natural foods (whereas the bureaucrat Murdock swills Coke), is close to nature, and is hostile toward bureaucracy, the State, and technology—precisely the position of many 1960s counterculturalists. But, as Russell Berman has pointed out in an article in *Telos* (1985), Rambo's real enemy is the "governmental machine, with its massive technology, unlimited regulations, and venal political motivations. Rambo is the anti-bureaucratic opposed to the state, the new individualist activist." Thus Rambo is a supply-side hero, a figure of individual entrepreneurism, who shows how Reaganite ideology is able to assimilate earlier countercultural figures.

Now this analysis suggests that Reaganism should be seen as revolutionary conservatism with a strong component of radical conservative individualism and activism, and that this fits in with *Star Wars, Indiana Jones, Superman, Conan,* and other films and television series that utilize individualist heroes who are anti-State and who are a repository of conservative values. And as Berman points out, this constitutes a major shift in the strategies of the culture industries, which celebrated conformity and a beneficent State in the 1950s and which has shifted to valorization of non-conformity and individualistic heroism in the new age of entrepreneurial glory.

Assertion of the individualist male hero in the public sphere is often conjoined with, or complemented by, reassertion of male patriarchal power in the family. Consequently, conservative sexual politics were also a prime theme of many popular films in the Age of Reagan. There was a return to celebration of the family and traditional values in the family farm films (*Places in the Heart, Country, The River*), abortion was attacked and adultery received harsh symbolic punishment in *Terms of Endearment,* and both teen films like *Risky Business* and social comedies like *Arthur, Trading Places, The Big Chill,* and *Brewster's Millions* celebrated wealth, yuppyism, and selling out.

Now, to be sure, Right-wing hegemony was not uncontested, either in society or film. Many films attacked Reaganite positions; for example, *Missing, Under Fire, Salvador,* and *Latino* presented views of Latin America at variance with the administration's; *Reds* presented a sympathetic view of the Russian Revolution and American communists; and liberal films like *War Games* and *2010* dramatized the dangers of nuclear war and the need for *détente* with the Soviets. Feminism and more liberal views of sexual politics survived in films like *Desperately Seeking Susan, Independence Day, Love Letters,* and, with reservations, *Tootsie* and *Victor Victoria.* The contestation during the Reagan era—about which much more could and probably should be said—and the striking differences between 1960s popular culture and popular culture in the Age of Reagan lead me to some concluding remarks about the nature and social functions of popular culture in the United States.

CONCLUSION

My two concluding studies suggest that, although popular culture in the United States has, by and large, served the interests of reproducing dominant values and beliefs, thus socializing individuals to fit into and accept dominant institutions, social practices, gender roles, and behavior, it should be seen as a *contested terrain* whereon the social conflicts within U.S. society are worked out. My studies suggest that popular culture should be seen as a field contested by liberals, conservatives, and representatives of the views of social movements of the Left and Right. Although most producers and representatives of the culture industries insist that their products are mere "entertainment" and devoid of political ideologies, I have argued that popular entertainment in the United States is deeply political and often represents precise political positions and views. To be sure, some popular culture attempts to be apolitical, and much entertainment contains compromises between liberal and conservative, traditional and new, views and values. Yet much popular entertainment does legitimate dominant values, institutions, and ideologies in the United States and thus can serve as a subtle means of indoctrination, an advertisement for the system, manipulating people into the belief that values, gender roles, and institutions, which are socially constructed, historically changeable, and frequently flawed and oppressive, are instead natural, good, beneficial, and unchangeable.

Indeed, to avoid manipulation in a media age, students should learn media literacyjust as they learn computer literacy. We are living in a media culture, increasingly dominated by the mass media of culture and communication. To avoid manipulation, it is increasingly important to learn how to read and criticize media, to be aware of their messages and impact, and to learn how politics and ideology permeates our entertainment media. This requires vigilance, development of a critical consciousness, and learning techniques of media criticism. To begin, when watching ads, ask: what are the ads trying to sell and how are they selling it? Before purchasing anything, ask: why am I buying this and do I really need it? When watching a television program or film, ask: what messages and values are being communicated and how are the media conveying them? In this way, one can begin undoing the political socialization to which we have been submitted and can begin the task of becoming a freer, happier, better, and more autonomous individual.

REFERENCES

Adorno, T.W., and Max Horkheimer. 1972. *Dialectic of Enlightenment*. New York: Seabury.

Aronowitz, Stanley. 1972. *False Promises*. New York: McGraw-Hill.

Barnouw, Erik. 1978. *The Sponsor*. New York: Oxford University Press.

———. 1975. *The Tube of Plenty*. New York: Oxford University Press.

Berman, Russell. 1985. "Rambo: From Counter-Culture to Contra." *Telos* 64:143–47.

Bordwell, David, Janet Staiger, and Kristin Thompson. 1985. *The Classical Hollywood Cinema*. New York: Columbia University Press.

Brenkman, John. 1981. "Mass Media: From Collective Experience to the Culture of Privatization." *Social Text* 1:94–109.

Cavell, Stanley. 1982. *Pursuits of Happiness*. Cambridge: Harvard University Press.

Center for the Study of Democratic Institutions. 1959. *Broadcasting and Democratic Regulation in a Free Society*. Santa Barbara, Calif.

Charney, Mitchell. 1948. *News by Radio*. New York: Macmillan.

Czitrom, Daniel J. 1982. *Media and the American Mind*. Chapel Hill: The University of North Carolina Press.

Dieterle, William. 1941. "Hollywood and the European Crisis." *Studies in Philosophy and Social Science* IX:96–103.

Ewen, Stuart. 1976. *Captains of Consciousness*. New York: McGraw-Hill.

Ewen, Stuart, and Elizabeth Ewen. 1982. *Channels of Desire*. New York: McGraw-Hill.

Fly, James, Clifford Durr, et al. 1959. *Broadcasting and Government Regulation in a Free Society*. Santa Barbara, Calif.: Center for the Study of Democratic Institutions.

Gitlin, Todd. 1980. *The Whole World Is Watching*. Berkeley: University of California Press.

Goldman, Robert. 1984. "We Make Weekends: Leisure and the Commodity Form." *Social Text* 8:84–103.

Goldman, Robert, and John Wilson. 1977. "The Rationalization of Leisure." *Politics and Society* 7, 2:157–87.

Habermas, Jurgen. 1962. *Struckturwandel der Offentlichkeit*. Berlin and Neuwied: Luchterhand.

Halberstam, David. 1979. *The Powers That Be*. New York: Knopf.

Herzog, Herta. 1941. "On Borrowed Experience." *Studies in Philosophy and Social Science* IX:65–95.

Jameson, Frederic. 1979. "Reification and Utopia in Mass Culture." *Social Text* 1:130–48.

Jewett, Robert, and John Lawrence. 1977. *The American Monomyth*. New York: Doubleday.

Jezer, Marty. 1982. *The Dark Ages*. Boston: South End Press.

Johnson, Nicholas. 1970. *How to Talk Back to Your Television*. Boston: Little, Brown.

Jowett, Gareth. 1976. *Film: The Democratic Art*. New York: William Morrow.

Kahn, Frank J., 1968. ed. *Documents of American Broadcasting*. New York: Appleton-Crofts.

Kellner, Douglas. 1979. "TV, Ideology and Emancipatory Popular Culture." *Socialist Review* 45:13–53.

———. 1980. "TV Images, Codes, and Messages." *Televisions* 7, 4:1–19.

———. 1981. "Network Television and American Society: Introduction to a Critical Theory of Television." *Theory and Society 10: 31–62*.

———. *1983. "Critical Theory, Commodities, and the Consumer Society." Theory, Culture, and Society 3:66–84*.

———. 1985. "Public Access Television: Alternative Views." *Radical Science Journal* 16, *Making Waves*: 79–92.

Kellner, Douglas, and Michael Ryan. 1986. *Camera Politica: The Politics and Ideology of Hollywood Film, 1967–1985*. Bloomington: Indiana University Press.

Key, Wilson Bryan. 1972. *Subliminal Seduction*. New York: Signet.

Klein, Paul. 1972. *Performance*: Feedback 5.

Kosinsky, Jerzy. 1982. "A Nation of Videots." In *Television: The Critical View*, edited by Horace Newcomb. New York: Oxford University Press.

May, Larry. 1983. *Screening out the Past*. Chicago: University of Chicago Press.

Mosco, Vincent. 1979. *Broadcasting in the United States*. Norwood, N.J.: Ablex.

Network Project. 1973. *Control of Information*. New York: Notebook Number Three.

Packard, Vance. 1960. *The Waste Makers*. Baltimore and London: Penguin.

Sayres, Sonya, Anders Stephenson, Stanley Aronowitz, and Fredric Jameson, eds. 1984. *The 60s Without Apology*. Minneapolis: University of Minnesota Press.

Schatz, Thomas. 1981. *Hollywood Genres*. Philadelphia: Temple University Press.

Schiller, Herbert. 1973. *The Mind Managers*. Boston: Beacon Press.

Shain, Russell E. 1974. "Hollywood's Cold War." *Journal of Popular Film and Television* 3:334–50.

Sklar, Robert. 1975. *Movie-Made America: A Social History of American FIlm*. New York: Random House.

Smythe, Dallas. 1977. "Communications: Blindspot of Western Marxism." *Canadian Journal of Political and Social Theory* 1,2:1–27.

Warshow, Robert. 1970. *The Immediate Experience*. New York: Atheneum.

Williams, Raymond. 1973. "Base and Superstructure in Marxist Cultural Theory." *New Left Review* 82:6–33.

Wright, Will. 1977. *Shotguns and Society*. Berkeley: University of California Press.

5

Education and Inequality

Michael W. Apple and
Kenneth Teitelbaum

INTRODUCTION

Behind the official rhetoric and the manipulated statistics constantly coming out of Washington, we are in the midst of one of the most serious crises we have ever experienced. It is a crisis that is having a differential impact on workers, on the poor, on people of color, on children, and on women. "Despite present-day appearances, there is a very high likelihood of an economic debacle in America's near-term future" (Mandle and Ferleger 1985). A facade of prosperity hides an increasing vulnerability. The vulnerability is not an abstraction, but is already being lived out as the gap between the haves and have-nots not only here in the United States, but worldwide, increases day by day. Already one out of every seven Americans lives in poverty as does one out of five children under 6 years old (Cohen and Rogers 1983; Apple 1987). The flight of capital promises even worsening conditions and the search for ever expanding profits ensures that an ethic of private gain, not of common good (Raskin 1986), will prevail in government discourse. Cohen and Rogers place these conditions in their larger context.

The powers of the American state are now deployed in a massive business offensive. Its basic elements are painfully clear. Drastic cutbacks in social spending. Rampant environmental destruction. Regressive revisions of the tax system. [Looming trade wars and high unemployment now considered "normal."] Loosened constraints on corporate power. Ubiquitous assaults on organized labor.

Sharply increased weapons spending. Escalating threats of intervention abroad (Cohen and Rogers 1983, p. 15).

While all of this *is* escalating currently, it is not something new. There has always been a real tension between "property rights" and "person rights" in the United States, between profits and democracy in its richest sense. All too often it has been the former, not the latter, that has gained the upper hand.

Where does education stand in this tension? Surely, it has been one of the major forces for democracy in this society. Surely, in a time when power is being centralized and the lives and hopes of millions of people are being shattered, the content, processes, and outcomes of our school system will enable people to critically examine what is happening all around them. Surely, it will provide paths to equality. Unfortunately, all of this may be less sure than we might common-sensically think.

Adults and children in thousands of classrooms across the country are engaged every week in the concrete practice of teaching and learning. In a variety of ways, the school experience represents an extensive component of people's lives. The typical sixth grade student, for instance, will have already spent about 7,000 hours in school. This corresponds to having attended an all-day religious gathering every Sunday for more than 24 years. An elementary school teacher, one study found, engages in about 1,000 personal interchanges with students during each school day (Jackson 1968, pp. 5–11). Simply put, schools play a central role in the lives of many American people. In fact, because of its universal, mandatory nature, the school as a social institution has become a dominant source of information and referral in the United States during the twentieth century. It has also generated numerous public debates and policies, so much so that it would hardly be possible for teachers, administrators, parents, and students to be unaware of many of the political and ideological tensions and pressures of their daily school lives.

But the everyday life of schooling is marked in particular by numerous practical considerations. The immediacy of classroom events weighs heavily on the minds of participants. Millions of inexperienced and experienced teachers alike, faced with classes of 20 to 35 eager and not-so-eager students, must focus their attention on such questions as "What do I do on Monday?" Similarly expressed concerns about classroom management are met by such practical advice as "Don't smile 'til Christmas" by sympathetic colleagues. The intensely practical concerns of everyday school life oftentimes can deflect attention from the goals of teaching and the values implicit in educational activities. It is hard to focus on education's place in the crisis because of this. Other forces contribute to this lack of clarity as well—especially the kinds of research done on the subject of schools.

The educational research community has been particularly attentive to the practical concerns of school participants and has focused much of its attention on the development of efficient methods of curriculum implementation and assessments of the effectiveness of given educational practice. Considerable work has gone into the formulation of a general set of technical procedures that would guide curriculum planning, instruction, and evaluation. Indeed, given that schooling is in part an eminently practical endeavor, this dominant research tradition makes sense. But its excessively prescriptive and psychological nature, and frequent adoption of process/product approaches, has serious negative consequences, as well. With its focus on the individualistic aspects of teaching and learning, the dominant research tradition in education has served to circumvent rigorous study of the broad and complex nature and social consequences of everyday school practice. In particular, it has functioned to obscure the significant linkages between the internal dynamics of U.S. schooling and the larger ideological, economic, and political context.

The stress on method and the evaluation of given curricular practice has thus resulted in an overly technical orientation for the field. This technocratic rationality that has predominated, with its acceptance of "common-sensical" givens, has served to coat with a neutral veneer an enterprise that in a fundamental sense "takes sides." This is the case in two broad, interrelated ways. The first concerns the *educational* choices that are made. For example, the continued adoption of narrowly conceived, easily measurable behavioral objectives as a logical and "scientific" starting point for the teacher's planning of daily lessons implicitly accepts one vision of educational practice over others. This vision includes: a passive role for students in the planning process; a lack of attention to the reasons for students' behavior; the notion that only that which is measurable is really worth learning; and the assumption that teachers can and should specify all the significant learning outcomes of an educational activity before engaging in it (Hyman 1974, pp. 45–49). For many educators, this perspective on planning and practice is accepted unproblematically. And yet a viable alternative vision could be easily suggested. It would include: an active role for students in the planning of lessons; a significant concern for the reasons for students' behavior; the belief that some important learning is simply not possible to measure easily; and the notion that teachers should not be expected to specify all learning outcomes before engaging in an educational activity. With reference to the last aspect, for instance, John Dewey (1922) wrote: "Ends arise and function within action. They are not, as current theories too often imply, things lying outside activity at which the latter is directed. They are not ends or termini of action at all. They are terminals of deliberation, and so turning points *in* activity" (p. 223, emphasis added). As Herbert Kliebard has more recently noted, "if ends arise only *within* activity it is not clear how one can state objectives before the activity (learning experience) begins." It then follows that "the most significant dimensions of an educational activity or any activity may be those that are completely unplanned and wholly unanticipated," an idea that has important implications for evaluation procedures (Kliebard 1977a, p. 64, emphasis added; Kliebard 1977b).

Another example of the unproblematic nature of the educational choices that are made is contained in Henry Giroux's recent discussion of Mortimer Adler's *The Paideia Proposal*, a proposal to have all schooling be based on the "great ideas" and books of the past. There would be no electives, no tracking; all students would study exactly the same material. As Giroux suggests, Adler's work (1982) accepts "a predetermined and hierarchically arranged body of knowledge...as the cultural currency to be dispensed to all children regardless of their differences and interests" (Giroux 1985, p. 25). This is somewhat of a departure from the common practice of a differentiated curriculum. But whether Adler's core curriculum is established or not, with whatever modifications might be made, there exists here the taken-for-granted assumption that the traditional canons of Western culture are appropriate storehouses of knowledge from which to dispense lessons to students. The chief concern then becomes the proper distribution, management, and measurement of such knowledge. Here again, educators tend to assume that curricula "work" if "they 'produce' higher test scores, for less money, in a measurable and relatively uncomplicated way" (Apple and Beyer 1983, pp. 425–26). The mode of operation alluded to in the previous example is maintained: knowledge is broken down into atomistic units of behaviors; pretests are designed; "ability" is determined; teaching takes place; and a test is given. The selection of the school knowledge itself is essentially viewed as a given, the result of a supposedly neutral, consensual and technical process. Our point is that the dominant models of educational theory and research have been unable to unravel the complexities of everyday interaction in schools or to clarify the choices implicit in dominant educational ideas and practices.

This is quite consequential to the issue of the relation of schooling to equality, for directly related to the role that seemingly neutral technical concerns and procedures play in the obfuscation of educational choices is the dominant research tradition's systematic mystification of the *political and ideological nature and social consequences* of everyday curriculum selection, transmission, and evaluation. The predominant concern is with the development of an effective method A to achieve result B or of an instrument to evaluate the achievement of B. Lost in such a concern is a rigorous consideration of "whether B, or the process of getting there, is ethically or politically just" (Apple and Beyer 1983, p. 426). And yet it is clear that schools do not and cannot function in isolation from "the structurally unequal society (and the conflicts this inequality engenders) of which they are a part" (Apple and Weis 1983, pp. 3–4). Ethical and political choices are fundamental to the educational enterprise (Huebner 1975).

There are alternative traditions that take these choices seriously, however. Strongly influenced by critical theory and the sociology of knowledge, as well as a kind of rebirth of Marxist and neo-Marxist dialogue, a new perspective on educational research has emerged during the last decade.[1] In the United States, Canada, England, Australia, Spain, France, Brazil, and elsewhere, there has been an ongoing attempt by increasing numbers of sociologists of education and curriculum researchers to clarify the complex relationship between the day-to-day meanings and practices of schools, which in the past were too often left by educational researchers as a kind of "black box," and past and current relations of domination and subordination outside the institution. Three significant areas of school life in particular have been and are continuing to be explored: 1) the day-to-day interactions and regularities of school life—what has been referred to as "the hidden curriculum"—and the covert ideological teaching that goes on because of them; 2) the formal corpus of school knowledge—the overt curriculum itself—that is planned and found in the various materials and texts that are mediated by teachers; and 3) the fundamental perspectives, procedures, theories, and commitments—for example, social labeling practices and industrial models such as systems management—that educators tacitly accept and use to plan, organize, and evaluate what happens in schools (Apple 1979, p. 14; Apple and Beyer 1983, p. 430).

While there are disagreements among many of the individuals who have investigated the ideological roles played by the hidden and overt curriculum, all agree that classrooms may often be less the instruments of help and more a part of the complex process of the reproduction of unequal class, race, and gender relations in our society. Thus, there exist specific patterns of intentions and behaviors in the institution of schooling, which are influenced by and in turn influence the unequal character of our economy and culture. The following sections of this chapter will explicate our view of this relationship between the daily practices of schools and the society in which they are situated. What schools do in creating some of the conditions that are necessary for the maintenance of dominance is very complicated, however. To understand this, we shall need to link our school systems and the teaching and curricula within them to the conflicts, power relations, and contradictions that surround them.

SCHOOLING AND THE REPRODUCTION OF INEQUALITY

Like other sectors of the State, schools are influenced by the conflictual nature of capitalist economic and cultural relations. Contradictory pressures are placed on schools, in particular, in assisting in the development of an efficient, hierarchically organized labor force while at the same time instilling a belief in democratic and egalitarian principles. Such conflicts are experienced by school participants both inside and outside of the classroom, generating a need for creative responses to the resultant tensions. At the same time, no set of ideological norms and practices is ever totally monolithic or determined by the mode of production. The school as a social institution remains partially autonomous from the direct demands of the capitalist imperative.

As a result of such tensions, schools do not just serve to reinforce dominant material relations and ideologies but function, as well, as an arena in which mediation, rejection, and active resistance to dominant influences also takes place. We shall return to this aspect of the character of schooling in the next section. First, we shall have to outline the ways in which schools, contrary to mainstream thinking, in large part serve social interests that are in opposition to the enhancement of democratic practice and economic and cultural equality.

In exploring the relationship between what schools do and the existence of unequal social relations, it is helpful to think of schools as assisting in three significant and interrelated social functions: accumulation, legitimation, and production. The accumulation function of schools is related to the interaction between knowledge and people in the institution. It refers to the ways in which educational institutions provide support for the social division of labor in our society and the relentless search for profit. First, schools are fundamentally concerned with the distribution of knowledge, norms, skills, values, and dispositions. As Pierre Bourdieu and others have pointed out, however, this "cultural capital" is not allocated equally (Bourdieu and Passeron 1977; Bernstein 1977; Bowles and Gintis 1976). There is ample evidence that different knowledge and ways of knowing are distributed to different groups of students in a way that reproduces economic and cultural inequality by race, class, and gender (Persell 1977; Karabel and Halsey 1977; Apple 1982). For instance, schools in higher income (typically, white) school communities are more likely to provide access to high status curricula, instructional activities, and enrichment programs than schools in less affluent communities. They also offer their students instruction that demands greater creativity and thinking skills than is the case for schools with a more working class clientele (Carnoy and Levin 1985; Anyon 1979). Very simply, they expect more from their students.

For example, one of the authors recently observed two first grade classes in the same city, one in a predominantly working class area and the other in a predominantly middle class area. In the first school, the students were doing "average" work in November if they were reading the first book of a four-book reading series. In the second school, students were considered to be doing "average" work in November if they were nearly done with the second book of the same reading series. A more systematic study conducted by Kathleen Wilcox and others found similar results. Significant differences were found between the first grades of an upper middle class school and a lower middle class school with reference to four general attributes: external and internal standards of authority; future vs. present orientation; verbal self-presentation skills; and emphasis on cognitive skills and achievement (Carnoy and Levin 1985, pp. 110N43).

A similar process occurs within schools and within classrooms. Tracking, labeling, ability grouping, counseling, and the like have often functioned to select and sort students in a way that adopts criteria based on an acceptance of the cultural forms of dominant groups (Keddie 1977; Rist 1970; Cicourel and Kitsuse 1963). For example, although it is sometimes an unconscious process, educators commonly utilize the exhibition of mainstream interactional skills, linguistic structures, and learning styles as the "norm" and, more significantly, as indicators of academic competence. Ethnic and racial minorities whose verbal and non-verbal communication patterns or attitudinal displays seem "different" are then grouped, labeled, and counseled as if they were of lesser ability or talent (Gilmore 1985; Heath 1983; Trueba, Guthrie, and Au 1981; Erickson 1975; Philips 1972). Although perhaps there has been considerable progress in this area (and this progress did not come easily; it had to be struggled for over a long period of time), a similar situation can also impact on the ways girls are treated in schools. Differential treatment has led, for example, to many girls being socialized into a kind of "learned helplessness." This can have significant implications for their expression of self-confidence and independence, their academic abilities, and their choices of study and occupation (Sadker and Sadker 1982).[2]

It would be wrong to simply blame individual teachers for this state of affairs, to claim, as one critic has, that teachers are essentially "mindless" about the implications of their practice (Silberman 1970). For in myriad essential ways, individual teachers are expected and indeed pressured by parents, other teachers and administrators, and state education officials to accept the nature of social relations as it is and to be "realistic" about students' chances for success. They are encouraged to assume that, since students from certain backgrounds "have a higher probability of access to and success in certain occupations than students from other backgrounds" (Carnoy and Levin 1985, p. 138), it is "natural" (and neutral) for them to prepare these different groups of youth differently. The results are school socialization patterns that generally conform to the occupational roles and social backgrounds of parents.

Schools thus not only allocate knowledge; they allocate people, as well. "Cultural capital" is distributed in such a way that students are allocated to their "proper" place in society. What this process does, of course, is to roughly reproduce a hierarchically organized labor force and class, race, and gender inequality. Despite what human capital theorists would have us believe about the possession of knowledge inexorably leading to greater personal economic power, the teaching and internalization of differentiated dispositions, norms, and values, through not just the overt educational content but also the tacit messages of day-to-day school practice, tends to lead to power remaining in the hands of those social groups who already have it.

But there is more to understand here than simply an unequal allocation of knowledge and people. By such practices, schools play another fundamental role in assisting the process of capital accumulation. This process demands a stratified and at least partly socialized labor force in order to function as efficiently and cost effectively as possible. While this does not occur as smoothly as employers and dominant groups would like, schools do provide some of the basic conditions (that is, the proper and differentiated norms, values, and dispositions—such as punctuality, individual achievement, moral conformity, and authority relations) necessary for the promotion of capital accumulation. By their everyday practices, schools partly socialize future members of the working class, who will work in low-level blue-, white-, and pink-collar jobs, to become used to a lack of control over their work activity; to expect little or no opportunity to express their own ideas, insights, and individuality; and to accept as natural a pyramid-shaped and fractured labor force (Carnoy and Levin 1985, pp. 54–56). By their internal sorting and selecting procedures, schools also reinforce an acceptance of the separation of mental and manual labor, which has played a crucial role in the development of the paid workplace during the twentieth century (Braverman 1974). And by their constant emphasis on the pursuit of an education for extrinsic rewards (for example, good grades, acceptance to college, or a decent job), schools also lay the groundwork for the later acceptance of the drudgery of work as necessary "to obtain a meaningful life in the sphere of buying and consumption" (Carnoy and Levin 1985, p. 55). Of course, such an emphasis on consumption, as a kind of light at the end of a week's travel through a monotonous and dreary tunnel, serves the requirements of capital accumulation, as well. The structure of capitalist economics rests on a constant demand for consumer goods and for individual ownership of them.

Schools also serve a second major social function, that of legitimation. One way in which this occurs is that schools act to legitimate certain knowledge and ways of knowing over others. Out of the virtually unlimited range of knowledge in history, science, culture, and so on, only certain traditions and meanings are kept alive and transmitted in schools (Apple 1979). This "selective tradition" exists as a result of, and at the same time functions to reinforce, dominant influences in political, economic, and cultural spheres. A crucial characteristic of this selective tradition is that it is not usually presented as a partial or limited account of the past or of culture, but rather as "*the* tradition, *the* significant past" (Williams 1977, pp. 115–16). An "effective, dominant culture" is produced in part through the ideological selection of "legitimate" knowledge in schools (Apple 1979).

The selective tradition works to include, to leave out, and to distort. The extent to which schools act as agents of this selecting process can be seen, in part, by an examination of the curricular materials utilized in schools. A number of studies of curriculum content have pointed out, for example, that whites, males, and the middle and upper classes dominate the histories, literature, and other curricula of the classroom. When presented at all, depictions of the contributions of racial and ethnic minorities, women, and laborers have often been minimized or distorted (for example, Christian 1984; Taxel 1981; Butterfield et al. 1979; Fitzgerald 1979; Taxel 1978–79; Stewig and Knipfel 1975; Reynolds and Reynolds 1974). For instance, in a study of 17 popular secondary history textbooks, Jean Anyon (1979) found a wholesale neglect of the dynamic struggles of labor groups in the United States, even though historians have clearly documented that our country has had one of the most contentious labor histories of any nation in the world. In effect, the working class is deprived—at least in school textbooks, whose influence is still quite significant in schools (Apple 1985)—of a history of itself as a working class. Anyon stresses that this glossing over of the true nature of labor history in the United States offers ideological support for the fundamental existing arrangements of political and economic power. In the content of the curricula adopted by schools, then, the traditions, history, and so forth, of certain groups are presented as much more significant than those of other groups. Subordinate groups tend to be portrayed, when at all, in less complimentary ways. Not only does this have much to say about the way we view ourselves, it no doubt effects the ways that we relate to each other as well.

But it is not just the content of the curriculum that should concern us here. The form of educational activities is also of significance. Independent, competitive learning activities and norm-referenced assessments are commonplace in schools. Such instructional and evaluative strategies serve to legitimate a vision of social relations that devalues the need for collective action.[3] Furthermore, the common division of school knowledge into separate disciplines, with little interdisciplinary work taking place, undermines the ability of students to see problems holistically, that is, relationally. (Of course, this discouragement of relational thinking is reinforced by other aspects of the educational enterprise, for example, the previously stated tradition of breaking down the knowledge to be taught into atomistic units of behavior.) Not only, then, are particular social groups and social movements given legitimacy in schools, but particular kinds of social relationships and thinking skills are legitimated as well.

Schools thus distribute particular social and cultural ideologies and at the same time help create the conditions for their acceptance. But they also function to legitimate *their own internal workings* as based on meritocratic criteria and as contributing to widespread social and economic justice. They foster the belief that schools and other major social institutions are equally responsive to individuals, regardless of their race, class, and sex. Whatever differences in life chances exist among these groups are portrayed as determined by an allegedly neutral conception of talent and ability. And yet a significant amount of data has recently cast considerable doubt on such claims. For example, in virtually every social arena from health care to anti-inflation policy, the top 20 percent of the population benefit much more than the bottom 80 percent (Navarro 1976, p. 91; O'Connor 1973). And while schools may offer avenues for individual mobility, there has actually been little consistent loosening of the ties between origins and educational attainments over time (Olneck and Crouse 1978). Finally, as Christopher Jencks and his colleagues (1979) found, high school graduation itself pays off primarily for students who are already economically advantaged; for example, the benefits that white students get from school are still twice as great as for blacks (pp. 174n75).

At the same time that schools legitimate themselves, they also legitimate the existent socioeconomic system. For example, in a study of the economics classes at one high school, it was found that the U.S. economic system was portrayed as consensual, efficient, and like a well-functioning machine, one worthy of citizens' trust and too remote for most of us to be concerned with beyond a few facts and technical terms or generalizations. Experts are to be relied on to solve "dysfunctional" problems that arise from time to time (McNeil 1977). Yet, it is not only the economy that is legitimated by schools. Democratic principles require that our state bureaucracy and government generate consent from the governed. Schools are thus invested with the responsibility of helping to legitimate the role of the State as a neutral and equitable arbiter of conflicting claims, a position on the State that our earlier quote from Cohen and Rogers clearly shows to be false. Since the need for political legitimacy may not always be consistent with the requirements of the economy, schools function to encourage a reservoir of popular support for the political institutions of our society. Indeed, a glorification of the U.S. Constitution, American patriots, and American social institutions takes place in virtually every school in the country. This especially occurs in times of crisis, fiscal and otherwise, for, as Gabriel Kolko (1970) has observed, "the true character and the efficacy of a political structure is revealed only under the test of pressure and crisis (pp. 207n08).[4]

Finally, schools also serve a production function. Along with universities, they produce the knowledge itself that is vital for cultural control, the expansion of markets, the artificial creation of new consumer needs, the control and division of labor, and the technical innovation that increases profit margins (Apple 1982; Apple and Beyer 1983, p. 428). A corporate economy requires the production of high levels of technical/ administrative knowledge to keep the economic apparatus running effectively and to become more sophisticated in the maximization of opportunities for economic expansion. Low levels of achievement by subordinate groups, such as racial minorities and children of the poor, are tolerable as long as the technical/administrative knowledge needed for the further expansion of the economy is generated. Production of a particular "commodity" (that is, high status knowledge) is of greater concern than the ways in which it is distributed. More equitable distribution patterns can be considered if they do not interfere with the production of the technical/administrative knowledge itself (Apple 1982; Apple 1979, pp. 36n37).

To understand how this process assists in the generation of inequality, it is important to emphasize the ways that technical/administrative knowledge is actually *used*. Historically, in economies like our own, technical knowledge has been produced and organized in a way that has tended to benefit corporate concerns. As Stephen Marglin has pointed out, the technical efficiency brought about by the production, accumulation, and control of technical/administrative knowledge has been extensively sponsored and introduced by corporate managers so that they could increase not only the efficiency of organization but also their share of economic profits (Marglin 1976; Noble 1977). As research and development centers whose costs are socialized (that is, spread among all of us so that capital need not pay the bulk of the expense) and as training grounds for future employees of industry, universities play an essential role in making available the technically useful knowledge on which so much of our science-based industries depend and on which the culture industry is based (Apple and Weis 1983, p. 6). This helps to explain why most school systems and the curricula within them are organized toward the university and why there is so much support from the business sector for the establishment of "gifted education" and science and math programs in a time of economic recession. Students who are perceived as able to contribute ultimately to the production of this technical/administrative knowledge are sponsored by the school. Other students are labeled as somehow deviant or are formally or informally selected out into various other levels, to receive the appropriately differentiated norms and values. They are essentially excluded from the knowledge necessary for both understanding and directing important aspects of the production process. Again, it is not essential that everyone have sophisticated technical knowledge, only that the conditions for the maximization of the production of this knowledge are satisfied (Apple 1982). The school is relatively efficient in this aspect of its productive function, although the current intense pressures placed on schools to teach more mathematics, science, and computer literacy documents the importance given to this kind of knowledge in times of crisis.

The production and control of technical/administrative knowledge is thus intimately tied to the division of mental and manual labor, a division that we suggested earlier is critical to the accumulation and control of economic capital. The school system as a whole ultimately helps to produce technical/administrative knowledge and is charged with the role of assuring that the most "talented" students receive the necessary experiences to be better able to play a role in the further production of this form of knowledge (as contrasted, for example, to the arts and humanities). But because origins and attainment continue to be linked, here again, in fulfilling this function, schools reinforce social inequities.

AGAINST A MECHANISTIC VIEW OF SCHOOLING

The foregoing discussion of the school's role in assisting in accumulation, legitimation, and production is intended to illuminate how schools, in part, reproduce unequal economic and social relations. As we have seen, part of this process involves schools fostering a belief in the efficacy of the social institutions that recreate the relations and of the actions of "helpers" within those institutions. When successfully socialized, individuals who fail to achieve the desired material success and social status blame the only "guilty" party left, themselves (or perhaps their families), for their lack of ability, motivation, effort, self-confidence, or whatever. The internal workings of the school's curricular and guidance programs help to make this situation appear as a "natural" outcome. These students later help fill society's need for service and/or manual labor (Apple 1982, pp. 50–51; Rosenbaum 1976), while a smaller number of students go on to help produce the kinds of knowledge seen as essential by dominant groups.

But by adopting a somewhat macroeconomic and macrocultural perspective, we do not mean to suggest that individual children are not often helped by the methods and practices of teachers or that the day-to-day actions of schools are always misguided. We want to emphasize this point. We, both authors, have been classroom teachers and we have observed enough schools and spoken to enough teachers, administrators, parents, and children to know full well that, viewed individually, there are worthwhile activities taking place in schools. And there are many caring and creative teachers and administrators, concerned and responsible parents, and motivated and bright students. However, focusing on those aspects does two things. It deflects us from the task of ferreting out the social interests embedded in the general patterns of school practice. And it serves to reinforce the overly psychologistic and technical mainstream vision of schools that we discussed earlier, a vision that is seriously myopic in its depiction of what schools do and why.

However, an important issue *is* raised by these points, one that we shall stress in this section of our discussion. We must guard against adopting a mechanistic view of schooling, one that is overly pessimistic and, in fact, partly incorrect about the relationship of schools to society. As we noted in our introductory remarks, schools function neither as totally economically determined social institutions nor as simply reproductive in nature. Indeed, there is considerable danger in adopting an overly economistic analysis and using the language of reproduction for this very reason. Educational institutions are simply not always successful in carrying out the three functions of accumulation, legitimation, and production that we discussed in the prior section. There are two major reasons for this: first, the social functions themselves are often *contradictory*; and second, the schools themselves, and the participants in them (and in all social institutions), have *agency*. They are relatively autonomous from the requirements of the economic and cultural spheres. It is important to consider both of these reasons so as not to leave an overly reductive picture of the complex character of schools in our society.

As an apparatus of the State, the school is subject to the same kinds of conflicting pressures experienced within our political institutions. One of the most significant tensions involves the school's role in reproducing ideological and material hegemony at the same time that it is fostering a belief in democratic and egalitarian ideals. It is also caught between selecting and sorting an "adequately socialized" work force while acting as if it were part of an open system. In attempting to carry out these dual roles, the school reflects and itself produces fundamental tensions within society. What is specifically in contradiction here are its legitimation and accumulation functions—for schools need to legitimate ideologies of social justice (as well as their own operation), a role that may be "objectively at odds with the equally (and given current economic conditions, now more) compelling pressure on schools to serve the changing needs of industry" (Apple and Beyer 1983, pp. 428–29). Manuel Castells (1980) has provided a helpful general description of how the contradiction of the legitimation and accumulation functions can give rise to difficulties:

Capital must develop productive forces in order to continue its accumulation. But the social conditions necessary for the development of productive forces are increasingly contradictory to capitalist social relationships. Since capital shapes society, the state is used more and more as a basic mechanism to absorb, smooth, and regulate the contradictions that emerge in the process of accumulation. However, the state is not a purely regulatory capitalist apparatus. It expresses the contradictions of society and must also fulfill the functions of legitimating the dominant interests and integrating the dominated class into the system. The growing state intervention to support the capitalist logic in all spheres of economic and social life undermines the basis for its legitimacy as the representative of the general interest (p. 58).

In their attempt to serve both U.S. capitalist expansion and the democratic political system, then, schools are caught in contradiction and conflict. Thus, in some instances, the production of technical/administrative knowledge is not always "functional" for capital but may be both reproductive and non-reproductive at the same time. For example, while there are times when the development of the productive forces of society makes necessary a "transformation" of both the labor process and human labor, such transformations may also demand social and technological conditions that may ultimately be less than totally compatible with capitalist logic (Apple 1982, p. 170). As Castells writes:

For instance, the development of scientific research requires a massive investment in education which is only profitable in the long term. So too the introduction of information as a productive force requires a good deal of autonomy in decision-making and produces a situation that is entirely contradictory to the discipline capital imposes on workers (1980, p. 51).

Capital's need for autonomy, then, is at odds with its need for tight control. This is very important, for, as this example indicates, our society is not "a system of structural self-reproduction" but rather an unstable and contradictory structure of "asymmetrical multidimensional relationships" (Castells 1980, p. 47). In less abstract terms, things are constantly going on that work both to support *and* undo dominant social and ideological beliefs and practices at one and the same time. This is exactly how we should interpret schooling.

In a recently published analysis, Martin Carnoy and Henry Levin (1985) have suggested three specific kinds of contradictions that are inherent in the nature of the democratic capitalist State and that are directly associated with the operation of schools. These contradictions exist: 1) in the political struggle over resources for schooling; 2) internal to the educational process itself; and 3) imported to the educational process through its relationship with the paid workplace (pp. 144–61). Each of these contradictions generate such conditions as to make it impossible for a simple reproduction process to take place.

The first contradiction refers to the struggle between the interests of capital and labor, and within capital and labor, over the use of State resources for the expansion of the profitability of capital or for an expansion of educational opportunities. This debate rages in the political arena and thus provides the opportunity for a political rather than just a technical debate on educational issues. In fact, State intervention has increased markedly during the last several decades. Although there is currently a partially successful attempt to reverse this trend, elements within both the business community and the labor community continue to look to the State for the resolution of conflicts. At the same time, there is evidence that capitalism and democracy may increasingly come into conflict (Edwards 1979, pp. 211–12). In the battle to maintain and extend the role of the State, and to defend and expand democratic practices in the political and economic spheres, schools and other social institutions become the battleground for ideological disputes. This opens up the terrain for a politicized struggle within as well as outside the school doors.

The second contradiction pertains to some of the complicated and more democratic activities that schools are entrusted to engage in, activities that may contradict the efficient reproduction of a capitalist work force. Carnoy and Levin identify five such goals that schools are asked to reach: democratic participation, social equality, social mobility, cultural development, and the independence of the educational bureaucracy from the direct control of capitalist firms. In other words, in attempting to address each of these goals, schools in part contradict their reproduction role and breed the potential for resistance to dominant influences. For instance, a teacher who takes seriously the messages of democratic participation attempts to introduce a more active participatory element in the classroom. Such an orientation would help prepare students for a participatory role in their lives, which would not be in keeping with what can be found in most paid workplaces. Yet the fact that these more participatory practices can and sometimes do occur in schools demonstrates that often the everyday life of the school does not always function as a passive mirror of the economy but rather is part of a "contested terrain" (Apple 1982). In a related way, the successful transmission of the message that education leads to social mobility raises expectations and generates "an expansion of educational enrollments and attainments that has exceeded the available number of jobs requiring those credentials" (Carnoy and Levin 1985, p. 152). This results both in an overeducated and sometimes frustrated labor force and in the serious potential for behavior that is disruptive to existing work arrangements.

The third contradiction refers to the education system's connection to the paid workplace to which, in Carnoy and Levin's words, schools "correspond structurally" (p. 155).[5] There are three sources of contradiction associated with this correspondence: the student as alienated labor; class (and we would add race and gender to the primary focus on class found in Carnoy and Levin) resistance to the school agenda; and teachers as alienated labor. First, although students may have greater freedom of expression than workers, like workers they have little direct influence over the shape of their own activities. This results in many students developing little attachment to the worth of what they are doing. Extrinsic payoffs motivate them. But in recent years, educational credentials themselves have lost some of their market value (for example, a good education will no longer insure a good job) and the lure of extrinsic rewards has lost some of its luster. A lack of motivation and effort by groups of students results. As the current outcry about lowered standards and the need to reemphasize "excellence" in schools would perhaps indicate, students learn less than what the modern labor force would appear to require and, in some cases, resist the messages and practices intended for them (Apple 1982; Valli 1986).

Second, groups of students perceive the futility of seeking an education for extrinsic payoffs in an economic structure that will probably not provide meaningful labor. These are students who are often labeled as "slow" and in need of some kind of "remedial" help (although such labeling practices are rarely informed by their linkages to the history of racial oppression and poverty). In most cases, it is, in fact, extremely difficult for a student placed in a remedial group to do markedly better, in large part because the disability label placed on the student turns out to be a real disability in itself (Apple 1979). Such students represent a constant potential for disruption in schools. They represent a constant threat to their socialization into the "appropriate" norms and values and thus to the reproduction of a compliant work force. Paul Willis's (1977) ethnographic account of a group of high school working class boys in a heavily industrialized city in England is revealing on this point. With a decidedly cynical eye, the youth he studied had come to realize that in essence they had been explicitly and systematically selected out of the best courses, the best tracks, and ultimately the best jobs. The school's relatively flexible environment, greater opportunity for freedom of expression, and less threatening sanctions provide such students with the opportunity to disrupt the smooth functioning of the educational system by their subtle and explicit rejection of the messages and practices of the schools, or by "dropping out" altogether. The youth in Willis's study rejected the "legitimate" culture of the school by affirming their affinity for manual work and for physicality, and by spending a good deal of their time finding ways to get out of doing schoolwork. The important point is that, in reality, their behavior is probably a realistic assessment that *as a class* this will not benefit very much by trying harder or graduating (Willis 1977; Everhart 1983; Valli 1986). Thus, students themselves act against, and contradict, the school's role in efficient sorting and teaching "appropriate" norms and values.

And third, the changing structures of the control of teachers' work in areas somewhat removed from the corridors and classrooms of schools have significant implications for the nature of teaching as an occupation and as a set of skilled and self-reflective actions. The same pressures currently affecting jobs in general are being felt increasingly in teaching. In the general sociological literature, the label affixed to what is happening is the "degradation of labor." This degradation is a result of our dominant economic arrangements (Edwards 1979; Braverman 1974). There have been two particularly profound consequences for the teaching profession: the separation of conception from execution, and de-skilling (Apple 1982). At the local, state, and federal levels, movements for strict accountability systems, competency-based education and testing, systems management, a truncated vision of the "basics," mandated curricular content and goals, and so on, are clear and growing. For example, the increasing adoption by school districts of commercially produced, prepackaged sets of curriculum materials, with such rigid instructional guidelines for teachers to follow that teachers essentially become managers of other people's curricula rather than creators and implementers of their own, serves to accelerate the trend of teaching as alienated labor. It also undercuts the floor of autonomy that teachers have struggled so long to achieve and on which progressive teachers depend in order to introduce more critically oriented materials (Apple and Teitelbaum 1985; Gitlin 1983).

Increasingly, then, teaching methods, texts, tests, and outcomes are being taken out of the hands of the people who must put them into practice. Instead, they are being legislated by state departments of education or in state legislatures, and are being either supported or stimulated by many of the national reports, such as "A Nation at Risk," which are often simplistic assessments of and responses to problems in education (Stedman and Smith 1983). As is too often the case, educational bureaucrats are borrowing the ideology and techniques of industrial management without recognizing what can and has happened to the majority of employees in industry itself (Gordon, Edwards, and Reich 1982; Edwards 1979; Apple 1979, pp. 105n22).

The fact that these management techniques are being increasingly applied to a profession that has historically been seen, especially at the elementary school level, as tied to *women's labor* should make us take notice. There has been a very long history both inside schools and in paid labor in general for what counts as "women's work" to be de-skilled and to be subject to external control. Thus, any analysis of what is currently happening to schools, teachers, and curriculum cannot simply focus on class and economic dynamics but must pay very close attention to *gender* dynamics as well (Apple 1987).

These trends may have consequences exactly opposite of what many authorities intend, however. Instead of professional teachers who care greatly about what they do and why they do it, we may have alienated executors of someone else's plans. Teachers become not only more dissatisfied with their work conditions but may also become less inspiring about learning and knowledge (Carnoy and Levin 1985, p. 158). The relatively low financial rewards and lessening status of the teaching profession during the last decade only exacerbate the situation. Amidst this growing dissatisfaction, the quality of the educational enterprise in general (and the socialization of proper norms, values, skills, and dispositions) can suffer. But at the same time, the potential for a broader politicization of the teaching force increases. A general questioning of the nature and role of schooling may take place and an increasing number of teachers may begin to consciously resist the shift of control over content, teaching, and evaluation to outside the classroom. They attempt to maintain control of their own labor, for example, by developing their own, perhaps more critically oriented, curriculum materials, or by utilizing the mandated curriculum only three days a week instead of the five days that are stipulated (Apple and Teitelbaum 1985). While such efforts continue to be made by teachers, the trend toward not just school-wide but *statewide* tests, textbook adoption lists, mandated goals, and "appropriate" teacher competencies signals serious obstacles in the way of teachers who attempt to transform the curriculum into something more socially critical and personally meaningful for themselves and their students. But it should be made clear that many teachers do try, and do realize what is happening to them, thereby threatening both the "smooth running" of the institution and its connections to the ideologies and procedures of capital.

This brief discussion of the contradictions and conflicts associated with everyday educational practice is intended to highlight the non-reproductive side of the institution of schooling. But there is another reason that schools do not simply reproduce unequal economic and cultural relations. Like all social institutions, schools are relatively autonomous because they lie at the very intersection of the economic, political, and cultural spheres. They have their own histories, organizations, and ideologies that cannot be simply "read off" from the logic of capitalism. Indeed, we want to argue that the social and psychological nature of social institutions, and of human existence, is too complex to be totally enveloped within dominant social forms. Even in the absence of a clearly defined crisis or conflict, individuals in social institutions develop creative responses to the injustices that they observe or experience. As Raymond Williams has noted:

No mode of production and therefore no dominant social order and therefore no dominant culture ever in reality includes or exhausts all human practice, human energy, and human interaction.... [It] is a fact about the modes of domination, that they select from and consequently exclude the full range of human practice. What they exclude may often be seen as the personal or the private, or as the natural or even the metaphysical (1977, p. 125).

Human actors, then, build on and interpret culture in different ways. They are not passive receptacles into which hegemonic meanings can be simply poured. This can be seen historically, in the past struggles of individuals and social groups to introduce more democratic and egalitarian content and form into social institutions, and at present, in the attempts by a host of critical educators to introduce more progressive practice into schools and universities (for example, Teitelbaum and Reese 1983; Schniedewind and Davidson 1983; Lind-Brenkman 1983; Shor 1980; Wolf-Wasserman and Hutchison 1978). As we have shown, students also often act in ways that make simple predictions about the social effects of educational practice difficult to make. They simply do not always accept what the school attempts to teach them. Ideological hegemony was (and is) a constant human struggle, the conclusion of which cannot be known in advance (Apple 1982).

CONCLUSION

In this chapter, we have provided an overview of many of the complex connections that tie our formal institutions of education to the production of inequality in the larger society. At the outset, we criticized the dominant tradition of interpreting education, arguing that it is unable to deal with the ways schools *are* actually connected to these unequal relations. We then moved to a discussion that examined the reproductive functions of education. Here the focus was on the manner in which education helps in capital accumulation, legitimation, and production through its selection of knowledge, its sorting of students, and its production of technical/administrative knowledge for use by powerful groups.

Yet we also claimed that limiting our perspective to how schools recreate dominance would tell only half the story, at best. Thus, we turned our attention to the utterly contradictory roles educational institutions perform, to the cultural and political conflicts between students and the overt and hidden curriculum, and to what is happening to teachers themselves, all of which may make it very difficult for education to fit in nicely with the hegemonic aims of an elite.

Finally, and this is one of our most crucial points, we argued that, by their very nature, people—as classed, raced, and gendered actors—will never be fully controlled. They will always find creative ways to assert their freedom, even in the most difficult and oppressive circumstances. Even in a time of conservative restoration (Short 1986; Apple 1987), when it is clear that the Rightist political, ideological, and economic project has had no small measure of success, we should not be pessimistic. There are counter hegemonic tendencies surfacing at every moment, in part stimulated by the very contradictory position schools, in fact, hold. Gramsci had a lovely way of putting some of this: "Pessimism of the intellect; optimism of the will (Gramsci 1971, p. 175). Schools were built not only to serve industrial needs, but to serve democratic purposes, as well. They were also created by the concrete struggles of working class, women and minority groups who often won important victories in what the curricular and teaching policies and practices should be (Reese 1986; Hogan 1982, 1985; Wrigley 1982). After all, if schools were such reliable defenders of the status quo, industry and Rightist groups wouldn't be attacking them so vigorously. If we helped build them, we can rebuild them as well. Schools have been the site of democratic struggle before. Our task is to help ensure that this history continues.

This cannot be done alone, however. Just as we argued that schools do not sit isolated from the relations of dominance and subordination of the larger society, so too must those of us who work so hard at democratizing the content, process, and outcomes of education not sit isolated, as well. Connections with groups who are working for equality in other arenas can and must be made. The concerted and organized efforts of these groups of women, men, people of color, progressive unions, and others in the media, health, welfare, and legal systems, in the home, and elsewhere *in coalition*—each one teaching and learning from the others—can provide "the will" to continue the history of the democratic project. Who knows, perhaps those who say "where there's a will, there's a way" may prove to be right after all.

NOTES

1. Of course, this more critically minded tradition is not without its antecedents in the United States. The work of George Counts, Harold Rugg, John Dewey, and others contained important ideas from which more recent scholars have drawn. Educators even less in the mainstream of educational scholarship and practice—for example, those who approached the institution from a more explicitly socialist perspective—also developed oppositional ideas and activities. For a clear sense of the latter, see Teitelbaum (1985).

2. We realize, of course, that the school is not alone in playing a significant role in the reproduction of unequal class, race, and gender relations. For example, the family, the paid workplace, peer groups, mass media, and so on, all contribute to the creation and reinforcement of inequality and injustice in our society (see other essays in this volume). In fact, as we suggest various times in this essay, they do so in ways that directly relate to the day-to-day activities of schools.

3. Alternative visions have been suggested by a number of educators. Elizabeth Cagan (1978), for example, advocates replacing the more individualistic approach that "generates competitive, egotistic, and atomized social relations" with group games, folk singing, group meetings, moral lessons, and community action programs that would instead emphasize "social consciousness, concern for others, group solidarity, and moral commitment" (p. 228).

4. For example, during and after World War I in the United States, an intense campaign was conducted by various federal, state, and local government officials (and Right-wing private citizen groups) to purge the nation of radical and foreign ideas and practices. Additionally, in the attempt to create order and homogeneity, "panegyrics celebrating our history and institutions were delivered regularly in almost every American school, church, and public hall in 1919 and 1920" (Cohen 1969, p. 108). Biographies of American heroes (statesmen, cowboys, and pioneers) appeared in great numbers and the superiority of American institutions was emphasized in countless pamphlets, films, and the like. The American flag became a more sacred symbol and those suspected of radical leanings were sometimes forced to show their loyalty by kissing it. Recent immigrants in particular were called upon to prove that they had truly converted to Americanism. They were expected to learn English quickly and to adopt American customs; alien non-conformists found themselves facing deportation orders.

5. The extent to which the economic sphere "determines" school practice—and schools "correspond" to the workplace—is a matter of some dispute among educational researchers. For a helpful general discussion of modes of determination, see Wright (1978, pp. 9–29). See also the more detailed discussion in Apple (1982).

REFERENCES

Adler, Mortimer. 1982. *The Paideia Proposal*. New York: Macmillan.

Anyon, Jean. 1979. "Ideology and U.S. History Textbooks." *Harvard Educational Review* 49:361n86.

Apple, Michael W. 1979. *Ideology and Curriculum*. London: Routledge and Kegan Paul.

———. 1982. *Education and Power*. Boston: Routledge and Kegan Paul.

———. 1985. "The Culture and Commerce of the Textbook." *Journal of Curriculum Studies* 17:147–62.

———. 1987. *Teachers and Texts: A Political Economy of Class and Gender Relations in Education*. Boston: Routledge and Kegan Paul.

Apple, Michael W., and Landon E. Beyer. 1983. "School Evaluation of Curriculum." *Educational Evaluation and Policy Analysis* 5:425–34.

Apple, Michael W., and Kenneth Teitelbaum. 1985. "Are Teachers Losing Control of Their Jobs?" *Social Education* 49:372–75.

Apple, Michael W., and Lois Weis. 1983. "Ideology and Practice in Schooling: A Political and Conceptual Introduction." In *Ideology and Practice in Schooling*, edited by Michael W. Apple and Lois Weis. Philadelphia: Temple University Press.

Aronowitz, Stanley. 1973. *False Promises: The Shaping of American Working-Class Consciousness*. New York: McGraw-Hill.

Bernstein, Basil, 1977. *Class, Codes and Control*. Vol. 3: *Towards a Theory of Educational Transmissions*. London: Routledge and Kegan Paul.

Bourdieu, Pierre, and Jean-Claude Passeron. 1977. *Reproduction in Education, Society and Culture*. London: Sage.

Bowles, Samuel, and Herbert Gintis. 1976. *Schooling in Capitalist America*. New York: Basic Books.

Braverman, Harry. 1974. *Labor and Monopoly Capital*. New York: Monthly Review Press.

Butterfield, Robin A., Elene S. Demos, Gloria W. Grant, Peter S. May, and Anna L. Perez. 1979. "A Multicultural Analysis of a Popular Basal Reading Series in the International Year of the Child." *Journal of Negro Education* 18:382–89.

Cagan, Elizabeth. 1978. "Individualism, Collectivism, and Radical Educational Reform." *Harvard Educational Review* 48:227–66.

Carnoy, Martin, and Henry M. Levin. 1985. *Schooling and Work in the Democratic State*. Stanford: Stanford University Press.

Castells, Manuel. 1980. *The Economic Crisis and American Society*. Princeton: Princeton University Press.

Christian, Linda. 1984. "Becoming a Woman through Romance." Ph.D. dissertation, University of Wisconsin–Madison.

Cicourel, Aaron, and John Kitsuse. 1963. *The Educational Decision-Makers*. Indianapolis: Bobbs-Merrill.

Coben, Stanley. 1969. "Postwar Upheaval: The Red Scare." In *The Impact of World War I*, edited by Arthur S. Link. New York: Harper and Row.

Cohen, Joshua, and Joel Rogers. 1983. *On Democracy*. New York: Penguin Books.

Dewey, John. 1922. *Human Nature and Conduct*. New York: Random House.

Edwards, Richard. 1979. *Contested Terrain*. New York: Basic Books.

Erickson, Frederick. 1975. "Gatekeeping and the Melting Pot: Interaction in Counseling Encounters." *Harvard Educational Review* 45:44–70.

Everhart, Robert. 1983. *Reading, Writing and Resistance*. Boston: Routledge and Kegan Paul.

Fitzgerald, Frances. 1979. *America Revised: History Schoolbooks in the Twentieth Century*. Boston: Little, Brown.

Gilmore, Perry. 1985. "Gimme Room: School Resistance, Attitude, and Access to Literacy." *Journal of Education* 167:111–28.

Giroux, Henry. 1985. "Critical Pedagogy, Cultural Politics, and the Discourse of Experience." *Journal of Education* 167:22–41.

Gitlin, Andrew. 1983. "School Structure and Teachers' Work." In *Ideology and Practice in Schooling*, edited by Michael W. Apple and Lois Weis. Philadelphia: Temple University Press.

Gordon, David, Richard Edwards, and Michael Reich. 1982. *Segmented Work, Divided Workers*. New York: Cambridge University Press.

Gramsci, Antonio. 1971. *Selections from the Prison Notebooks*. Edited and translated by Quintin Hoare and Geoffrey N. Smith. New York: International Publishers.

Heath, Shirley Brice. 1983. *Ways with Words: Language, Life, and Work in Communities and Classrooms*. Cambridge, Eng.: Cambridge University Press.

Hogan, David. 1982. "Education and Class Formation." In *Cultural and Economic Reproduction in Education*, edited by Michael W. Apple. Boston: Routledge and Kegan Paul.

———. 1985 *Class and Reform*. Philadelphia: University of Pennsylvania Press.

Huebner, Dwayne. 1975. "Curricular Language and Classroom Meanings." In *Curriculum Theorizing: The Reconceptualists*, edited by William Pinar. Berkeley: McCutchan.

Hyman, Ronald T. 1974. *Ways of Teaching*. New York: Harper and Row.

Jackson, Philip W. 1968. *Life in Classrooms*. New York: Holt, Rinehart, and Winston.

Jencks, Christopher, et al. 1979. *Who Gets Ahead?* New York: Basic Books.

Karabel, Jerome, and A. H. Halsey, eds. 1977. *Power and Ideology in Education*. New York: Oxford University Press.

Keddie, Nell. 1977. "Classroom Knowledge." In *Curriculum and Evaluation*, edited by Arno A. Bellack and Herbert M. Kliebard. Berkeley: McCutchan.

Kliebard, Herbert M. 1977a. "The Tyler Rationale." In *Curriculum and Evaluation*, edited by Arno A. Bellack and Herbert Kliebard. Berkeley: McCutchan.

———. 1977b. "Bureaucracy and Curriculum Theory." In *Curriculum and Evaluation*, edited by Arno A. Bellack and Herbert M. Kliebard. Berkeley: McCutchan.

Kolko, Gabriel. 1970. "The Decline of American Radicalism in the Twentieth Century." In *For a New America: Essays in History and Politics from "Studies on the Left," 1959–1967*, edited by James Weinstein and David W. Eakins. New York: Random House.

Lind-Brenkman, Jean. 1983. "Seeing beyond the Interests of Industry: Teaching Critical Thinking." *Journal of Education* 165:283–94.

McNeil, Linda. 1977. *Economic Dimensions of Social Studies Curriculum: Curriculum as Institutionalized Knowledge*. Ph.D. dissertation, University of Wisconsin–Madison.

Mandle, Jay R., and Louis Ferleger. 1985. "Achieving Full Employment." *Socialist Review* 84, 6:77–90.

Marglin, Stephen. 1976. "What Do Bosses Do?" In *The Division of Labour*, edited by Andre Gorz. New York: Humanities Press.

Navarro, Vincente. 1976. *Medicine under Capitalism*. New York: Neale Watson Academic Publications.

Noble, David. 1977. *America by Design: Science, Technology, and the Rise of Corporate Capitalism*. New York: Alfred A. Knopf.

O'Connor, James. 1973. *The Fiscal Crisis of the State*. New York: St. Martin's Press.

Olneck, Michael, and James Crouse. 1978. *Myths of the Meritocracy: Cognitive Skill and Adult Success in the United States*. Madison: University of Wisconsin Institute for Research on Poverty, Paper 485–78.

Persell, Caroline H. 1977. *Education and Inequality*. New York: The Free Press.

Philips, Susan U. 1972. "Participant Structures and Communicative Competence: Warm Springs Children in Community and Classroom." In *Functions of Language in the Classroom*, edited by Courtney B. Cazden, Vera P. John, and Dell Hymes. New York: Teachers College Press.

Raskin, Marcus. 1986. *The Common Good*. Boston: Routledge and Kegan Paul.

Reese, William. 1986. *Politics and the Promise of School Reform*. Boston: Routledge and Kegan Paul.

Reynolds, Diane A. Troubetta, and Norman T. Reynolds. 1974. "The Roots of Prejudice: California Indian History in School Textbooks." In *Education and Cultural Process: Toward an Anthropology of Education*, edited by George D. Spindler. New York: Holt, Rinehart, and Winston.

Rist, Ray C. 1970. "Student Social Class and Teacher Expectation: The Self-Fulfilling Prophecy in Ghetto Education." *Harvard Educational Review* 40:411–51.

Rosenbaum, James. 1976. *Making Inequality: The Hidden Curriculum of High School Tracking*. New York: John Wiley.

Sadker, Myra Pollack, and David Miller Sadker. 1982. *Sex Equity Handbook for Schools*. New York: Longman.

Schniedewind, Nancy, and Ellen Davidson. 1983. *Open Minds to Equality: A Sourcebook of Learning Activities to Promote Race, Sex, Class, and Age Equity*. Englewood Cliffs, N.J.: Prentice-Hall.

Shor, Ira. 1980. *Critical Teaching and Everyday Life*. Boston: South End Press.

———. 1986. *Culture Wars*. Boston: Routledge and Kegan Paul.

Silberman, Charles. 1970. *Crisis in the Classroom*. New York: Random House.

Stedman, Lawrence C., and Marshal S. Smith. 1983. "Recent Reform Proposals for American Education." *Contemporary Education Review* 2:85–104.

Stewig, John, and M. L. Knipfel. 1975. "Sexism in Picture Books: What Progress?" *The Elementary School Journal* 76:151–55.

Taxel, Joel. 1978–79. "Justice and Cultural Conflict: Racism, Sexism and Instructional Materials." *Interchange* 9:56–84.

———. 1981. "The Outsiders of the American Revolution: The Selective Tradition in Children's Fiction." *Interchange* 12:206–28.

Teitelbaum, Kenneth. 1985. *Schooling for 'Good Rebels': Socialist Education for Children in the United States, 1900–1020*. Ph.D. dissertation, University of Wisconsin–Madison.

Teitelbaum, Kenneth, and William J. Reese. 1983. "American Socialist Pedagogy and Experimentation in the Progressive Era: The Socialist Sunday School." *History of Education Quarterly* 23:429–55.

Trueba, Henry T., Grace Pung Guthrie, and Kathryn Hu-Pei Au, eds. 1981. *Culture and the Bilingual Classroom: Studies in Classroom Ethnography*. Rowley, Mass.: Newbury House.

Valli, Linda. 1986. *Becoming Clerical Workers*. Boston: Routledge and Kegan Paul.

Williams, Raymond. 1977. *Marxism and Literature*. Oxford, Eng.: Oxford University Press.

Willis, Paul. 1977. *Learning to Labour: How Working Class Kids Get Working Class Jobs*. Westmead, Eng.: Saxon House.
Wolf-Wasserman, Miriam, and Linda Hutchinson, eds. 1978. *Teaching Human Dignity: Social Change Lessons for Everyteacher*. Minneapolis: Education Exploration Center.
Wright, Erik Olin. 1978. *Class, Crisis and the State*. London: New Left Books.
Wrigley, Julia. 1982. *Class Politics and Public Schools*. New Brunswick, N.J.: Rutgers University Press.

6

Ideology at Work

Alan Draper and Richard Guarasci

INTRODUCTION

Our image of how society is organized and the way it should be organized comes from many different sources. Schools, the media, and our families all help forge the ideologies we hold. The workplace, however, is not often included on this list. Allegedly, the workplace is where commodities, not consciousness, is produced. Orthodox Marxists have done much to reinforce this idea that the workplace is irrelevant to ideological formation when they distinguish between the base and the superstructure. Material production is reserved for the base and ideological production for the superstructure. The base and superstructure are treated as if they were separate and functionally distinct arenas that people engage in (Bottomore 1983, p. 43). But this is too schematic. More subtle and, we believe, more accurate readings of Marx have rejected the sharp distinction between base and superstructure (Williams 1977) for various reasons.

First, it is clear that both ideological as well as material production takes place at work. Lenin argues that trade union consciousness among workers is the natural result of capitalist work relations. That is, Lenin felt that the capitalist workplace creates a spontaneous recognition of irreconcilable differences between managers and workers over workplace issues, such as wages and working conditions, but not necessarily over political or cultural issues. Trade union consciousness emerges directly from the workplace because it is here that surplus value is extracted from workers, and the antagonism between labor and capital is experienced in its starkest form (Lenin 1963).

On the other hand, Burawoy argues that consciousness is created at work—not a consciousness of workplace resistance as Lenin argues, but one of accommodation. Burawoy claims that "whatever consent is necessary for the obscuring and securing of surplus value is generated at the point of production rather than imported into the workplace from outside" (Burawoy 1982, p. 135). According to Burawoy, workers view their work as a game in order to invest interest into the trivial tasks they must perform. At the same time that game playing makes tolerable the dreary labor workers must perform, it does nothing to alter the alienating conditions that make game playing necessary. Burawoy thus concludes that "as long as workers are engaged in a game involving the relations of production, their subordination to the process of production becomes an object of acquiescence" (Burawoy 1982, p. 82).

Although Burawoy and Lenin disagree on whether the workplace yields accommodation or resistance to capitalist hegemony, neither theorist accepts the rigid distinction between base and superstructure. Both Burawoy and Lenin view the workplace as a site of ideological construction.

A second problem with the stark distinction between base and superstructure is the dependent position accorded the superstructure as a mere "effect" of the base. Rather, we see the base and superstructure as relatively autonomous. That is, you cannot read a particular set of ideologies that labor and capital might have from a particular base. Alas, things are not so neat. Social relations at work constrain but do not determine the types of ideologies that might emerge. To return to the differences between Burawoy and Lenin: whether the ideological consequences of capitalist relations at work are accommodative or conflictual cannot be determined from the social relations of production alone. Indeed, Armstrong, Goodman, and Hyman argue that ideology affects what happens at work as much as it is affected by it. They argue that relations between managers and workers are defined by the ideas each group brings to work with them. For instance, labor representatives will only contest workplace issues that the dominant ideology has deemed appropriate to raise with management. The dominant ideology defines what workplace issues are legitimate to contest, not only because labor representatives subscribe to these approved limits, but their members— also subject to the dominant ideology—do, as well (Armstrong, Goodman, and Hyman 1981, pp. 45–50). The rigid separation between base and superstructure cannot be sustained.

This chapter will review how managers have sought to create hegemony at work, that is, to create a consciousness in which managerial norms of productivity and efficiency are internalized by workers. This has not been easy for managers to accomplish, nor have they succeeded fully. Workers have their own estimate of what constitutes a "fair day's work," which differs from that of management. For managers, this discrepancy is not a trivial matter. Inasmuch as the profits of the firm, or their firm's competitive position, depend on increasing output, managers have an interest in replacing a worker's estimate of what constitutes a fair day's work with their own. Moreover, workers may view attempts to increase productivity quite differently from managers. Increased productivity may mean increased profits to managers but speedup or impending unemployment to workers.

This chapter reviews the various strategies managers have used to create hegemony at work and the resistance by workers to managerial norms of productivity and efficiency. We first analyze how managers altered the labor process to destroy the apprentice system in the early 1800s in order to take advantage of new business opportunities. As a result, workers came to appreciate the power of capital in new ways. They organized trade unions to defend themselves and reinterpreted their ideology of republicanism to account for the class conflict now emerging in their trades.

The destruction of the apprentice system and the creation of an American proletariat proceeded unevenly across the trades. In some trades, skilled workers still controlled the process of production, and they used their shopfloor power to make their labor tolerable and to restrict output. Managers, after trying many different strategies to break the shopfloor power of skilled workers, sought to establish their own hegemony on the shopfloor through two approaches. One strategy, named after its most famous exponent, Frederick Winslow Taylor, was Taylorism. This strategy sought to destroy the shopfloor power of skilled workers by altering the production process itself. Conception and execution of tasks were to be separated. The former was to be reserved for management, and the latter for employees. Only in this way, argued Taylor, could managers ensure that their goals were respected on the shopfloor. The second strategy emerged from the human relations school identified with the work of Elton Mayo. This strategy sought to manipulate the informal culture created by workers on the shopfloor to serve managerial goals. Whereas Taylorism sought to destroy the informal culture of workers that supported such norms as output restriction, the human relations school sought to work through that culture and mold it to serve managerial ends.

Finally, this chapter reviews recent management-inspired work reforms and their impact on the politics and ideology of the contemporary U.S. workplace. The democratic impact of quality circles and the quality of worklife programs appear problematic at best. Management's intent is clearly oriented to profit and competitiveness while attempting to compel the allegiance of employees by offering them symbolic participation. The result of attempts to win the hearts and minds of modern workers will turn, finally, on the political contest for control over authority and resources both within and outside the workplace.

REPUBLICANISM

Capitalist ideology—a belief in markets, individualism, and competition—was more firmly established in the United States by 1810 than was capitalism. Production for profit that utilized wage labor was the exception rather than the rule. Most citizens were independent farmers. In the South these farmers used slaves to cultivate their fields. In the North farmers used the labor provided by their families, rather than hire employees, to satisfy their needs and produce a surplus for the market. Nor could the economic elite of the period, the Southern gentry who used slaves on their plantations or Northern commercial traders, be labeled capitalists accurately. Neither utilized wage labor in the production of commodities. Even manufacturing, which engaged only 3 percent of the population in 1810, was not organized on capitalist lines. Rather, the apprentice system prevailed.

Under the apprentice system, masters hired journeymen and apprentices to work for them and, in exchange, taught their helpers all of the techniques involved in the production of a particular product. Control over the process of production was in the hands of skilled master craftsmen who initiated journeymen and apprentices into the mysteries of their trade. Production required only hand tools and was performed in small groups in small workshops near the master's house where the apprentice sometimes lived. As a member of the master's household, the bonds between the master and his helpers were as much personal as contractual. This mitigated some of the sense of exploitation that journeymen and apprentices felt at the hands of masters, who kept for themselves the profits derived from the sale of finished products. The social distance between journeymen and master craftsmen was also lessened by the fact that the masters worked alongside their helpers and conditions at work were shared. Finally, at the end of an apprenticeship a journeyman could expect to become a master craftsman, self-employed and independent. Thus, despite the differences in status and income between journeymen, apprentices, and their masters, all saw themselves as part of a trade and a member of a distinct artisan class that was separate from the unskilled poor below them and the commercial traders above them. Loyal to their particular trade, the class interests of this artisan class were expressed in the ideology of republicanism.

Republicanism envisioned society as divided between producers and accumulators, not employers and employees. Producers included such groups as masters, journeymen, and farmers, who personally performed labor that created wealth; while parasitical accumulators, like bankers and merchants, lived off the wealth created by others. Ideologically, republicanism preached the gospel of self-improvement, but it never supported an untrammeled individualism in which the needs of the individual took precedence over those of the community. Rather, individuals were to "repress their personal desires for the greater good of the whole" (Kasson 1976, p. 4). An artisan should seek personal success, but not at the expense of the customs and traditions of his trade. Republicanism also upheld such ideals as the dignity of labor in which pride in work and craftsmanship were respected, as well as frugality and independence. Finally, republicanism favored a division of wealth according to one's contribution to the wealth of society. Thus, republicanism rejected the ideal of social equality, but it also rejected artificial inequality in which "some attained high position through special favors...or... others were reduced to poverty and subservience by those possessed of such favors" (Siracusa 1979, p. 126).

Artisans traced these republican ideals back to the revolutionary heritage of 1776, which rejected the idle decadence and corrupt privilege of aristocratic Europe. Artisans identified themselves completely with republican ideals because republicanism "exalted the productive classes" (Foner 1976, p. 102), especially their "honest labor." Artisans were attracted to republicanism not only because "their very social situation, their lives as cooperative yet independent craftsmen, made them preternatural republican citizens" (Wilentz 1983, p. 50), but republicanism condemned bankers and merchants who manipulated artisans through their control over the credit artisans needed. Republicanism's rejection of artificial inequality reflected the artisans' disdain of accumulators as well as their vulnerability to them.

The identification of artisans with republicanism was never more clear than at Independence Day celebrations when masters and journeymen marched together to stress the harmony of their trade and their fealty to republican ideals (Wilentz 1983, pp. 46–51). But with the decline of the apprentice system and the introduction of new work relations in the shops in the 1820s, masters and journeymen marched separately and July 4th celebrations became "declarations of class consciousness" (Wilentz 1983, p. 53). Changes in social relations at work shattered the community of interest in republicanism that prevailed within the trades.

The industrial revolution, which introduced changes in social relationships at work, was "aggressive, revolutionary, and destructive" (Ware 1959, p. 98). Employers changed the organization of work in their shops in order to take advantage of the business opportunities created by easier credit terms, a cheap supply of unskilled immigrant labor, and larger markets. The result was the destruction of the apprentice system, the development of a permanent American proletariat, and the demise of the ideology of republicanism.

The industrial revolution profoundly affected the organization of work and disrupted workplace social relations. Once, workers needed to know all of the techniques involved in the production of a product. Now, as a result of the industrial revolution, task differentiation split the production process into discrete tasks. Each worker needed to know only part of the production process and needed little training to master it (Hirsh 1978, p. 22). Some tasks, such as cutting in shoemaking, still required skilled labor, but others could be farmed out to "green" workers (Dawley 1976, p. 94).

Once, artisans owned their own tools and could set the pace of their work and decide how the work was to be performed. Now, simple machines owned by the manufacturer intensified the pace of work, and the production process was laid out before the artisan entered the shop.

Once, shops were small, and the employer worked alongside the help. Now, production took place in factories and the manufacturer no longer performed "honest" labor. The personal bond and shared life-style that had connected the journeyman and master was lost. The social distance between the two groups increased and their only ties were through "the cash nexus."

Once, journeymen could look forward to self-employment, to their independence, once they had mastered a "competence." Now, due to the new technology and an increase in the scale of industry, self-employment was beyond the reach of laborers. Opening one's own shop required control of wealth rather than control of skill. In 1840, 17.3 percent of the heads of households in the eight crafts studied by Hirsh were self employed. By 1860, only 8.7 percent of the artisans were independent (Hirsh 1978, p. 78). The narrowing of conventional paths of mobility from journeyman to independent master "created an expanding class of journeymen destined either to spend their lives in the employ of masters in degraded work conditions or as industrial workers toiling in the mills of the burgeoning cities" (Laurie 1980, p. 164).

These changes proceeded unevenly, some trades experiencing them earlier and more profoundly than others. But their collective result was to create an American proletariat, a class of permanent wage workers. A report of the Massachusetts House of Representatives took note of the effect that these changes in the organization of work and the social relations of the shop had on this new proletariat:

Instead of that manly and sturdy independence which once distinguished the mechanic and the workingman, we have cringing servility and supineness. Instead of self-respect and intelligence, we have want of confidence and growing ignorance. Instead of honest pride in the dignity of labor, we have the consciousness of inferiority. Instead of a desire to enter the mechanic arts, we have loathing and disgust of their drudgery and degradation. Instead of labor being the patent of nobility, it is the badge of servitude (quoted in Siracusa 1979, p. 205).

Journeymen experienced the changes that occurred in the shops as a catastrophe. They had lost, in their own minds, status and independence, "and no comfort gains could cancel this debt" (Ware 1959, p. X). In response, some journeymen abandoned republicanism in favor of religious revivalism (Laurie 1980, p. 122). Others, however, now interpreted their republican beliefs through the changes at work that had taken place (Wilentz 1983). Once part of the army of republicanism, manufacturers were now the target of a republican critique by this new proletariat. In the eyes of journeymen whose conditions at work had deteriorated and whose hopes of independence had evaporated, manufacturers were a new aristocracy. They prospered off the labor of others while personally creating no wealth themselves. Moreover, they failed to demonstrate "public virtue" when they selfishly pursued their own interests at the expense of the community's welfare.

This new "class" reading of republicanism, which identified a conflict of interest between manufacturers and artisans, was expressed in the formation of trade unions that excluded the self-employed. Unions among shoemakers, stonecutters, and saddle and harness workers were formed. The trades where the reorganization of production along these new, capitalist lines had proceeded fastest and deepest were the trades where unions were most likely to arise (Hirsh 1978, p. 84).

The ideology of republicanism gave ground slowly to the reality of class division and class conflict. An example of the tension between this new class awareness formed at work and the class harmony between and within trades expressed by republicanism occurred in the midst of the largest strike prior to the Civil War. During this violent strike, which idled 20,000 New England shoemakers, workers were so unsure of the rupture that had occurred that they "solicited contributions from the bosses to the strike fund" (Dawley 1976, p. 84). But it was clear that an ideology such as republicanism, which perceived a community of interest between employer and employee, could not be sustained under the new workplace conditions. The employers knew it: only one manufacturer delivered on his pledge to assist the strikers. Such experiences drove home to workers the antiquarianism of republicanism. Ideological change to a militant craft unionism whose goals were narrowly confined to shopfloor issues of wages and job control took place slower than the rate of change on the shopfloor would warrant, but it did take place.

As much as changes in the labor process and in the social relations of production provoked ideological change, they did not determine the ultimate form the new ideology would take. The process of proletarian- ization did not determine the content of the ideology that finally emerged; at most, a trajectory toward increasing awareness of class di- vision was set. As we argued in our introduction, there is no particular ideology that accords with a particular "base"; rather, ideology is relatively autonomous from the relations of production. For instance, the process of proletarianization was similar in Britain, France, and the United States, but the ideological response of U.S. workers to this experience was less radical than in the European cases. A socialist movement never devel- oped among U.S. workers to the extent it did in Britain or France.

Two points explain why proletarianization did not elicit an alternative, oppositional ideology among U.S. workers, but rather a militant—not radical—trade unionism. First, workers may have shared a common ex- perience at work, but (with the establishment of Irish, German, and nativist communities) not outside it. Politics and social life were organized around ethnic and religious identities, as opposed to class. As a result, workplace grievances did not penetrate the political arena and political issues were not reflected in workplace conflicts. Social and political life were organized on a different axis than the workplace. For this reason, ethnic politics and a narrow, militant trade unionism confined to issues of wages and job control went hand in hand (Hirsh 1978, p. 109).

Second, the ideological response to proletarianization never got be- yond a militant trade unionism to a consciousness of "parallel conflicts" (Dawley 1976, p. 70) in the economic, political, and cultural arenas be- cause workers tended to identify with the State. The republican revo- lution to free the State from aristocratic privilege had already been won. The forces of democracy had triumphed in 1776. This, too, kept the grievances generated by proletarianization confined to workplace issues rather than broadening them into a critique of politics or society as a whole. The State did not have to be emancipated from aristocratic priv- ilege, only the workplace did.

MONOPOLY CAPITALISM

Proletarianization proceeded apace from 1820 to 1870. By 1870, "two out of three productively engaged Americans" (Montgomery 1967, p. 30) satisfied their daily needs by selling their labor to an employer. Fierce competition forced employers to further reduce wages and de- grade working conditions in order to cut their costs. Skilled workers countered these measures through their trade unions, which sought to maintain the dignity of the trade by supporting work rules that restricted output (Montgomery 1979, p. 16) and by regulating the supply of labor in the craft (Yellowitz 1976). But what fortified skilled workers most against attacks on their living standards and working conditions was their monopoly of knowledge of the processes of production. They knew how to make finished steel or glass products from primary materials, and management did not. This permitted them to exercise control over their work. Frederick Winslow Taylor, who mounted an assault against skilled workers' control of production, acknowledged, "[The] foremen and superintendents know, better than anyone else, that their own knowledge and personal skills fall far short of the combined knowledge and dexterity of all the workmen under them" (quoted in Montgomery 1979, p. 9).

But the structure of business was changing. Only the fittest survived the cutthroat competition among capitalists. The market was now divided among fewer but larger companies. The large trust had replaced the small shop. The factory would not look the same again. The establishment of big business brought new developments in industrial architecture (Nelson 1975, p. 33). But the changes that took place inside factory walls were even more profound.

Prior to 1880, most factories were "congeries of craftsmen's shops rather than an integrated plant" (Nelson 1975, p. 4). Despite the advantages that accrued to managers as a result of the industrial revolution, the manner in which work was to be performed was still in the hands of skilled workers who knew far better than managers how to do it. Management's absence from the shopfloor was reflected in the degree to which the flow of work was left in the hands of inside contractors to organize. Inside contractors were skilled workers employed by the company who agreed to deliver a product to the company at a negotiated price. As employees of the company, inside contractors worked inside the company's building and sold their output to the company, which supplied them with material, equipment, and power. But technical and social control of the workplace was in their hands. Inside contractors hired and fired their own workers, were responsible for motivation and discipline, set wages, organized the flow of work and introduced technical changes (Clawson 1980, pp. 28–30).

In factories where inside contractors did not organize the labor process, work was organized according to the "drive system." The drive system combined "authoritarian rule and physical compulsion" by foremen over the workers (Nelson 1975, p. 4). Foremen had authority in their departments over the flow of work and personnel issues, much as inside contractors did in the factories where they worked. The workplace was the foremen's empire and they used their prerogatives to "drive" the workers and extract as much effort from them as possible.

Both systems of management, however, could not escape their dependence on skilled workers to use their discretion and judgment in performing the work. Clawson writes, "Many of the decisions about the details of the labor process" still required skilled workers who were "usually on their own...in deciding how to do the work, and their initiative and cooperation were necessary to get the goods produced" (Clawson 1980, p. 28). And skilled workers continued to use the control they exercised at work to make their labor less oppressive by restricting output. If employers were going to increase their profit through greater production, they would have to break the power skilled workers exercised on the shopfloor.

Several strategies were used by employers to increase output. First, employers introduced piecework. They hoped that payment by results would stimulate greater effort from workers. But as workers responded to this incentive, employers cut the piece-rates so that workers ended up earning what they had before but working harder to do so. Such experiences with piecework bred suspicion among workers, who continued to restrict output. Taylor, who had worked as a skilled machinist, admitted that piecework was flawed as a strategy to prevent output restriction: "After a workman has had the price per piece of the work he is doing lowered two or three times as a result of his having worked harder and increased his output, he is likely entirely to lose sight of the employer's side of the case and become imbued with a grim determination to have no more cuts if soldiering can prevent it" (quoted in Clawson 1980, p. 215).

Another strategy to prevent output restriction was to gain the confidence of skilled workers and instill in them a sense of loyalty and identity with the firm. Employers offered recreational opportunities and housing to skilled workers, and public amenities for their use. But skilled workers had their own vibrant cultures and rejected what employers handed down (Gutman 1976). Other plans to win the hearts and minds of skilled workers, such as profit sharing and industrial democracy schemes met similar fates. Profit sharing could not "alchemize wage working into something close to proprietorship" (Rodgers 1978, p. 50), and industrial democracy experiments made workers feel more like colonized natives than industrial citizens.

Finally, management tried to create within the factory a political consensus based on the authoritarian foundations of managerial authority, through the establishment of company unions. General Electric's Lynn Plan established limited and pseudo-participation for workers, through joint committees restricted to the interpretation of management-determined work rates, pay scales, and work routines. The plan was conspicuously devoid of any bargaining mechanisms. After continued labor unrest, the system faded from corporate organization.

Only when employers turned their attention to the production process itself did they encounter more success in their struggle against skilled workers. One strategy, articulated by Frederick Taylor, sought to overcome the work culture of skilled workers, which supported norms of output restriction by altering the labor process. Management would create hegemony on the shopfloor by destroying the work culture of skilled workers. Another strategy utilized by management took the opposite tack to achieve the same ends. Rather than attack the work culture of employees, the human relations school argued that managers should try to work through the work culture created by employees to achieve management's aims. Both strategies sought to establish the hegemony of management at work. But each strategy gave rise to contradictions or inherent limits that mitigated its effectiveness. Taylorism created conditions that gave rise to industrial unions, which utilized collective bargaining to define and contest the boundaries of managerial authority. The human relations school, represented by the work of Elton Mayo and his colleagues, was limited in the extent to which it could humanize work without undermining its goal of supporting managerial authority. Neither strategy could create a consensus around the managerial norms of productivity and efficiency that they sought to strengthen.

TAYLORISM

Frederick Winslow Taylor felt that output restriction would persist so long as workers made decisions about how the work was to be performed. To prevent this, Taylor argued that management needed to monopolize the conceptual aspects of work so that workers did no creative thinking, exercised no judgment or discretion at work, and simply executed the instructions given them by management. But Taylorism had more influence on management's thinking about the shopfloor than on what actually occurred there. Few employers implemented the changes that Taylor's "systematic management" called for. To implement the changes in the physical layout of plants that Taylorism demanded was expensive. In addition, workers, as well as foremen and plant superintendents whose arbitrary rule of the shopfloor was threatened by systematic management (Nelson 1975, pp. 75–76), fought Taylorism whenever it was introduced. Employers liked the idea of systematic management but found the obstacles in its way daunting. Taylorist ends would have to be pursued through other, more oblique, means.

Taylorism, the separation of conception from execution, would occur through technological innovation. Employers instructed engineers to design machines in such a way as to build the operations that skilled workers would have performed right into the machines (Noble 1977). In 1912, a report by the American Society of Mechanical Engineers noted how machines were designed to de-skill labor. "The transference of skill by the machine designer from the operators to the machine has embodied in the latter much of the accumulated experience of many mechanics working in simpler and more primitive tools" (quoted in Meyer 1981, p. 23). In industry after industry—shoemaking, stonecutting, and printing—machinery was introduced that reduced the employer's reliance on skilled labor (Yellowitz 1976, pp. 75–94). In the iron and glass industries, technological breakthroughs "eliminated intricate hand procedures . . . and reduced dependence on skilled workers" (Nelson 1980, p. ii). The skilled trades retreated before the formidable alliance of employers and science.

As machine work became more varied, human work become more routine (Meyer 1981, p. 27). Once skill had been transferred to machines, cheaper unskilled workers could be hired to run them. Workers found themselves in a situation similar to that the first astronauts encountered. According to Tom Wolfe in *The Right Stuff* (1979), the first astronauts were not selected on the basis of their ability to pilot or fly because their spacecraft would be controlled from earth, but on their physical ability to endure space flight. Similarly, machine operators did not have to know how a job was to be performed, because that knowledge was built into the operation of the machines they tended, but had to be able to suffer the tedium and monotony of their jobs. As de-skilling proceeded, the work force became more homogenous, no longer so separated by income level, skill level, or work experience as it had been in the past (Gordon, Edwards, and Reich 1982). In 1920, a political economist who worked in Detroit's auto plants remarked, "The consequence of the rigid application of standardization in production has been the standardization of labor. Along with the interchangeability of parts goes the interchangeability of producers" (quoted in Meyer 1981, p. 42). These changes on the shopfloor, the destruction of the skilled trades and the creation of a homogenous work force, led to a new challenge to managerial authority, reflected in the formation of industrial unions during the 1930s.

The industrial unions that formed the Committee of Industrial Organizations in 1935 organized all workers in a plant, regardless of their particular trade. Homogenized labor made industrial unionism possible, and created a powerful vehicle to contest managerial authority. Control over the workplace was now subject to negotiation between management and unions through collective bargaining. While some analysts have lamented the displacement of shopfloor conflict to the bargaining table and the formalism implicit in collective bargaining, this is, perhaps, too simple. As bureaucratic and legalistic as collective bargaining is, it constitutes a check on managerial authority and broadens worker loyalty beyond the immediate work group. Mechanized Taylorism created the conditions for the growth of industrial unions, which continued to contest managerial hegemony through collective bargaining.

HUMAN RELATIONS SCHOOL OF MANAGEMENT

Vocational psychology appeared in the 1920s. It was one of the first recognizable indications that some business leaders, instead of reshaping attitudes toward management by destroying worker norms and culture as prescribed by Taylorism, believed that worker restriction of output—and control over productivity—could be achieved through less coercive techniques.

This new psychological approach argued that workers were motivated by factors other than income. Workers' attitudes, feelings, emotional outlook, and inter- and intra-group dynamics were seen as quite important. As it was expressed in one management journal, "People are tractable, docile, gullible, uncritical—and wanting to be led. But far more than this is deeply true of them. They want to feel united, tied, bound to something, some cause, bigger than they, commanding them yet worthy of them, summoning them to significance in living" (Bendix 1974).

However superficial such platitudes may appear during a period of militant business resistance to labor unions and workers' organizations, this statement reflected a change in strategy by some industrial leaders. For them it was a partial movement away from rule by coercion and toward rule by consensus. Quite distinct from systematic management's attempt to break the existing work culture by eliminating output restriction, the new approach acknowledged workplace norms and factory culture by acknowledging, at least, that workers had feelings, goals, and expectations. Henceforth, managerial ideology would include this new approach, no longer based on the elimination of the informal groups of workers' culture; rather, these groupings became the centerpiece of attempts to increase efficiency and combat unions, by manipulating the feelings of workers (Bendix 1974).

In the mid–1920s, under the auspices of management theorists and industrial psychologists on the Harvard Business School faculty, another new managerial ideology emerged. In 1927, joining a corporate experiment begun three years earlier, Elton Mayo, North Whitehead, and F. F. Roethlisberger from Harvard, and other social scientists conducted a series of industrial relation experiments at the Hawthorne (Chicago) plant of the Western Electric Company. Since 1924, the company, in combination with the National Research Council, had been studying the effect of illumination on worker productivity. These researches found that productivity increased regardless of lighting levels. Control groups as well as test groups increased their productivity. With the addition of the Harvard theorists, the experiments were broadened into a series of tests among a chosen group of the employee population—tests ranging from the manipulation of break periods and their contents, to the length of the work day and work week, and other features of general work conditions. These research activities became known as the Hawthorne Experiments.

The Harvard team in conjunction with Western Electric executives designed a series of experiments in the Relay Assembly Room and the

Bank Wiring Room of the Hawthorne facility. The direction of the experiments was carefully scrambled, including the original conditions and alternations. The workers were consulted and interviewed regarding each change or experiment. Quite interestingly, the results of these tests were not significantly distinct from the lighting experiments. Productivity increased with each innovation regardless of the direction of the test! As Mayo later reported it, "These periods, 12 and 13, made it evident that increments of production could not be related point for point to the experimental changes introduced. Some major change was taking place that was chiefly responsible for the index of improved conditions—the steadily increasing output" (Mayo 1945, p. 71). Many social scientists contend that the critical variable producing a steady increase in production was the lack of experimental objectivity due to the continuous consultation with the subjects. To many critics, the "Hawthorne effect" resulted from prejudicing the workers toward cooperation by advising them of the changes introduced at each stage of the project and, unfortunately, artificially enlisting their interest in corporate production.

But was this really the essential lesson of the experiment? Mayo concluded on the basis of his research that the Hawthorne experiments yielded a critical feature of worker motivation. "What actually happened was that six individuals became a team and the team gave itself wholeheartedly and spontaneously to cooperation in the experiment. The consequence was that they felt themselves to be participating freely and without afterthought, and were happy in the knowledge that they were working without coercion from above or limitation from below" (Mayo 1945, p. 72). Like Taylor, Mayo discovered that, in the work world, workers established their own culture within the capitalist factory; but unlike Taylor, Mayo concluded that productivity, profit, and industrial stability depended on recognizing workers' habits and culture while directing them toward capitalist goals. The human relations approach establishes the existence and necessity of workers' culture, as expressed in peer groups and teams, for the maintenance and growth of successful industrial enterprise. Mayo stated this position clearly. "Management, in any continuously successful plant, is not related to single workers but always to working groups. In every department that continues to operate, the workers have—whether aware of it or not—formed themselves into a group with appropriate customs, duties, routines, even rituals; and management succeeds (or fails) in proportion as it is accepted without reservation by the group as authority and leader" (Mayo 1945). Mayo understood that managerial success rests with the legitimization of managerial authority within the workers' own culture.

Mayo's emphasis on the informal work group rested on a sophisticated theoretical and philosophical analysis, which drew upon the social and psychological analyses of Freud, Durkheim, Piaget, and Pareto. Using their theories, Mayo argued that obsessive, neurotic social maladjustment is not only characteristic of individuals devoid of secure infantile experiences but typical of any social reality that is "anomie." "That is to say, when a code or tradition, that has been sufficiently adequate to its material problems and to its social controls is faced with a situation that it cannot meet, the individuals of the group will turn from nonlogical to irrational action. They will lose their capacity for disciplined cooperation" (Mayo 1933, p. 158). Mayo's analysis of modern industrial society was founded on this description of a distressed world of social relations, characterized by atomized individuals, naturally susceptible to neurotic and undirected behavior patterns when unmediated by group demands, identities, and norms. Such groupings were seriously imperiled by the continuously changing patterns of industrial life in and around the modern workplace and, consequently, social disorganization and unnatural behavior would increase significantly. In the workplace this process was evident by "the failure of workers and supervisors to understand their work and working conditions" and, with this, "the belief of the individual in his social function and solidarity with the group—his capacity for collaboration in work—these are disappearing, destroyed in part by rapid scientific and technical advance" (Mayo 1933, p. 158).

Mayo proposed that it was incumbent upon management to recognize and recreate, if possible, the important social codes of group behavior in order to establish what Mayo would term confidence, morale, and loyalty on the part of the worker. To Mayo the legitimization of group identities counteracted the irrational tendencies of both workers and managers inherent in the modern workplace. The manager required the participation of workers with each other, as well as with managers, for the subordination of modern society's neurotic and anomic characteristics. However Mayo was not calling for the *democratic* participation of workers in the design and management of these workplaces to counteract the despair and captiveness of modern industrial life. Simply put, Mayo advised acknowledgment of the worker and the establishment of teams and groups as prerequisites for increased morale, organizational cooperation, and increased productivity.

From this philosophic perspective Mayo interpreted the Hawthorne experiments. The worker brings now-displaced inner conflicts to the workplace, which are inherent in the general "anomie" of industrial society, and these anxieties are increased by the demands of shopfloor mobility, isolation, and atomization in deference to technological necessity and increased productivity. The response of workers will be "irrational or ill-founded" in the normal course of workplace events. To Mayo the Hawthorne experiment illuminated these behavioral tendencies and presented the direction for their resolution. What was required for economic growth and industrial peace was the recognition of group formations, the emergence of group norms, and a properly trained managerial elite who would harness the satisfaction of workers' emotional needs to managerial goals.

But how was Mayo's recognition of teams and group culture to be reconciled with Taylor's recognition that workers' culture supported output restriction? At Hawthorne the interview turned up the following evidence, "Now the interviewers had discovered that this working group claimed a habit of doing most of their work in the morning period and 'taking things easy' during the afternoon...and the attention of the research group was redirected to a fact already known to them, namely, that the working group as a whole actually determined the output of individual workers by reference to a standard, predetermined but never clearly stated, that represented the group conception of a fair day's work. This standard was rarely, if ever, in accord with the standards of the efficiency engineers" (Mayo 1933, p. 125).

Mayo concluded that output restriction was a function of employee fear of managerial intentions concerning wage rates, productivity levels, and job security. The recognition of work teams and "skilled" management communication with them will lead to worker loyalty to the team and team loyalty to management. As previously quoted, "the girls became a self-governing team [at Hawthorne], and a team that cooperated wholeheartedly with management." Mayo realized that workers suffering from "anomie" will not bind themselves directly to management. They are "injured" individuals in need of smaller scale identities and loyalties. The groups and teams provide that necessary social psychological linchpin for corporate success. "This is the beginning of the necessary double loyalty—to his own group and to the larger organization" (Mayo 1945, p. 84).

Mayo understood "teams" as therapeutic resolutions of the broad-based social ills of an industrial civilization. Rather than confront the structure of authority in the workplace, Mayo sought mechanisms for "emotional release." His work omitted any discussion of unionization or other institutions of worker representation. He accepted the political authority granted to management and he sought the development of a "spontaneous consent" of workers generated by group loyalties. Apparently union sympathies were excluded as a "therapeutic" form of worker identity with team goals.

THE SIGNIFICANCE OF MAYO AND THE HAWTHORNE EXPERIMENTS

The major analytic contribution of the Hawthorne experiments was the recognition of the importance of the "informal group" to the work process. Quite opposite the methods of Taylor, Mayo and the Hawthorne experimenters elevated the informal groups of workers, countering their image as obstacles to productivity with a view of these groups as the means for increased output with peaceful labor relations within the modern factory. Workers needed informal groups as psychological outlets and sociological foundations in their realization of their role in the technologically advanced but highly atomized modern factory system. Rather than "break them," Mayo and the Hawthorne experiments made work groups the focus of successful modern management technique.

Modern-day applications of human relations ideology and practice are divided into several schools of thought but united in their exclusion of calls for substantive democratic participation by workers. Indeed some of them embrace some form of worker participation, but these schemes are quite distinct from genuine democratic participation in the conception and execution of work. Either as individual "job enrichment" approaches or as collective "work teams" programs, contemporary humanistic management schemes are based fundamentally on pseudo-participatory reforms, where the essential distribution of authority remains with management but where the forms of control "appear" more flexible. Their philosophic origins dating to the Hawthorne experiments and Mayo, contemporary human relations programs seek personal adjustments in worker personality behavior and alterations in managerial form rather than a democratic restructuring of the workplace. This bias of the human relations school of management theory was present in the initial experiments at the Hawthorne plant and it is the continuing focus of contemporary management schemes for "worker participation" and "job enrichment." In the name of "humanizing" the workplace, human relations theorists have omitted the most "human" of all aspects of workplace reality, the nature and scope of power and authority within the work world.

PARTICIPATORY CORPORATISM AND WORK REFORM

The orthodoxy of Frederick Taylor's "systematic management" no longer compels the managerial imagination, although it remains the foundation for the industrial division of labor, albeit, in "new clothes." Distinct from mechanized Taylorism, the new ideology may be termed, somewhat enigmatically, "participatory corporatism." This new initiative aims at defining managerial roles and binding workers to a reinvigorated structure of authority on the shopfloor by creating a rhetoric of "participatory management" amidst a limited broadening of the division of labor. This new "participatory corporatism" aims less at controlling an unsatisfied and insurgent working class and more at addressing market-directed imperatives that require more specialized and higher quality production in the face of fierce international competition. Participatory corporatism seeks to legitimize managerial prerogatives and market exigencies by wedding workers' values and cultures more closely to the competitive realities of the market. This strategy requires the uncoupling of labor from the state; namely, the host of worker protections legislatively garnered by U.S. unions stand as obstacles to managerial control over the redesign and redeployment of the contemporary division of labor. The new "participatory corporatism" fashions an increase in "employee involvement" as a means to better respond to increasing market demands and, consequently, the need for controlling the costs of capital stock changes. This new attempt to establish managerial hegemony celebrates worker knowledge on the shopfloor while limiting worker initiative be separating it, as much as possible, from State power.

The new participatory corporatism has led to a large number of participatory reforms by U.S. enterprises. These generally take the form of one or more of the following: job enrichment, quality circles, autonomous work groups, and employee stock ownership plans (ESOPs). A 1982 New York Stock Exchange study estimated that 44 percent of all companies with more than 500 employees maintained quality circle programs, roughly 90 percent of the Fortune "500" (Lawler and Mohrman 1985). Numerous businesses have adopted job enrichment schemes, and autonomous work groups remain the least popular reform in the United States (Walton 1985). By 1983 over 6,000 U.S. corporations adopted employee stock ownership plans, involving approximately half a million workers (Russell 1984). Most recently the General Motors Saturn Corporation agreement with the United Automobile Workers (UAW) calls for extensive labor-management joint committees and work groups, from the shopfloor to higher supervisory levels.

While the extent of these reforms appears dramatic, the actual shift in workplace authority remains less significant. Instead of a wholesale redesign of the division of labor, management's participatory corporatism offers only the patina of political alterations at any level within the modern enterprise. Drawing from the human relations school, particularly Elton Mayo, the new ideology exalts the group over the individual. Distinct from this earlier tradition of managerial reform, the contemporary movement celebrates the veneer of shifts within the division of labor coupled with participative schemes arranged along the lines of nineteenth century "protective democracy." Worker participation appears extensive and is not insignificant in the immediate context of workplace regulations and personalities. The problem remains that supervisory vetoes preserve managerial prerogatives and, just as important, these changes bring workers more closely into the orbit of marketing needs, production "necessities," and competitive ethics. After all, that is the whole point: to increase productivity and American competitiveness.

Whether or not managerially initiated changes will empower workers to pursue greater issues involved in de-skilling and other forms of managerial order, work reform revolves around the political, cultural, and economic dynamics of workplace sociology. It remains problematic as to whether U.S. business leaders are engaged in a significant gamble by fooling with deep-seated American images of managerial prerogatives and fundamental visions of the property rights of U.S. capital. What becomes obvious is the need for many U.S. firms to alter labor-management relations founded upon a new managerial ideology: the reasons for these changes rest with corporate responses to marketing exigencies, the need for more flexible production functions, the need for productivity gains, and the intensified desire for a non-union environment with reduced state control over the shopfloor. In short, the motive force for change rests with forces external to the enterprise as opposed to worker unrest within.

Participatory corporatism calls for a "new industrial relations" based upon increased worker participation for solving managerial problems while satisfying the logic of enterprise self-interest. It introduces worker responsibility for the quality and productivity of production but it preserves managerial authority, infusing market ideology into both the informal and formal work groups of the enterprise.

The actual experience of the "participatory corporatism" involves a very low level of "democratization." Most programs are "quality circle" (QC) experiments; some are slightly more ambitious (plantwide) and are entitled "quality of worklife" (QWL) programs. The QC enrolls 6 to 12 workers from the same work area, who are trained in "problem solving, statistical quality control and group process" (Lawler and Mohrman 1985; Simmons and Mares 1983). Such groups meet approximately four hours per month on company time, receive little or no financial awards, and recommend suggestions to management. They aim to improve quality and productivity. Often they are parallel to existing lines of supervision and control, creating little incentive for middle managers to work with them or absorb the costs of their recommendations. They become isolated, draining, disappointing to workers, and ultimately threatening to middle-level managers. Higher levels of integration into plant authority might involve the establishment of a QWL program, which increases the level and rhetoric of employee involvement beyond the smaller group. The latter attempts to collapse intermediate managerial functions and increase worker participation by developing "an atmosphere of mutual trust" (Walton 1985). The most ambitious managerial reforms include autonomous work groups that yield the previously held prerogatives of station supervisors to the work group, including their immediate division of labor *within* the group (Bluestone 1983; Guest 1979).

Participatory corporatism follows Mayo's incisiveness. Recognizing the alienating impact of mechanized Taylorism on workers, along with the loss of the benefits of worker knowledge in speeding production and improving its quality, the new ideology seeks to regain those aspects of both worker culture and the informal group compatible with new market necessities. As Grzyb points out, Taylorism desired a certain fragmentation and "decollectivization" of the work force as a means to realize increased managerial and technical control. Now the diminishing returns from this design become obvious. Management covets worker initiative and increased responsiveness to market changes. The means to this end is a limited "recollectivization" of workers founded upon corporate goals fueled by a new celebration of competitive and market ethics at the point of production (Grzyb 1981). Participatory corporatism attempts a redefinition of workers' common sense about "how to live on the job." Quality circles and work teams increase worker sociability and cohesiveness, previously denied under mechanized Taylorism. Atomized workers don't talk, at least not so much as management realizes they must in order to get them to share their ideas and observations, which increase accumulation and valorization. In short, if degradation costs and participation pays, then managers must get workers talking even if it obscures the role of lower management.

Participatory corporatism represents an attempt at fashioning a new legitimacy for managerial authority in an age of intensified competition and technological innovation. An insurgent worker culture limits corporate flexibility and control. Taylorism may have increased productivity but it ultimately undercuts its advantages by degrading work and alienating too many workers. In the face of Taylorism, many workers desire what Heckscher has termed "responsible autonomy," more control over their immediate tasks and less susceptibility to close managerial supervision (Heckscher 1981). He may be correct insofar as the overwhelming majority of American workers remain outside any effective alliance with state power regarding job security. While managers may envy a corporatist scheme of worker participation, workers may bring less enthusiasm than might be expected in the face of degradation, only because their "common sense" indicates that autonomy affords them more control than the ideological illusions of participatory corporatism. As underscored by Mike Parker's critique of worker participation and the quality of worklife plans in the automobile industry, management's latest initiatives in control are less respected than feared (Parker 1985).

CONCLUSION

The history of cultural hegemony within the American workplace remains characterized by the nexus of market imperatives, class politics (both within and outside the factory and the office), and the disposition of State power. This said, it would be a significant error to understand the dynamics of workplace politics in mechanical formulations. At all historical turns, work culture is always made by real workers and real managers acting as both the subjects and objects within their own biographies. The complexities of class conflicts are compounded by the enormity of intra-class struggles at all levels of the sociological ladder, and, most notably, framed within racial, gender, and ethnic categories on the American scene. Caught within this political prism, managerial authority must always be legitimized and renewed in the refraction of labor politics and workers' attempts at securing autonomy. Cultural hegemony, like commodities, proves to be a necessary outcome of the production process. Ideology at work, itself, must be produced in order for work to be produced. Ironically, such attempts always yield to the central contradictions involved in any human enterprise that requires appeals for conformity to institutional needs amidst the inevitable mercury of market competition. The result will always produce new ideologies at work.

REFERENCES

Armstrong, P. J., J.F.B. Goodman, and J. D. Hyman. 1981. *Ideology and Shopfloor Industrial Relations.* London: Croon-Helm

Bendix, Reinhard. 1974. *Work and Authority in Industry.* Berkeley: University of California Press.

Bluestone, I. 1983. "Labor's Stake in Improving the Quality of Worklife." In *The Quality of Worklife in the 1980's,* edited by Harvey Kolodony and Hans van Beinum. New York: Praeger.

Bottomore, T. B., ed. 1983. *A Dictionary of Marxist Thought.* Cambridge, Mass.: Harvard University Press.

Burawoy, Michael. 1982. *Manufacturing Consent Changes in the Labor Process under Monopoly Capitalism.* Chicago: University of Chicago Press.

Clawson, Dan. 1980. *Bureaucracy and the Labor Process.* New York: Monthly Review Press.

Dawley, Alan. 1976. *Class and Community: The Industrial Revolution in Lynn.* Cambridge, Mass.: Harvard University Press.

Foner, Eric. 1976. *Tom Paine and Revolutionary America.* New York: Oxford University Press.

Gordon, David, Richard Edwards, and Michael Reich. 1982. *Segmented Work, Divided Workers: The Historical Transformation of Labor in the U.S.* New York: Cambridge University Press.

Grzyb, J. 1981. "Decollectivization and Recollectivization in the Workplace: The

Impact of Technology on Informal Work Groups and Work Culture." *Economic and Industrial Democracy* 2:455–82.

Guest, R. 1979. "The Quality of Work Life—Learning from Tarrytown." *Harvard Business Review*, July, pp. 76–87.

Gutman, Herbert G. 1976. *Work, Culture, and Society in Industrializing America*. New York: Random House.

Heckscher, C. 1981. "Democracy at Work: Whose Interest?" Ph.D. Dissertation, Harvard University.

Hirsch, Susan E. 1978. *Roots of the American Working Class: The Industrialization of Crafts in Newark, 1800–1860*. Philadelphia: University of Pennsylvania Press.

Kasson, John F. 1976. *Civilizing the Machine: Technology and Republican Values in America, 1776–1900*. New York: Grossman.

Laurie, Bruce. 1980. *Working People of Philadelphia, 1800–1850*. Philadelphia: Temple University Press.

Lawler, E., and Mohrman, S. 1985. "Quality Circles after the Fad." *Harvard Business Review*, January, pp. 64–71.

Lenin, V. I. 1963. *What Is to be Done?* Oxford: Clarendon Press.

Mayo, Elton. 1933. *The Human Problems of an Industrial Civilization*. New York: MacMillan.

———. 1945. *The Social Problems of an Industrial Civilization*. Cambridge, Mass.: Harvard University Press.

Meyer, Stephen. 1981. *The Five Dollar Day: Labor Management and Social Control in the Ford Motor Company, 1908–1921*. Albany, N.Y.: State University of New York Press.

Montgomery, David. 1981. *Beyond Equality: Labor and the Radical Republicans, 1862–1872*. Urbana: University of Illinois Press.

———. 1979. *Worker's Control in America: Studies in the History of Work, Technology, and Labor Struggles*. New York: Cambridge University Press.

Nelson, Daniel. 1975. *Managers and Workers: Origins of the New Factory System in the U.S., 1880–1920*. Madison: University of Wisconsin Press.

———. 1980. *Frederick W. Taylor and the Rise of Scientific Management*. Madison: University of Wisconsin Press.

Noble, David F. 1977. *America by Design: Science, Technology and the Rise of Corporate Capitalism*. New York: Oxford University Press.

Parker, M. 1985. *Inside the Circle: A Union Guide to QWL*. Boston: South End Press.

Rodgers, Daniel T. 1978. *The Work Ethic in Industrializing America, 1850–1920*. Chicago: University of Chicago Press.

Roethlisberger, F. J. and William Dickson. 1939. *Management and the Worker*. Cambridge, Mass.: Harvard University Press.

Russell, R. 1984. "Using Ownership to Control: Making Workers Owners in the Contemporary United States." *Politics and Society* 13:253–94.

Simmons, J., and W. Mares. 1983. *Working Together*. New York: Knopf.

Siracusa, Carl. 1979. *A Mechanical People's Perceptions of the Industrial Order in Massachusetts, 1815–1880*. Middletown, Conn.: Wesleyan University Press.

Walton R. 1985. "From Control to Commitment in the Workplace." *Harvard Business Review*, March, pp. 76–84.

Ware, Norman. 1959. *The Industrial Worker, 1840–1860.* Boston and New York: Houghton Mifflin Company.

Wilentz, Sean. 1983. "Artisan Republican Festivals and the Rise of Class Conflict in New York City, 1788–1837." In *Working Class America,* edited by Michael H. Frisch and Daniel J. Walkowitz. Urbana: University of Illinois Press, pp. 37–77.

Williams, Raymond. 1977. *Marxism and Literature.* Oxford, Eng.: Oxford University Press.

Wolfe, Tom. 1979. *The Right Stuff.* New York: Farrar, Straus and Giroux.

Yellowitz, Irwin. 1976. *Industrialization and the American Labor Movement, 1850–1900.* Port Washington, N.Y.: Kennikat Press.

7

Alternative Cultures, Autonomous Institutions

Calvin F. Exoo and Alan Draper

America is God's crucible, the great Melting Pot where all the races of Europe are melting and re-forming! Here you stand, good folk, think I, when I see them at Ellis Island, here you stand in your fifty groups, with your fifty languages and histories, and your fifty blood hatreds and rivalries. But you won't be long like that, brothers, for these are the fires of God you've come to—these are the fires of God. ... Germans and Frenchmen, Irishmen and Englishmen, Jews and Russians—into the Crucible with you all! God is making the American. Yes, East and West, and North and South, the palm and the pine, the pole and the equator, the crescent and the cross—how the great Alchemist melts and fuses them with his purging flame! Here shall they all unite to build the Republic of Man and the Kingdom of God.

Israel Zangwill, The Melting Pot

Of course, not all Americans were "born liberal,"[1] even if America was. Nor are all American institutions dominated by those who were.

For example, one particular group of Founding Fathers made their pilgrimage to America locked in cargo holds. They found their homesteads while standing on auction blocks. Later, they were emancipated

---

Professor Exoo wrote the first half of this chapter, "The Immigrant Story"; Professor Draper is author of the second half, "The Black Experience."

into a land that lynched thousands of them, widely denied them the vote until quite recently, and still consigns almost half of all their children to growing up in poverty. The culture black Americans forged out of these illiberal experiences was not capitalist individualism.

Then, between 1895 and 1910, wave upon tidal wave of immigrants washed over America—about a million each year. More than three-fourths of them came from southern and eastern Europe, carrying, along with their weathered crates of threadbare belongings, an undaunted culture that was the antithesis of American individualism.

The institutional arks that carried black and southern European culture—especially church and family—are not owned or even visibly dominated by the upper class white Anglo-Saxons whose culture preponderates in American workplaces, media, schools, and parties. What has become of these autonomous institutions? Have they stood as bastions of resistance to the dominant culture? Or at least as "havens from the heartless world" of capitalist individualism? Or have they, in the end, surrendered? This chapter is the story of those different peoples, their different cultures, and their encounter with single-minded America.

The chapter is divided into two sections that tell two very different tales. The first part analyzes the encounter of southern Europeans with the dominant culture. This group, over many generations and after much struggle, has reached an uneasy accommodation with capitalist individualism. The second part examines the relationship of black Americans to the hegemonic culture. Separate treatments are necessary because the reception and treatment of these two groups by dominant groups in the United States have been so different. These separate treatments reflect our view that the racial divide is one that the dominant culture has not completely overcome. Politically and culturally, black Americans remain what James Baldwin called them many years ago—"another country."

THE IMMIGRANT STORY

The "melting pot" was a grand illusion. Those Americans who came from Ireland and from eastern and southern Europe did not find a place where all "races and nations" could contribute ways of feeling, believing, and behaving to a new, eclectic culture. The new land was not a melting pot, it was a mold—a bed of Procrustes built by the northern Europeans who preceded the southerners to this country, who held its power, who demanded that newcomers succumb to their mold, and who, in the end, had their way.

What the Immigrants Brought to America: Familism

In Europe after 1800, a population explosion, combined with the desire of landlords and governments to take advantage of new, more efficient agricultural technology, drove peasants off the land their families had tilled for centuries. The first of these disinherited wanderers to find America came from northern and western Europe. They sailed in the holds of wind-driven cargo vessels, which made frequent trips to northern Europe from the United States, but not to eastern or southern Europe. Later, when steam made the crossing shorter and less expensive for passenger ships, the "golden door" opened to the south: by 1907, over 80 percent of American immigrants were from eastern or southern Europe. Together with the group of "new immigrants," this section will include the Irish, even though their immigration peaked in the 1840s and 50s, because they share a number of important cultural traits with southern Europeans, which made them the first to feel the lash of American ethnocentrism.

What, about the culture of these newcomers, was "foreign" to America? "The value deepest in the psyche of Southern and Eastern Europeans," Novak asserts, "is an instinct for family and community" (1971, p. 209). Most of the European territories of interest to us had long known, by the nineteenth century, the status of the conquered province. Prior to 1873, the Ottoman Empire had dominated Greece for four centuries. Poland had been divided by Russia, Prussia, and Austria in 1790. It was not independent again until 1918. Serbia was conquered by the Ottoman Empire in 1459. By the nineteenth century the Habsburg Empire had made inroads into parts of Serbia and Croatia, and remained there until 1918. Ireland had suffered under the British penal laws since 1651. Southern Italy (which provided most of America's Italian immigration) stood under the Bourbons and under the peculiar oppression of their northern "countrymen" (Krickus 1976, p. 65). What might the social character of a permanently invaded people be? "Outsiders" are regarded with intense suspicion and hostility. Who are "outsiders"? Agents of the oppressive state, certainly. But in a conquered province, anyone whose fidelity to the native people is not assured might be, actively or passively, an agent of the state. And how can that fidelity be communicated, in this hostile environment, except in intimate acquaintance? This group of close acquaintances would be tightly bound indeed: theirs would be the *simpatico* of the commonly oppressed and the mutually dependent. Who are these "insiders"? Who can be known intimately enough? Family and friends. Close friends. The invaded people, then, has two social characters: suspicion for outsiders, kinship among insiders.

Greeley goes so far as to ascribe the peculiar style of Irish speech to the turning inward of the invaded people. The constant ironies, the interrogative inflections, the answering of questions with questions are all directed toward creating double meanings—one meaning for the outsider, another for the insider (Greeley 1972). In Italy, Gambino tells us, *la famiglia* is the fundamental social norm. This suggests both the importance of blood ties and, because *la famiglia* is also a metaphor that includes close friends, the intimacy and power of those friendships (Gambino 1974, p. 294; also, Bodnar 1982, p. 94).

The family may have been fundamental, the model for other relationships, not only because of the need to turn inward but also because "the family was the keystone to Catholic social doctrine. Even where the church's influence was less manifest . . . traditional family systems survived the trauma of immigration. The Polish and Italian families were not altogether similar but closely knit families were vital to both groups. . . . The integrity of the family was central to the welfare of all of its members, so individual expression which threatened family cohesion was deemed a serious offense. One of the first things a child learned was that the individual's fate was inextricably tied to the family and his first loyalty was to it" (Krickus 1976, pp. 71–72).

In the American city, one scenario has it,[2] village solidarity was easily and naturally translated into ethnic group solidarity. There were just too few immigrants from the old village to sustain a social network; the immigrant had to find a new "family." He neither had, nor did he need, much selection. There were only so many in the community who spoke his language. With most of these people, he shared his religious faith. Perhaps most important of all, the ethnic community was identified, feared, and mistreated *as a group* by the natives of the new land. Here was a familiar basis, the basis the immigrant had always known, for brotherhood: the brotherhood of the oppressed (Herberg 1955, p. 14).

Familism, Socialism, and Capitalism

What did the immigrant's cultural compass, this ethos of familism, tell him as he stood at the crossroads to the industrialized world? Was his path to be acceptance of the dominant culture, capitalist individualism; resistance, in the form of socialism; or retreat into the private, familiar world of "old ways"?

Competitive individualism was not just different from the southern European way of life; it was antithetical to it.[3] "Formerly, the peasant's life had been guided by standards he accepted as fixed and immutable." The New World "made a mockery of those very standards." Here, "the loyal dutiful man," faithful to tradition and family, the one who remained in the household, returning his check to *paterfamilias*; or who at least remained in the neighborhood, a solid rock of "reciprocal goodness" in the network of family, friends, and neighbors—that man was not respected, but derided. The one whose head was not so turned by *hubris* as to try to accumulate more wealth for himself than was enough for a gift to the church—he was not esteemed; he was a failure. Meanwhile, "shrewd, selfish, unscrupulous upstarts thrived. Clearly the attributes the immigrants held in high esteem were not those that brought success in America. The idea of success was itself strange; to thrust oneself above one's station in life called for harsh competitive qualities the peasant had always despised" (Handlin 1952, pp. 79–80).

On the other hand, the road from familism to socialism was not smooth or straight either. Indeed, one scholar has argued that the inward-turning circle was a closed circle—precluding a larger, class solidarity by fostering division between ethnic groups and even kinship networks (Vecoli 1978, p. 231).

What is more, the fixity of the peasant's legal, economic and political life, together with Catholic doctrine, had made the southern European fatalistic. He understood himself as in "the inscrutable world of an unfathomable God" (Kleppner 1967, p. 110), where the human lot is not to make the world over, but to "remain in the state in which [we are] placed," as the Catholic Bible still translates 1 Corinthians 7:17.[4] The world is certainly imperfect, but the answer is not a political Tower of Babel; the secret is to endure and be reconciled. Clearly, such a habit of mind would not be immediately open to what must have seemed the grandiose schemes of the socialists.

Nevertheless, the immigrants did find their way to collective social action, again and again. Their own mutual aid societies, ubiquitous in immigrant communities, were just an organizational step from the way familism had always worked. In these, the immigrants pooled their resources, huddling against the elements, so that when death, disability, eviction, or unemployment found one of their families, the others were there for them. As their members moved away from the margin of existence, these circles opened to embrace the newly arrived immigrants or the longer settled poor (Handlin 1952, p. 175).

In the circle beyond the mutual aid societies were the labor unions. To join them, immigrants often had to surmount the outspoken nativism of their leaders. Samuel Gompers, for example, argued that "the maintenance of the nation depended upon the maintenance of racial purity," that immigrants "could not be Americanized," and he called for restrictions on immigration (Leinenweber 1984, p. 245). Nevertheless, southern/eastern Europeans did join, and became the "backbone" of the early industrial unions (Vecoli 1984, p. 278; Bodnar 1985, pp. 88 ff.).

But what of the last circle, the one so wide it stood outside the sphere of "American" institutions: what of socialism? Several writers have argued that southern Europeans had already met this new thought in the old country—that ethnic socialism was transplanted as a "sturdy sapling" from Europe (Vecoli 1984, p. 279). "Recurring periods of repression (in Europe) drove many leading theorists and agitators of the radical persuasion into exile, some to America" (Vecoli 1984, p. 274). Because these radicals were usually of the intelligentsia, they were often among the leaders of their ethnic communities in America. But in addition, by the early 1900s "many thousands" of immigrant artisans, industrial workers, and even peasants had participated in European socialist parties or peasants' leagues. "By the outbreak of World War I, the spectrum of European radicalism . . . had been transplanted in microcosm to the United States" (Vecoli 1984, p. 274; see also Bodnar 1985, pp. 86 ff.).

Once here, the cause of immigrant socialism had to contend with the ambivalence of American socialists toward the newcomers. In 1908, for example, the Socialist Party's National Committee rejected a platform resolution calling for the organization of immigrants, and instead supported the exclusion of workers from "backward" countries (Leinenweber 1984, p. 248). On the other hand, when organizing efforts were made, and especially when they were made by organizers from within the target community, they were often successful (Bodnar 1985, pp. 104 ff.). By 1919, over half the 109,000 members of the Socialist Party of America were to be found in the party's foreign-language federations (Leinenweber 1984, p. 261). That relatively small total tells us that most southern Europeans did not rush to resist the dominant culture, any more than to embrace it. Most of them retreated from the fray altogether, into the ethnic coffeehouses, churches, taverns, the ethnic newspapers, theatres, and households where the old ways held sway, and the debate over the direction of a larger society was unheard. But the significant minority who did turn to socialism demonstrates that the circle of the oppressed could grow wider. At least one of the ways that a people familiar with "collective responses to survival and need" could turn, at the crossroads of industrialized society, was to socialism (Bodnar 1985, p. 88).

And yet, socialism among southern/eastern Europeans only declined after these early successes. Why? The rest of this section will focus on one of the answers to that question, not pretending that it does not neglect others. It argues that the vituperative, seductive power of the hegemonic culture goaded and beckoned the immigrant toward an ineluctable conformity.

What the Immigrant Found in America:
Nativism, Racism, and the Americanization Movement

What we have called the dominant culture is really the culture of upper class Anglo-Saxon Protestants, mainly those "Yankees" of New England descent whose "dominion dates from colonial times and whose cultural domination in the U.S. has never been seriously threatened" (Gordon 1964, p. 73). It was their doctrine of the calling (Weber 1958, p. 77), their Lockian liberalism, their experience on the frontier (Kleppner 1967, p. 537), and, later, their dominance over the economy that ran as tributaries to the one great river of American social thought: capitalist individualism (see also Chapter 1). Because Yankee culture is so deeply rooted in Yankee religion, the Catholic culture carried into this country by increasingly large numbers of immigrants after the 1830s was not just different—it was "sinful." And it may also be true—as Louis Hartz suggests—that a society that had long been unanimous did not know how to disagree tolerantly (1955, p. 12).

For whatever reasons, one of the first lessons Catholic newcomers to the promised land learned was that many of the natives hated them. As early as the 1790s, fear of a contagion from the "licentiousness" of the French revolutionaries to their supporters among French and Irish immigrants produced the Alien and Sedition Acts (Higham 1955, p. 8).

Within 30 years, the fervor of the Second Great Awakening had conjured another nativist hobgoblin: the "obsequious papist," whose submission to the Roman despot was irreconcilable with and dangerous to American political liberty (Kleppner et al. 1981, p. 105; Higham 1955, p. 6).

Together, these somewhat contradictory bugbears, the foreign radical and the foreign submissive, called forth incredibly deadly anti-Catholic race riots, the large "Native American" movement of the 1830s and 40s and then the "American" or "Know-Nothing" Party. The party platform was rabidly anti-Catholic, calling for restriction of immigration and restriction of immigrants from such activities as officeholding. By the 1850s, the American Party had captured six governorships and controlled several state legislatures. Although it faded soon afterward, xenophobia lived on. Two of the major political issues of the post-Civil War era were the banning of parochial (Catholic) schools and the prohibition of that "Roman affliction," the demon rum (Kleppner et al. 1981, p. 137).

Toward the end of the nineteenth century, as the source of immigration changed from north to south, "a new . . . chord from the nativist lyre began to sound—the ugly chord, or discord, of racism" (Gordon 1964, p. 97; see also Higham 1955, pp. 9 ff.). This was the historically groundless, scientifically ludicrous notion that the "old Americans" of northern European descent were a physically and culturally superior race. Variously called Teutons, Anglo-Saxons, Aryans, or Nordics, their genetic heritage was not only blonde hair and blue eyes, but also "a gift for political freedom" (Higham 1955, p. 10). Alpine and Mediterranean peoples on the other hand, were "docile, lacking in self-reliance and initiative, [and the] Anglo-Saxon conception of righteousness, law and order, and popular government" (an educator of the period, quoted in Gordon 1964, p. 98). In 1916, *The Passing of the Great Race*, by Madison Grant, an anthropologist at the American Museum of Natural History, gave literary voice and weight to these doctrines. "[In the] competition between the lowest and most primitive elements and the specialized traits of Nordic man; his stature ... fair skin and light-colored hair, his straight nose and his splendid fighting and moral qualities will have little part in the resultant mixture" (quoted in Novak 1971, p. 102). The scientific community could only applaud. A review in *Science* magazine commended Grant's "work of solid merit." Studies at Yale and Columbia "proved" the intellectual inferiority of the "darker races" (Novak 1971, p. 100; Bowles and Gintis 1976, p. 196). The federal government's own contribution was a "summary" of scientific knowledge about the newcomers' shortcomings: a 42-volume boulder that would later be pressed to the chest of the immigrants.

The final triumph of xenophobia began with World War I, when all the fears of the last 100 years came together in a crucible of patriotic urgency. In the shadow of the war, prominent Americans began to see diversity as disloyalty. In the presidential campaign of 1916, Theodore Roosevelt made "100-percent Americanism" a major issue in his campaign for the Republican nomination. "Anything less, including any ethnic tie, was 'moral treason.' " Woodrow Wilson went Roosevelt one better. His Democratic platform proclaimed "the indivisibility of the nation" to be "the supreme issue." It denounced alleged "conspiracies" in "the interests of foreign countries," and condemned ethnic associations as "subversive" (McClymer 1982, pp. 97–98). With the entry of the United States into the war in 1917, followed by the departure from the war effort of the Soviets after the Revolution, anti-foreignism again resonated with an old companion theme—anti-radicalism. Such critics of the war as the Socialist Party and the Industrial Workers of the World (IWW) quickly found that just beyond the pale of a people whose tolerant talk had come too easily lay a violent intolerance. The backlash against radicals now known as the "Red Scare" focused on the new immigrants, assuming, as had the whole anti-radical tradition, that militant discontent must be a foreign import (Higham 1955, p. 219). In July 1917, the attorney general of the United States ordered the internment of all German aliens found to be IWW members. Two months later, his Justice Department officers invaded every IWW hall in the United States, seizing natives for trial and aliens of all nationalities for deportation. Also during this period, 23 state governments enacted criminal syndicalism laws under which "a vigorous program of prosecution for [radical] organizational membership or for opinion ensued; in a three-month period the state of Washington convicted eighty six individuals of membership in the IWW" (Higham 1955, p. 227). Businessmen seized the day in a massive advertising campaign, declaring radicalism and even unions guilty by association with "foreign subversion." Finally, in 1919, Attorney General A. Mitchell Palmer began his blitzkrieg of "Palmer Raids," rounding up thousands of members of the already beaten and balkanized communist parties, separating out the aliens for deportation hearings, often holding them for weeks in overcrowded, unsanitary conditions without preliminary hearings (Higham 1955, pp. 230–31). About a third of them were found guilty and deported, often leaving their families impoverished and ostracized. Their crime was membership in a party whose opinions were not free to be spoken in the land of the free.

While one hand of the American establishment crushed those immigrants who chose the "wrong" path, the other prodded and coaxed the rest to the right course—the way of "Americanization." The Americanization movement was a massive marshaling of the "means of intellectual production" on behalf of one unabashed, oft-stated goal: "[the foreign-born] must be induced to give up the languages, customs and methods of life which they have brought with them across the ocean, and adopt instead the language, habits, and customs of this country...the standards and ways of American living" (National Americanization Committee pamphlet, in Gordon 1964, p. 101).

Participants in this movement included the federal government, most of the state governments, the U.S. Chamber of Commerce, thousands of school systems, thousands of employers, and more than 100 private organizations. Their molding pots included adult education courses in English, patriotism, and "the American Way of Life," the banning of parochial schools and of speaking foreign languages in the public schools, regulation of the home lives of immigrants by social workers, punitive tax and wage rates for aliens not working to become citizens, and surveillance of aliens to prevent strikes and other "disruptive" activities (Higham 1955, ch. 9; McClymer 1982).

The final solution of the Americanization movement came in 1924, with congressional passage of the national origins formula. The law assigned to each country an immigration quota proportionate to its members among the U.S. population of 1920. The flood of southern and eastern Europeans was now a trickle. Those who had always come to reinvigorate and rebuild immigrant institutions and values came no more. Now it was only a matter of time before those institutions and values would be worn away by the relentless waves of hegemony. We might better understand both this Americanization movement (usually dated from about 1914–25) and the demand for Anglo-conformity that preceded and postdated it by revisiting several of the engines of hegemony that occupied earlier chapters and asking, "What was their contribution to making America unanimous again?"

The Immigrant in the Fires of Hegemony

The Schools

From the outset, acculturation was one *raison d'etre* of the American system of compulsory public education. Here is a typical argument for this, the Horace Mann idea, from one of its early apologists:

No one at all familiar with the deficient household arrangements and deranged machinery of domestic life of the extreme poor and ignorant, to say nothing of ...all the vicious habits of low bred idleness, which abound in certain sections of all populous districts—can doubt, that it is better for children to be removed as early and as long as possible from such scenes and examples.... The primary object [of this removal was] not so much... intellectual culture, as the regulation of the feelings and dispositions... the formation of a lovely and virtuous character (Henry Barnard, quoted in Katz 1971, p. 31).

The arrival of the southern Europeans only increased the urgency of teaching these lessons, and not only to children. From 1914 to 1925, more than a million foreign-born adults were enrolled in formal Americanization classes run through the public school system (McClymer 1982, p. 103). But recent studies have shown that, in the schools at least, the work of Americanization is an ongoing concern. In its curriculum, its grading system, its classroom rituals, the school system continues to teach the eternal verities: patriotism, meritocracy, and workplace docility (Bowles and Gintis 1976). This is partly for the benefit of the "newest immigrants," the blacks and Hispanics who came to U.S. cities after 1940. A Boston assistant school superintendent recently wrote of their "potentials which have for too long been submerged by parental lack of values" (Tyack 1974, p. 281). Partly, these lessons are for working and lower class children—even whites of long American standing—to whom the dominant culture will never be completely native.

The Workplace

Corporate America was in the vanguard of the Americanization movement. And why not? After all, Americanization meant acceptance not just of a political, but also of an economic system—the capitalist's own economic system.

In return for an increase in pay, Ford Motor Company workers, for example, surrendered to prescription in every area of their lives by the Ford Sociological Department: where to live, how to furnish a home, how frequently to bathe, how to raise children, how to use table utensils, how to be a responsible consumer, and so on. "In particular, they learned those habits of life which resulted in good habits of work," such as diligence, promptness, and docility (Meyer 1981, p. 156). But of course, these lessons were not unique to a ten-year period. They were the same lessons work supervisors had always taught, and continue to teach. And they are powerful lessons. Survival, after all, depends on learning them. In the Amoskeag Textile Mill, for example, workers

understood the paternal role of the "boss." They learned quickly that currying favor with the boss was important for survival or advancement and that obedience and discipline were the keys to their relationship with bosses. Letters that new immigrant workers wrote to their bosses . . . reveal their perception of the bosses as paternalistic figures and their own position as obedient "children" (Hareven 1982, p. 51).

This is not to say that immigrants went gentle into the good night of the modern workplace. After 1911, the new gospel of scientific management decreed the speedup of assembly lines, the rending of workplace kin groups, a hardening in the face of the boss—a change from patron to supervisor. Workers responded with slowdowns, sabotage, unionization (Hareven 1982, pp. 138 ff.; Gutman 1976). But as long as the contest took place only in the factory, as long as workers were unsupported by political parties, the fight between capital and labor was not a fair one. That was true not only because employers held hiring and firing in their hands. Two recent studies have tapped immigrant workers' blood-vivid memories of the ministrations of corporate goon squads and police departments. Workers at Jones and Laughlin's Aliquippa plant, for example, called the place "Little Siberia." One of them cannot forget the "aggressive little Serbian" unionizer who was beaten so badly by a huge company goon that he later died: "He busted his ear drums, kicked him in the head, kicked him in the stomach so bad. . . . And the police were standing right there and they wouldn't move, because they had orders not to interfere" (Bodnar 1982, p. 125; Hareven 1982, p. 66). How much more compelling the velvet glove of cultural hegemony must have been, because it sometimes came off, revealing the mailed fist of state or corporate violence. Forcing them to be free.

Political Parties

The familism and paternalism of southern/eastern European culture led naturally to the building of political machines. Unfortunately, in most cities, while machines went about winning the small personal battles of the immigrants—the patronage job, the fixed ticket, the hod of coal—the great social war of the poor was lost by default, was never, in fact, joined at all.

This may have had something to do with a Catholic peasant fatalism, which saw the call for social change as *hubris* (Exoo 1983). It also had something to do with the siren song of corporate money. "In the 1880s and 90s, several financial syndicates made millions of dollars by gaining control of the street railway franchises in New York, Philadelphia, and scores of other cities.... The Bell Telephone Company launched its drive for monopoly in this period, offering bribes to officials in city after city" (Judd 1979, p. 64). Similar opportunities emanated from control of business licensing and regulation, public works contracts, the police power over illicit enterprises, and so forth. Obviously, being indentured to large corporations truncates a city government's reform agenda.

On the other hand, a number of immigrant-supported party organizations did wage fundamental fights against corporate power (Judd 1979, pp. 76 ff.). The demand for such programmatic parties might well have grown among immigrants, as the fatalism born of a peasant economy gave way to the only choices offered in a capitalist economy: individual or collective striving. After all, the sons and daughters of immigrants were anything but fatalistic in the workplace. In fact, they were the cornerstone of some of the more militant unions (Krickus 1976, ch. 3; Bodnar 1985, p. 88).

But by their time, it was too late. The middle class Protestant counterattack against the immigrants' machines had broken the potential of political parties. The direct primary, civil service, non-partisan elections, the city manager, and so on had done their job: making the organization and political power of working and lower class people a thing of the past (see Chapter 2).

The Press

Although a foreign press exists even today, it is surprising how quickly American newspapers were able to lure away the loyalty of so many immigrant readers (Handlin 1952, p. 200). But perhaps, on second thought, it is not surprising that a foreign press whose purpose was to advance a point of view should be out-sold by an American press whose purpose was to sell papers.

Especially alluring to the immigrant were the tabloids of Hearst and Pulitzer. Their kaleidoscope of headlines, large type, and illustrations were tailor-made for those still not at ease with the new language. Even less resistible to the immigrant than their format were the mesmerizing subjects of these papers. These included opulent portraits of the wealthy and glamorous, "women's" pages with their cavalcades of splendid consumables, and, of course, the sensationalized "news" of crimes, disasters, scandals, and bizarre or sentimental "human interest." For the newcomer, the city was a chaotic and threatening world, but one that also beckoned with tales of "rags to riches" and with the rising castles of robber barons to prove those tales true. Here then was a screen of newsprint, onto which were projected all the fears and dreams of the new land. And as he held them in his hand, the immigrant's nightmares and daydreams became safe and accessible. What a psychically compelling pageant it must have been. But it was more. The triumph of the American commercial press over the ethnic press and the socialist press represented, for the immigrant, a turn away from the hard new political and social questions, a turn toward the anesthetic balm of consumerism.

An Entertainment Medium: The Movies

The low-budget potboilers churned out by a host of independent producers in the early days of film appealed mainly to working class Americans, who, for a nickel, "could be enveloped in a new world, a magical universe of madness and motion" (Ewen and Ewen 1982, p. 87). *Survey* magazine, the journal of social work, reported that "in the tenement districts the motion picture has well-nigh driven other forms of entertainment from the field" (quoted in Ewen and Ewen 1982, pp. 86–87). These silent films, with their accessible mimed interpretations of American life, were especially important to the immigrant, who found in them a Rosetta stone to this new culture. In fact, many of the early films were about working class immigrant life. Some even rendered that life as a challenge to middle class ideology. In one, scenes of courthouse injustices toward the poor presage the unmasking of blind Lady Justice to reveal an eye fixed on the gold tossed into her scales. In another, a baby grows sick from the impure milk sold in the slums and dies, after his parents fail to raise money from the heartless rich to buy the high-priced pasteurized milk. The comedies of Chaplin and Sennett often feature underdog heroes who prick the pompousness and hypocrisy of middle class life (Ewen and Ewen 1982, pp. 89–92).

But by 1920, the movie business had become big business. Centralized in large, well-financed Hollywood studios, it reached out to a new middle class audience. The man who found it was Cecil B. deMille, who "withdrew the curtains that had veiled the rich and fashionable and exhibited them in all the lavish and intimate details of their private lives" (Benjamin Hampton, quoted in Ewen and Ewen 1982, p. 100). His films became the formula for cinematic success by giving voice "to a crucial myth of modern culture: metamorphosis through consumption" (Ewen and Ewen 1982, p. 100).

Especially for the now-maturing sons and daughters of the immigrants, a new myth was exactly what was needed. This second generation had watched their parents cling desperately to the old ways, and fall into discredit for it. Unmoored in this way, chartless, the child of immigration might well have found his course in the opulent movie palaces that were now beginning to replace the neighborhood nickelodeons. One of their architects called them "social safety valves in that the public can partake of the same luxuries as the rich." And so they were. For here was not only luxury, but luxury enwrapping the religion of capitalism: "success" was its message, happiness through commodities; and the theatre was its "temple of daydreams" (Ewen and Ewen 1982, p. 104).

The Response of Immigrant Institutions

The Foreign-Language Press

For the most part, the foreign-language press advocated neither resistance nor surrender to capitalism. Instead, it advocated retreat into the sphere outside politics and the workplace, into the closed circle of the old ways—faithfulness to family, neighbors, parish, tradition. Its pages were filled with sad rhapsodies to the old country, and dire warnings of the betrayal that awaited those who fell into the hands of the strangers of the new land. Perhaps this faithfulness was no accident. After all, the passing of the old culture would also mean the demise of the immigrant press.

But of course, even this retreat into ethnic havens was not enough for the dominant culture, which demanded total surrender. Finally, when these ethnic enclaves were invaded by the Americanization movement, the ethnic press fought back valiantly. A Polish-language paper, for example, denounced "this foolish Americanization, similar to the Prussian system of denationalization," which has in it, chimed another, "not the smallest particle of the true American spirit, the spirit of freedom, the brightest virtue of which is the broadest possible tolerance" (quoted in McClymer 1982, p. 110).

But by the end of the Americanization era, demoralized by the long years of vilification and near-insolvency, the members of the American Association of Foreign Language Newspapers allowed the Committee for Immigrants in America to flood their pages with jingoistic anti-radical editorials and with advertisements solicited from corporate retailers designed to sell "American ideals ... products and standards of living" to the foreign born (Chair of the Committee Francis Kellor, quoted in Kivisto 1984, p. 182).

The Catholic Church

The nineteenth century was, for the Catholic Church in the United States, one crisis of cohesion after another. The first was largely resolved by the middle of the century. By that time, the Irish, by sheer dint of numbers, had established dominance in the church, the resistance of earlier Catholic arrivals notwithstanding.

This resolution cleared the way for a second struggle, this time between the Irish and the groups that followed them, mainly the Germans and the Italians. This became known as the fight over "Cahenslyism," after the German Catholic who proposed that the U.S. church be organized into ethnic dioceses, instead of the usual geographic divisions. The U.S. hierarchy vehemently opposed this plan, for two reasons. Obviously these U.S. bishops, Irish to a man, would cling to their rank and to Irish supremacy for all the dioceses.

But Cahenslyism was not just a power squabble between the Irish, Italians, and Germans. It was also the landmark question of whether the church would be a force for cultural pluralism or for Anglo-conformity. As we have already seen, the immigration of the post–1880 period had refueled a long-standing American tradition of anti-Catholicism. The New York *Times*, for example, wrote ominously of a group of determinedly unmelted German Catholics, "it is not too much to say that, if the spirit of the Roman Catholic Church were expressed in the proceedings of [this group], that church would be a public enemy" (quoted in Cross 1958, p. 92). The mostly-Irish church hierarchy knew this nativism as only victims can; by the 1880s, they had already been its captives for half a century. Their response to its redoubled strength was a sort of hostage syndrome—a zealous identification with the demands made on the new immigrants for "Americanization." Archbishop John Ireland, for example, denounced Cahenslyism as "the impudence of foreigners." Any immigrant, he opined, "who did not rejoice in the American way of life 'should in simple consistency betake his foreign soul to foreign shores, and crouch in misery and subjection beneath tyranny's scepter.' " He alerted the Associated Press to monitor the meetings of the German Catholic Assembly for its "general un-American character" (quoted in Cross 1958, pp. 89, 92, 93). The effect of such patriotic piety was the best a hostage can hope for—a softening of the hostage takers. President Harrison commended the archbishop's compatriot, Cardinal Gibbons, for his own stand against "foreigners." The press warmly applauded him for his "stern warning to the German nationalists in their own stronghold" (Cross 1958, p. 94).

Inevitably, Cahenslyism was defeated. The yearning of the newcomers to rebuild the village parish was too strong to be denied altogether, but ethnicity was accommodated only at the parish level. The hierarchy, the diocese, remained "American." This assured that when the immigrants' English-speaking children came of age, the old languages would begin to fade from the church. Later, as these children, or their children, moved from the old neighborhood, they would enter homogenized suburban parishes with no distinctive saints, language, or clergy. At last, they would be American.

At about the same time, Leo XIII translated the Catholic Church's long-standing symbiosis with the dominant classes into the new language of capital vs. labor. *Rerum Novarum* of 1891 strongly supported the doctrine of private property, rejected socialism out of hand, and suffered the existence of only such labor associations as did not jeopardize the "prerogatives of property." U.S. prelates were especially enthusiastic in seconding the papal bull. In separate pronouncements, the three U.S. cardinals declared,

"Socialism is the heresy of the hour."

"There cannot be a Catholic Socialist."

"An anxious capitalistic world looks to the Church, nervous with gratitude for the ... setback that Catholicism is to give to socialism" (quoted in Karson 1984, pp. 84–85).

Although there were exceptions, bishops and priests also took up the cudgels vigorously, among their congregations, at American Federation of Labor (AFL) conventions, and in the Catholic press (Karson 1984). Catholics ignored the church position at the peril of their immortal souls. The Knights of Labor, which advocated public ownership of some industry, was censured; its members were denied the sacraments. A prominent advisor to Henry George, the socialist writer and candidate for mayor of New York, was excommunicated (Cross 1958, pp. 109, 121). Somehow, "none of the American prelates ever developed the passion for reform" that the European church cultivated (Cross 1958, pp. 109, 218).

Even the Catholic schools, which began as one more enclave where the old ways could hide and be nurtured, were eventually co-opted. By the end of World War I, the Catholic hierarchy had joined in the attack on the "ethnic" Catholic school, forbidding, as had 15 states, the use of non-English materials there (Galush 1977, p. 95). By the 1960s, sociologists could look back and report that the Catholic schools had "accelerated the acculturation of the Catholic immigrant groups—partly because they have consciously promoted 'Americanization' in a fashion that public schools could not have done without stirring up trouble from the ethnic communities" (Greeley and Rossi 1966, pp. 154–55).

Call it poetic injustice. In Europe, the Catholic church had often been strong enough to write orthodoxy into civil law. In the United States, Will Herberg has argued, the situation is reversed. Here, the civic doctrine, "the American Way of Life," capitalist individualism, has imposed itself on all the other churches, Catholic included, becoming the "common religion of Americans" (Herberg 1955, p. 85).[5] The Catholic faithful themselves have testified to their conversion, challenging those reactionaries who assert "that the bourgeois virtues of enterprise and thrift were somehow incompatible with true Catholicism, pointing out that the three men Christ restored to life were all men of wealth ... [and that] the ability to make 'frequent and handsome donations' indicated 'that a man has the right sort of zeal' " (an article in the *Catholic World*, quoted in Cross 1958, pp. 163-64). "There may be, after all, something in the American publicist's prophecy, Father Thomas Jefferson Jenkins noted contentedly, that, if the church modify the state, the state here will modify the views of the church" (in Cross 1958, p. 163).

The Immigrant Family

Recent scholarship has dethroned the thesis that the family disintegrated on impact with modern society. (For the thesis, see Handlin 1952; Thompson 1966; for debunkers, see Hareven 1977, p. 188; Bodnar 1985, ch. 2). Instead, the world of machines created a need for a haven from it, and so strengthened the family. What is more, the family was able to mediate the transition to capitalist life, and so cushion its blow. Kin integrated kin into the economy, welcoming newcomers with information about where to live, what jobs could be had, and how. Even at the gargantuan Amoskeag Textile Mill, for example, the family was able to protect itself as a circle of subjects against the objectifying tendency of the modern factory, by acting as a principal source of recruitment for the company, and even exercising some control over the placement of its members in the same workrooms (Hareven 1977, p. 194). Later, when the company demanded faster work, the network of kith again cushioned the blow: "Workers assisted relatives and friends in meeting their quotas, even if it meant a loss in their own piece-rate work. The presence of relatives reinforced the workers' collective strength in resisting corporation pressure, especially when the demand for speedup became overwhelming" (Hareven 1977, p. 195).

In such fashion, families could sometimes adjust so that the world was not out of control. But the world was never again to be in control, as it had been in the village. When family recruitment and placement together turned into worker solidarity at Amoskeag, the company simply disallowed the practice (Hareven 1977, p. 195).

Outside the workplace, the family was a refuge from impersonality, where the old ways were taught and lived. A good example is the surrender of paychecks even by adult immigrant children to the parents, like blood flowing to the heart, and thence to the organs. This ritual said, "the family is an organism, not a confederation."

Precisely because it was a refuge, private ground, the immigrant family was viewed by established Americans as the *sanctum sanctorum* of a pagan culture. And so they proceeded to invade it. One prong of their attack focused on removing the children from the home. Ellen Richards, a founder of the social work profession, wrote "[The school is] fast taking the place of the home, not because it wishes to do so, but because the home does not fulfill its functions" (quoted in Lasch 1977, p. 14). It was during this period that the penal system was reformed to treat the juvenile delinquent not as a criminal but as a "victim of circumstances." This made it possible to sentence juvenile offenders, without trial, to the custody of probation officers, who then assumed the mantle of parenthood. Parents who resisted this benevolence were easily dismissed. "When my son is so ruthlessly torn away from me it gives me much pain," wrote one mother, seized, no doubt, by the hysteria of the deranged (quoted in Lasch 1977, p. 16).

As the children were being led out of the immigrant household, the "helping professions" marched in. Government and industry together deployed an army of social workers, home economists, and visiting nurses to "counsel" the foreign born on almost every imaginable aspect of life. Predictably, immigrants resisted this invasion. Amoskeag workers "were actually reluctant to expose their children to the [company's social] programs. They preferred to center their social activities around their churches and ethnic clubs (Hareven 1982, p. 64). "Ford workers grumbled and griped, and knocked and kicked about Ford sociological investigations" (Meyer 1981, p. 165).

But a third prong of the invasion was not so easy to resist as these frontal assaults. The media of a consumptive economy—newspapers, magazines, later radio—did not so much attack the old culture as display the silken, ineluctable promise of the new. And between every line of scintillating copy was a single message: you are what you buy. Relentless repetition of this subliminal message, each time with subtle seductive changes, eventually monopolized the concept of "success." Given that standard, it is little wonder that the children of the immigrants rebelled against the ways of their fathers, who failed so miserably to measure up.

Thus bereft of parental standards, it is also no wonder that the second generation should have gravitated to the new lessons of life recently invented for them. The same army of helping professionals that had failed to convert the foreign born continued to proselytize among the foreign stock during caseworkers' home visits, parent-teacher conferences, marriage counseling sessions, in magazine articles, and, later, on radio and television talk shows. They began with an implicit assumption not surprising for persons of their station: that the culture is a healthy one. Anyone not getting along in it, therefore, needs to "adjust." Cannily, these counselors saw that the successful man would be an "organization man," one able to "interface" with his "team" in "buzz sessions." Accordingly, the means to the well-adjusted person was the new science, the new religion of "interpersonal relations." It replaced the "old morality of 'right and wrong,' 'guilt and sin,' " with a family whose goal was a socialization in the ability to "relate." "Today it requires more than mere enveloping love to prepare a person for a specifically challenging world. The child must learn practical social techniques of affiliating himself to others outside the family, neighborhood, and parish" (Margaret Lantis, in Lasch 1977, p. 105).

Such socialization may explain something of why the tradition-bound personality has been replaced, in our time, not by the unbound, autonomous personality, but by the conformist personality: "men and women who can be 'guided without force and led without leaders.... Modern man lives under the illusion that he knows what he wants, while he actually wants what he is *supposed* to want.' His 'free choice' is the consumer's choice of brands" (internal quotation from Erich Fromm, in Lasch 1977, p. 89).

The End of Ethnicity

It is hard to let go of a way of life. Even if one wanted to, so much of culture is "unconveyed, like melody or witchcraft" (Emily Dickinson, quoted in Luce 1978, p. 47). It is learned, not by formal instruction, but by intuiting and following behaviors that are often not cognized, much less questioned (Hall 1959).

So, remnants of southern European differences have endured, even into the third and fourth generations. Writing in the 1960s, Gerhard Lenski found white Protestants more likely to identify with "individualistic, competitive patterns of thought"; Catholics with the more "collectivistic, security-oriented, working-class patterns of thought... historically opposed to the Protestant Ethic and the spirit of capitalism" (1963, p. 113).

But those differences, as Lenski himself noted but did not emphasize enough, were statistically, not fundamentally, significant: "It is amazing how strong a hold the Protestant Ethic... has on all segments of the American population" (p. 90). Despite a 10-percentage-point lead by white Protestants, majorities of all groups surveyed, including working class Catholics (and blacks), believed in the Horatio Alger myth. Although Catholics were found less likely than Protestants to migrate away from their families in search of the American Dream, still, a majority of Catholics had done so (pp. 214–15). Later studies pronounced even such differences as exist between Protestants and Catholics "declining" (McCready and Greeley 1972; Holloway and George 1979, p. 120). By 1984, Italians and Poles evinced "social and political attitudes that scarcely distinguish them from English, Germans, and Scandinavians" (Glazer 1984, p. 2). Never asked to melt in, ethnicity has, at last, melted away. But this is no surprise. Even in the 1920s, the serene faith of the Americanizers had presaged it. For example, the spectacular ceremony of graduation from the Ford English School was:

a pageant in the form of a melting pot, where all the men descend from a boat scene representing the ᵥ₋essel on which they came over; down the gangway...

into a pot 15 feet in diameter and 7 feet high, which represents the Ford English School. Six teachers, three on either side, stir the pot with ten foot ladles representing nine months of teaching in the school. Into the pot 52 nationalities with their foreign clothes and baggage go.... Presently, the pot [begins] to boil over and out [come] the men dressed in their best American clothes and waving American flags (descriptions by DeWitt and Marquis, in Meyer 1981, pp. 60–61).

Of course, the real process of melting and remolding was not so neat, or so picturesque. It did not happen without leaving subliminal memories of the old culture. It did not happen quickly. It did not happen without suffering, or without resistance. But it did happen. And in the process, America lost something.

THE BLACK EXPERIENCE

Blacks have been more resistant to hegemonic institutions and ideas than other American ethnic groups. This is due to the very different experience that blacks, as opposed to white ethnic groups, have had here. First, color was a marker for blacks that distinguished them from society in a way that nationality did not distinguish white ethnics (Lieberson 1980). Other minority groups may also have been readily identified, such as Asians, but none posed the threat to dominant groups in society that blacks did due to their numbers. As an easily distinguished minority large enough to pose a threat, blacks found acceptance and entry into the dominant culture harder than white ethnics.

A second factor that distinguished the experience of blacks from that of white ethnics was the legacy of slavery. Both groups came in ships, but only blacks came in chains. Slavery was especially important as a point of difference between the two groups because a developed ideology of black inferiority emerged along with it (Frederickson 1971). The racism directed at blacks was more virulent and developed as an ideology than the prejudice that white ethnics encountered. Moreover, blacks were more vulnerable to these myths than other groups because they lacked political and economic power that other groups eventually accumulated to defend themselves. All groups, the Irish, the Jews, the Italians, the Poles, suffered humiliation and shame at the hands of dominant groups when they arrived. But no group found its dignity and humanity so assaulted by myths of inferiority as blacks.

Third, the economic and social conditions the two groups faced were very different. Newly arrived immigrants who started out on the social ladder of success could count on finding blacks below them. At the turn of the century in the North, blacks had fewer occupational choices open to them than newly arrived Europeans. Blacks were concentrated in service-sector jobs that paid less and offered fewer chances for generational mobility than manufacturing jobs that newly arrived white ethnics filled. In addition, blacks were banned from unions and thus had little job security. Finally, living conditions were worse for blacks as can be seen by the higher mortality rates they suffered (Lieberson 1980, pp. 41–47). Lieberson concludes his comparison of the life chances of urban blacks and newly arrived immigrants in the North at the turn of the century thusly: "It is a serious mistake to underestimate how far the new Europeans have come in the North and how hard it was, but it is equally erroneous to assume that the obstacles were as great as those faced by blacks or that the starting point was the same" (Lieberson 1980, p. 383).

Lastly, the immigrant and black experience differed with regard to how quickly and completely each group was included within the political community. Immigrants who had been in the United States for five years had rights of citizenship that were denied blacks whose families had been in this country for five generations. For instance, white ethnics had the right to vote, while blacks found themselves disenfranchised. While the law was used to harass and persecute new immigrant groups, they were at least included under the body of law that applied to the rest of society. Not so for blacks. In Southern states, where 75 percent of all blacks lived prior to World War I, their legal status was set by "Jim Crow" laws that applied exclusively to them. Not until 1965, 100 years after the abolition of slavery, were the full rights of citizenship extended to blacks and guaranteed by the federal government.

This distinctive history of blacks in the United States is "the solid core, the hard rock, non-mystical aspect of Negro American culture" (Blauner 1970, p. 147). It is the ambiguity of their history, being part of a culture that they recognize as their own but which rejected them in ways white ethnics never experienced, that has afforded blacks a certain distance from hegemonic institutions. On the one hand, blacks were more vulnerable and more exposed to American values than other ethnic groups because they were stripped of their African culture and have a longer history of settlement here. The only national identity they have is American. They are truly native sons.

On the other hand, American culture did not permit blacks "to share fully and participate equally" in it (Blauner 1970, p. 152). Unless blacks distanced themselves from American culture they would be scarred and disfigured by the racism to which they were exposed (Valentine 1971). Native sons were treated like invisible men. Maintenance of self-respect and dignity required aloofness from American culture because that culture was unwilling to grant them any.

Thus, history has created a "double consciousness" within blacks that W.E.B. Du Bois described eloquently: "One ever feels his twoness—an

American, a Negro; two souls, two thoughts, two unreconcilable strivings; two warring ideals in one black body" (1969, p. 17). As a result of this double consciousness "blacks have assimilated American values from a unique perspective, that of the outsider" (Blauner 1970, p. 152). Like whites, blacks are subject to the message that hegemonic institutions impart. Therefore, it is not surprising to find that blacks believe in individualism, believe that social mobility is available to all who apply themselves (Hamilton 1982), and that opportunities for success are evenly distributed (Schlozman and Verba 1979), almost as much as whites do. But it is the failure of the United States to live up to its own ideals—which blacks experience profoundly—that creates a critical perspective among blacks toward the values they hold. Being part of American culture, blacks believe in "American dreams of comfort, respectability and security as rewards for conventional individual effort" (Valentine 1972, p. 33). But for blacks those dreams have "Whites Only" signs attached to them.

Blacks perceive it to be the role of government to resolve the tension between the real (racial exclusion) and the ideal (equal opportunity) that they experience. As a result, blacks are more likely to support government activism and regulation—to make the American Dream available to them—than other groups (Nie, Verba, and Petrocik 1976, p. 255). To put it another way, blacks perceive that the only way they can achieve "American" ends, equal opportunity where people are judged by their merits not their color, is through "European" means, social regulation by the government. American blacks are our native social democratic movement.

The first section will trace the origins of the double consciousness of American blacks by reviewing the ambiguous relation blacks have had to American society. Unable to participate in American society as equals, humiliated due to their color, blacks developed separate institutions to create their own ties of community and sustain their self-confidence. These institutions, especially the black church, reflected as well as tried to ameliorate the distinctive tensions blacks felt—belonging to an American culture that held them in contempt.

The second section examines the consequences of this ambiguous relationship for black political attitudes and behavior. Politically excluded, socially isolated, victimized by racism and finding solace in their own institutions outside of white society, blacks formed a distinctive political community once they gained their civil rights. Due to their distinctive experience, their voting patterns and political attitudes diverge from the rest of the nation. The second section examines some of these differences.

Toward an Afro-American Culture

The double consciousness of American blacks arose originally out of the slave experience. Slavery created a separate black culture that drew on African origins but was thoroughly American. This double consciousness was shaped by the overweening paternalism of Southern planters and the effort by slaves to forge a separate culture within it.

Slaves in the American South were more vulnerable to the culture of their masters than other slave forces in the New World for three reasons. First, of all the slave forces in the New World, only the slave force in the American South was able to reproduce itself. The slave trade to the American South peaked between 1730–70 (Curtin 1971, p. 97). Additions to the slave labor force after those years occurred mainly through the natural growth of the slave population already present as opposed to new slaves brought from Africa. Thus, African influences were not continually renewed by the importation of new slaves. Rather, black slaves in the United States had many generations to assimilate the culture of their masters.

Second, Southern planters made a greater effort to acculturate their slaves than did other master classes in the New World. Relations between master and slave in the Old South were paternalistic. Paternalism held that, in exchange for the involuntary labor the slaves performed, the master was obliged to extend protection, direction, and care to his slaves (Genovese 1974, p. 4). Paternalism was designed to "confirm blacks to perpetual slavery and make it possible for them to accept their fate" (Genovese 1974, p. 51). Paternalism required masters to take an active interest in the welfare of their slaves. Southern planters tried to shape the sexual, religious, and cultural lives of their slaves as part of their paternalistic duty. In addition, the master's close living quarters to his slaves led to frequent personal and intimate contact between the two groups.

Third, slaves in the South did not see a chance to escape the exploitive paternalism of the planter class. Conditions in the South were not so favorable to revolt as they were for slaves in the Caribbean or in South America (Genovese 1974, p. 588). Contrary to conditions slaves encountered in other parts of the New World, slaves in the American South were surrounded by a hostile white majority, the master class was not internally divided, and slaveholding was decentralized—the average slaveholder in the South had 20 slaves, not 200 as in the Caribbean— which made collective organization for slaves difficult (Genovese 1974, pp. 588–93). A separate identify would have to be forged within the paternalism of the master class. There was no chance to forge one outside it.

Paternalism was a strategy the planters used to coax slaves to work hard and morally justify slavery to themselves. But the privileges that masters granted paternalistically, slaves accepted as their rights. Genovese writes:

> If the law said they had no rights to property, for example, but the local custom accorded them private garden plots, then woe to the master or overseer who summarily withdrew the "privilege." To those slaves the privilege had been a right, and the withdrawal an act of aggression not to be borne (1974, pp. 30–31).

Slaves did not passively accept the slaveholders' paternalism, but reinterpreted it to serve their own ends. Levine argues, "For all its horrors, slavery was never so complete a system of psychic assault that it prevented the slaves from carving out independent cultural forms" (Levine 1978, p. 30). By holding masters to the terms of their paternalistic exchange, slaves gained protection from the arbitrary rule of their masters and asserted rights. Within the terms of paternalism, blacks began to build a separate slave culture. A double consciousness was born.

One area in which slaves carved out their own folkways within the limits of paternalism was family structure. What made black family structure distinctive during slavery was not its brittle, matrifocal character as is commonly believed. Both these phenomena are recent, and today afflict only the low-income segment of the black community (Wilson 1980). On the contrary, Herbert Gutman found that black slaves enjoyed long, stable marriages (Gutman 1977). This marriage ideal was not simply copied from their masters, but was sustained by religious and moral codes from within the slave community. Some of the family practices of the slave community differed from the customs of their masters. For example. whereas it was common for whites to marry their cousins, it was unusual for blacks to do so (Gutman 1977, p. 9). Naming practices among slaves also differed from those of their masters. Slaves did not name infant daughters for their mothers, while whites did so frequently (Gutman 1977, p. 190). Finally, slave family structure was distinctive for its enlarged kin network. It was not unusual for the kin network to include people who were not blood relatives (Gutman 1977, pp. 217–19). For slaves, where forced separation from their family could occur at any time, fictive kin relations made the environment more stable and secure.

Slaves also sought to carve out a separate culture for themselves through folktales and music, the development of an oral tradition. The sharing of this oral tradition created a group consciousness among blacks that excluded whites. The shared oral tradition not only set blacks apart, but was a vehicle through which slaves could express their hopes and resentments.

Slave folktales, such as the trickster tales of Brer Rabbit, featured the victory of the weak over the strong. In the stories of Brer Rabbit, the universe is full of danger and Brer Rabbit must use his guile and cunning to escape the clutches of Brer Fox. Such tales encouraged contempt for the powerful and the search for ways to escape their control (Levine 1978, pp. 102–36). Carried forward to the present, these folktales continue to preach a strategy of subterfuge and caution toward whites.

The oral tradition also helped create group solidarity through song, especially spirituals. The "sorrow songs" told of suffering and disappointment, but also expressed a trust in the ultimate justice of things when "men will judge men by their souls and not by their skins" (Du Bois 1969, p. 189). The songs of the slaves expressed solidarity and nourished hope; they described in word and texture a misery that all slaves shared, but tempered this with the hope of future deliverance.

Another expression of a distinctive slave culture was religion. Slaves took their masters' Christian beliefs and made them over. Religious practice created a sacred world apart for the slaves. Slaves derived different lessons from the Christianity they had been taught than their masters intended them to learn. The Christianity that white preachers taught told slaves to obey their masters, that God's grace could be won only through faithful service, and that the enslavement of blacks fulfilled the biblical curse on Ham. But the slaves heard different messages coming from the Bible. For them, Christianity held that all men, black and white, were equal in God's eyes, that all men descended from Adam and Eve and thus shared a common brotherhood, that God was available to all who claimed him regardless of their race, and that God will redeem the righteous who suffer and will punish their oppressors, just as God helped the Hebrews defeat the Egyptians (Genovese 1974, pp. 209–80; Levine 1978, pp. 30–55). Slaves turned the master's theology of submission into a theology that granted the slaves dignity and provided them a moral standard with which to judge their actions and those of slaveholders.

When the slaves were emancipated, the ambiguity of the black's relationship to the rest of society remained as real in freedom as it had in slavery. On the one hand, Reconstruction saw blacks embrace white cultural practices in dress, manners, and public behavior (Williamson 1971). This, after all, was the culture they were familiar with through their long and intimate contact with it during slavery. On the other hand, they sought as little contact with white society as possible (Smallwood 1981). They sought to insulate themselves from the racism of whites, to live apart, but on their own terms. However, the end of Reconstruction, the return to political power of the planters in the Old South, meant that blacks would live apart, but on terms set by whites and not by themselves.

The apartheid system of the South created by "Jim Crow" laws, the separation of public facilities for blacks and whites, had the effect of throwing blacks on their own resources. Cut off from white society, a black middle class of lawyers, doctors, teachers, ministers, and entrepreneurs developed that catered to the needs of the black community now that the surrounding white society in the South would not. Ironically, "the wall of separation" created by Jim Crow laws "became a wall of protection" for the black middle class (Marable 1983). Institutions and organizations run by and for blacks appeared. Newspapers, publishing houses, an entertainment industry, schools and colleges, and voluntary organizations arose to serve the needs of the black community. Within such structures, gossip and ideas could be exchanged, the oral tradition passed on, and communal social ties established.

The spiritual and social center of this activity was the black church. The church performed countless tasks within the black community, from providing spiritual and moral guidance to organizing dances and picnics. "For the Negro masses in their social and cultural isolation, the Negro Church was a nation within a nation" (Frazier 1969, p. 7). Ideologically, the black church's commitment to the "equality of all persons under God regardless of race or any other natural quality" was categorical and unconditional (Paris 1985, p. 11). It spoke of the brotherhood and common humanity of all men and supported the integration of blacks into American society as the fulfillment of this prophetic principle. At the same time the black church espoused brotherhood, it justified its separate organizational existence with reference to how white churches violated this principle in practice. Blacks were either placed in the back of white churches or were permitted to pray only after the service for whites had concluded. In 1900, Bishop Tanner of the African Methodist Episcopal Church articulated the reasons for a separate black church:

The difference ... between our Church and the churches of the other race today is ... in a fundamental Christian principle: The question of the substantial oneness and brotherhood of all men. ... It is the policy of their churches to discriminate between their members on account of their color and conditions. They refuse to judge men by their merits but made color and conditions a test of acceptance. ... We hold, teach and practice that God is no respecter of persons. This may be spoken of as the distinctive note of African Methodism. ... Either the darker races, who are vastly stronger than the white race numerically, are brothers or they are not. For one to admit it in words and deny it in practice is hypocrisy (quoted in Paris 1985, p. 19).

In the contrast between the assimilationist ideas it espoused and the racial separatism of its institutional existence, the black church embodied the double consciousness of the community it served.

The great migration of blacks from the South to the urban centers of the North and the success of the civil rights movement in the 1960s have brought blacks into closer contact with hegemonic institutions. Compared to just 20 years ago, tremendous progress has been made in integrating blacks into American society. Southern cities, like Birmingham,

Alabama, that had prevented blacks from exercising their right to vote in the 1960s now have black mayors. Despite these gains, however, blacks remain concentrated in certain schools, sectors of the job market, and residential neighborhoods. This racial exclusion continues to fuel critical and antagonistic elements within black culture today as it has in the past.

Blacks continue to pray separately from whites in their own churches. Few blacks have chosen to become members of white churches now that those churches accept blacks as full and equal members. For instance, black Baptists and Methodists prefer to remain separate from their white counterparts although white Baptist and Methodist Churches are now open to them. Nor has the integration of churches led to any switch by blacks from their current Protestant affiliations to "higher status" Protestant denominations such as Episcopalianism or Presbyterianism (Glenn and Gothard 1977, p. 55). Blacks continue to be attracted to separate black churches because of the message of brotherhood they preach and the expressive forms of worship they encourage.

While white churches are losing their hold on their parishioners to other diversions, this is not true of the black church. From 1966 to 1973, the church attendance of white Protestant church members declined, while it increased for blacks. One analysis of religious trends in the United States argues that "black religion provides a reservoir of strength and perseverance which has not been maintained by white majority religious groups" (Carroll, Johnson, and Marty 1979, p. 107). The black church is more successful than white churches in competing with secular institutions for the commitment of its parishioners because it continues to express the hope of the black community for complete integration and to serve as a haven for blacks from the racism they encounter outside.

Another part of the cultural infrastructure of the black community that continues to persist despite strides toward integration is the black press. The black press "includes more publications than any other racial minority group press in this country" (Wolseley 1971, p. 10). It consists of approximately 225 newspapers and 65 magazines with a combined circulation of 4,000,000 readers (p. 10).

Substantively, the black press preaches the gospel of success. Magazines like *Ebony* portray successful blacks and describe their achievements. Responding to this, E. Franklin Frazier, a black sociologist, criticized the black press for presenting an unrepresentative picture of black society, conjuring up "a world of make believe" for its readers and promulgating "bourgeois values" (Frazier 1957, p. 146). It may be argued that this selective picture of achievement presented by the black press promotes black self-esteem. But it does so in a way fully consonant with the dominant values of American society.

At the same time that the black press is socially conservative and politically moderate, they cannot avoid performing the function that called them into being: to protest and expose racism and to present a viewpoint on the news that is sensitive to blacks, which the white press cannot be trusted to present (Barrow 1977). The black press was vehement in its opposition to the lynching of blacks and the segregation of the armed forces, and threw its support behind such black heroes as Jackie Robinson and Joe Louis who were vilified in the white press. While the black press extolled the American Dream of success, the press was also forced to play a protest role and expose the dark side of that dream because racism prevented blacks from achieving it.

Finally, despite the increasing social acceptance of blacks, music is a racial divide that shows few signs of being crossed. Radio programming is directed at racially different markets, record purchases break down along racial lines and, while some black musicians have been able to cross over and attract white listeners, it is very rare for a white musician to attract a black audience. Moreover, whenever whites have tried to appropriate and assimilate black music, for example when swing music emerged from jazz or rock music from rhythm and blues, blacks invented new musical forms to preserve the racial singularity of their music. With regard to jazz, "no sooner had some whites learned the special techniques of black music than Negro musicians developed new, more difficult, techniques to replace them" (Sidran 1981, p. 60). Musical innovation was the result of blacks trying to devise a music "they [whites] couldn't play" (Kofsky 1970, p. 32). This unceasing attempt to develop exclusively black musical idioms and techniques was necessary to prevent whites from profiting from black music. But it was also necessary to preserve the distinctiveness of black music if it was to continue to play its historical role as an expression of the black experience (Sidran 1981). This is where black music derives its emotional power. Slaves sang spirituals to give them faith in their eventual delivery from bondage. The blues expressed the despair and helplessness black sharecroppers felt under the Jim Crow system of the segregated south. Where change was impossible due to racial oppression, the blues offered a cathartic release from life's burdens by singing about them (Haralambos 1975). Jazz, on the other hand, was an urban sound (Sidran 1981, p. 33) that developed as blacks migrated North. Black music was constantly renovated in order to retain its racial exclusivity, its function as an expression of the black experience.

Black music derived its emotional power not only from its connection to black history, but also from the alienation it expressed. As a result of its origins, black music could not help but express the distance blacks felt from the dominant culture. When jazz first appeared, its dissenting qualities were so apparent that clergy, ladies clubs, and music teachers tried to prevent it from being played (Leonard 1962). Jazz's raw, emotional, bawdy, improvisational qualities were at odds with upper class Puritanical values of restraint, propriety, and control (Sidran 1981). Its discordant sound implicitly rejected assimilation; and, every time jazz risked being tamed, the idiom was redefined to preserve its rejection of upper class values and its identification with the black experience. Thus, despite greater cultural approval of black art forms, black music continues to give voice to the hopes and tensions of the black community and express the distance blacks feel from dominant cultural norms.

The institutional and artistic expressions that blacks developed under the imposed isolation of the "separate but equal" doctrine have not disintegrated with the end of that pernicious doctrine. These institutions continue to support a separate, critical black culture that is reflected in daily life (for instance, church membership and musical taste) and in political attitudes and behavior. It is to the latter we now turn.

Black Political Culture

United by a common history of slavery and legal segregation, sustained by a separate black culture with its own institutions, and socialized by their concentration in certain schools, jobs, and residential areas, blacks developed their own political culture. Black political behavior and attitudes diverge from the mainstream. Deprived of their political rights for so long, blacks now make use of them with a sophistication and unity few groups can match. Two analysts of black political behavior aver that "No other group identifies its self-interest so well, or promotes it so forcefully or consistently" (Lewis and Schneider 1983, p. 13). The distinctiveness of black political culture is evidence that blacks have resisted incorporation into the dominant culture more than other groups.

Ethnic groups tend to identify with one of the two major parties, but no group is so united in its partisanship as blacks. Between 1964 and 1980, Democratic presidential candidates received between 87 and 99 percent of the black vote. Support for the Democratic Party persists at these extraordinarily high levels even when one controls for ideology and class position. While support for Ronald Reagan in the 1980 election broke down along ideological lines for whites, this was not true of blacks. Only 6 percent of those blacks who identified themselves as conservative voted for Ronald Reagan. Nor did class position disturb solid support for Democrats among blacks. As one went up the class structure, support for Democratic candidates did not decline as it did among whites, but remained over 90 percent even among blacks in high class positions. Black voting is bloc voting (Lewis and Schneider 1983).

The political attitudes of blacks are as distinctive as their voting behavior. Both show a great deal of divergence from the rest of the population. In their examination of black political attitudes, Nie, Verba, and Petrocik found that "no other group is as distinctively liberal as American blacks" (1976, p. 255). In each of the issue areas used by the authors to measure ideology, blacks consistently preferred the liberal position. In fact, an extraordinary 60 percent of all blacks preferred the most liberal position across all five issue areas. Nie, Verba, and Petrocik comment that to find such a uniform pattern of response within a group is "an unusual phenomenon in survey data (1976, p. 254).

Controlling for the effects of class does not disturb the extreme liberalism of American blacks. Blacks in higher class positions are almost as liberal in their issue preferences as lower class blacks. The liberalism of this group can be explained by their sensitivity to racial injustice. Blacks in higher class positions are more skeptical and cynical about equal opportunity than lower class blacks. Schlozman and Verba found "an extraordinary 94% of blacks in the highest occupational categories feel that whites enjoy unfair advantages" (1979, p. 171). Yet when probed about their own lives, blacks in high class positions were quite sanguine about opportunities available to them and predicted still greater opportunities for their children. Taking into consideration how high status blacks feel about their own lives, Schlozman and Verba attribute the liberalism of higher status blacks to the "residual inequalities" this group perceives between blacks and whites (1979, p. 173). But it may also be that this group is so liberal because their political views are not derived from their personal experiences. Race consciousness, identification with the black community, is very strong among high status blacks (Schwartz and Schwartz 1976, pp. 158–59). As a result, their views are "based on a perception of the black community as a whole to the political system and not just the impact of personal experience" (Friedrich, quoted in Abramson 1983, p. 223). Thus, their liberalism derives from their perception that blacks in general lack equal opportunity, although they may not feel this is true of their own lives. Due to their strong race consciousness, that is, their perception that the black community as a whole suffers from racial discrimination, high status blacks are likely to hold very liberal views.

Since the 1950s, blacks have moved consistently left on the political spectrum to the point that they can uniformly be considered extreme liberals. They firmly believe that it is the responsibility of government to provide jobs for the unemployed, health care, and a decent standard of living for all its citizens. The social democratic character of black political attitudes has pushed them further and further from the modal point of public opinion (Nie, Verba, and Petrocik 1976, p. 255). No fact speaks as loudly as this in supporting our view that blacks have resisted incorporation, that the pull of hegemonic institutions is weaker among blacks than among any other American ethnic group.

Racism and Incorporation

This chapter has argued that blacks evince a dual consciousness. That is, like other Americans subject to hegemonic institutions, they receive the values and ideas those institutions impart. But they are more skeptical and critical of the messages they receive than other ethnic groups, due to their history of political exclusion and cultural isolation. As a group that is poorer and has suffered more discrimination than any other, blacks are more cynical and have less stake in believing the myths that society generates about itself.

It is possible that as racism wanes, as racial barriers to mobility recede, and as parallel black institutions lose their vigor, blacks will succumb to the hegemonic culture like other ethnic groups before them. The political and social inclusion of blacks in American society is fairly recent. Perhaps, with time, integration will bring acculturation as it did with other groups. This, of course, is an optimistic view of race relations and there is no reason to believe that it will be achieved.

But even if our optimism is satisfied and race relations do improve, it does not necessarily mean that the distrust and skepticism blacks feel toward hegemonic institutions will subside. It depends upon how integration is achieved. If equal opportunity for blacks requires a social movement to achieve it, as civil rights did, then race consciousness will increase and reinforce distrust and cynicism toward the dominant culture.

Moreover, while integration may erode the skepticism blacks feel toward society's own claims, history provides a long memory for a people. Like the Jews, the history of racial oppression that blacks have suffered may create timeless feelings of alienation and vulnerability, regardless of the economic success and integration that blacks achieve.

If race relations do not improve, there is no reason to believe that black resistance to the dominant culture will subside. If race relations do improve, the consequences may not be any different.

CONCLUSION

The ethnic cultures that insulate people from the pull of capitalist individualism are eroding. The institutions that sustained these cultures could not compete with institutions that propounded the dominant culture and were either better funded or state supported. White ethnics found their island communities give way to the influence of the schools, the media, and the State. While black culture, too, has flirted with incorporation into the dominant ethos, the ongoing fact of racism prevents it from decaying to the same extent.

The loss of these ethnic cultures should not be romanticized. They were, after all, often parochial and intolerant of others. The diversity they contributed to American life surely made American society more vibrant and exciting, but their passing should not be mourned for this reason. Rather, the decay of these ethnic cultures is a loss because they offered protection and respite from the lonely and incessant struggle for success that capitalist individualism requires. And for this reason, we are poorer without them.

NOTES

1. The allusion is to Hartz's argument (1955, p. 5; see Chapter 1 for a discussion of this argument).

2. Herberg's scenario seems to imply that southern and eastern Europeans had no sense of ethnic and national identity prior to their immigration. There is considerable evidence to the contrary. Several sources suggest that a national identity *was* fostered and preserved in these areas by the indigenous church. Abramson puts the point generally: when a conqueror brings a new church to the land he occupies, then faithfulness to the indigenous church is somehow an assertion of the peoplehood of the natives (Abramson 1973, p. 132).

3. For a rejoinder to Thomas Sowell's suggestion that immigration was for many a rejection of the old ways and an embrace of competitive individualism, see Thomas Bodnar, who points out that the goal of most immigrants was to return to the old country. Indeed, celebrants of the American Dream have made us forget how high the return rate was (Sowell 1981, pp. 283–84; Bodnar 1985, pp. 52 ff.). From 25 to 60 percent did return, and more would have, had they not been "immobilized" by their closeness to "the margin of existence" (Handlin 1952, p. 82).

4. Max Weber, whose account of Protestant-Catholic cultural differences is still the most erudite, points out that Luther translated this verse (somewhat redundantly): "Let each man remain in that calling to which he was called" (Weber 1958, p. 80).

5. I do not mean to slight the importance of a recent greening of the Catholic Church, as reflected, for example, in the recent Pastoral Letter on Economic Justice from the American Conference of Bishops. But here is another poetic injustice: the very unanimity that the church helped to create is now unassailable, even by the church. A member of the staff that prepared the pastoral letter has told me that the authors could not consider an indictment of capitalism itself, because "we wanted to be taken seriously."

REFERENCES

Abramson, Harold. 1973. *Ethnic Diversity in Catholic America.* New York: John Wiley and Sons.

Abramson, Paul R. 1983. *Political Attitudes in America: Formation and Change.* San Francisco: W. H. Freeman and Co.

Barrow, Dr. Lionel C. Jr. 1977. "The Role of the Black Press in Liberation Struggle." In the *Black Press Handbook–Sesquicentennial: 1827–1977,* National Newspaper Publishers Association, pp. 32–36.

Blauner, Robert. 1970. "Black Culture: Lower Class Result or Ethnic Creation?" In *Soul,* edited by Lee Rainwater. New Brunswick, N.J.: Transaction Books.

Bodnar, John. 1985. *The Transplanted.* Bloomington: Indiana University Press.

———. 1982. *Workers' World.* Baltimore: Johns Hopkins University Press.

Bodnar, John, Roger Simon, and Michael P. Weber. 1982. *Lives of Their Own.* Urbana: University of Illinois Press.

Bowles, Samuel, and Herbert Gintis. 1976. *Schooling in Capitalist America.* New York: Basic Books.

Carroll, Jackson W., Douglas W. Johnson, and Martin E. Marty. 1979. *Religion in America: 1950 to the Present.* New York: Harper and Row.

Cross, Robert D. 1958. *The Emergence of Liberal Catholicism in America.* Cambridge, Mass.: Harvard University Press.

Curtin, Philip D. 1971. "The Slave Trade and the Atlantic Basin: Intercontinental Perspectives." In *Key Issues in the Afro-American Experience to 1877*, vol. I, edited by Nathaniel I. Huggins, Martin Kilson, and Daniel M. Fox. New York: Harcourt, Brace, Jovanovich.

Du Bois, W.E.B. 1969. *The Souls of Black Folk.* New York: Fawcett Books.

Ewen, Stuart, and Elizabeth Ewen. 1982. *Channels of Desire.* New York: McGraw-Hill.

Exoo, Calvin F. 1983. "Ethnic Culture and Political Language in Two American Cities." *The Journal of Ethnic Studies* 11:79–105.

Frazier, E. Franklin. 1957. *Black Bourgeoisie.* Glencoe, Ill.: The Free Press.

———. 1969. *The Negro Church in America.* New York: Schocken Books.

Fredrickson, George M. 1971. "Toward a Social Interpretation of the Development of American Racism." In *Key Issues in the Afro-American Experience to 1877*, vol. I, edited by Nathaniel I. Huggins, Martin Kilson, and Daniel M. Fox. New York: Harcourt, Brace, Jovanovich.

Galush, William J. 1977. "Faith and Fatherland: Dimensions of Polish-American Ethnoreligion." In *Immigrants and Religion in Urban America*, edited by Randall M. Miller and Thomas D. Marzik. Philadelphia: Temple University Press.

Gambino, Richard. 1974. *Blood of My Blood: The Dilemma of the Italian American.* Garden City, N.Y.: Doubleday.

Genovese, Eugene D. 1974. *Roll, Jordan, Roll: The World the Slaves Made.* New York: Vantage Books.

Glazer, Nathan. 1984. "The Structure of Ethnicity." *Public Opinion*, October/November, pp. 2–6.

Glenn, Norman D. and Erin Gothard. 1977. "The Religion of Blacks in the United States: Some Recent Trends and Current Characteristics." *American Journal of Sociology* 83:433–51.

Golab, Caroline. 1977. *Immigrant Destinations.* Philadelphia: Temple University Press.

Gordon, Milton M. 1964. *Assimilation in American Life.* New York: Oxford University Press.

Greeley, Andrew. 1972. *That Most Distressful Nation: The Taming of the American Irish.* Chicago: Quadrangle Books.

Greeley, Andrew, and Peter Rossi. 1966. *The Education of Catholic Americans.* Chicago: Aldine.

Gutman, Herbert. 1976. *Work, Culture, and Society in Industrializing America.* New York: Random House.

———. 1977. *The Black Family in Slavery and Freedom: 1750–1925.* New York: Vintage Press.

Hall, Edward. 1959. *The Silent Language*. Garden City, N.Y.: Doubleday.

Hamilton, Charles V. 1982. "Integrating the American Dream." *Public Opinion*, June/July, pp. 45–47.

Handlin, Oscar. 1952. *The Uprooted*. Boston: Little, Brown.

Haralambos, Michael. 1975. *Right On: From Blues to Soul in Black America*. New York: Drake.

Hareven, Tamara K. 1982. *Family Time and Industrial Time*. New York: Cambridge University Press.

————. 1977. "Family Time and Industrial Time: Family and Work in a Planned Corporation Town, 1900–1924." In *Family and Kin in Urban Communities, 1700–1930*, edited by Tamara K. Hareven, pp. 187–206. New York: New Viewpoints.

Hartz, Louis. 1955. *The Liberal Tradition in America*. New York: Harcourt, Brace.

Herberg, Will. 1955. *Protestant–Catholic–Jew*. Garden City, N.Y.: Doubleday.

Higham, John. 1955. *Strangers in the Land*. New Brunswick, N.J.: Rutgers University Press.

Holloway, Harry, and John George. 1979. *Public Opinion*. New York: St. Martin's Press.

Judd, Dennis R. 1979. *The Politics of American Cities*. Boston: Little, Brown.

Karson, Marc. 1984. "Catholic Anti-Socialism." In *Failure of a Dream*. rev. ed., edited by John H. M. Haslett and Seymour Martin Lipset, pp. 82–102. Berkeley: University of California Press.

Katz, Michael B. 1971. *Class, Bureaucracy, and Schools*. New York: Praeger.

Kivisto, Peter. 1984. *Immigrant Socialists in the United States: The Case of Finns and the Left*. London and Toronto: Associated University Presses.

Kleppner, Paul. 1967. "The Politics of Change in the Midwest." Unpublished Ph.D. dissertation, Univ. of Pittsburg.

Kleppner, Paul, Walter Dean Burham, Ronald D. Formisano, Samuel P. Hays, Richard Jensen, and William G. Shade. 1981. *The Evolution of American Electoral Systems*. Westport, Conn.: Greenwood Press.

Kofsky, Frank. 1970. *Black Nationalism and the Revolution in Music*. New York: Pathfinder Press.

Krickus, Richard. 1976. *Pursuing the American Dream*. Garden City, N.Y.: Anchor Press.

Lasch, Christopher. 1977. *Haven in a Heartless World: The Family Besieged*. New York: Basic Books.

Leinenweber, Charles. 1984. "Socialism and Ethnicity." In *Failure of a Dream*, rev. ed., edited by John H. M. Haslett and Seymour Martin Lipset, pp. 285–90. Berkeley: University of California Press.

Lenski, Gerhard. 1963. *The Religious Factor*. Garden City, N.Y.: Anchor Press.

Leonard, Neil. 1962. *Jazz and the White Americans: The Acceptance of a New Art Form*. Chicago: University of Chicago Press.

Levine, Lawrence W. 1978. *Black Culture and Black Consciousness*. New York: Oxford University Press.

Lewis, I. A., and William Schneider. 1983. "Black Voting, Bloc Voting, and the Democrats." *Public Opinion* 6, 5:12–15.

Lieberson, Stanley. 1980. *A Piece of the Pie: Blacks and White Immigrants since 1880*. Berkeley: University of California Press.

Luce, William. 1978. *The Belle of Amherst*. Boston: Houghton-Mifflin.

McClymer, John F. 1982. "The Americanization Movement and the Education of the Foreign-Born Adult, 1914–25." In *American Education and the European Immigrant: 1840–1940*, edited by Bernard J. Weiss, pp. 96–116. Urbana: University of Illinois Press.

McCready, William, and Andrew Greeley. 1972. "An End of American Catholicism?" *America* 125:334–38.

Marable, Manning. 1983. *How Capitalism Underdeveloped Black America*. Boston: South End Press.

Meyer III, Stephen J. 1981. *The Five Dollar Day*. Albany: State University of New York Press.

Nie, Norman H., Sidney Verba, and John R. Petrocik. 1976. *The Changing American Voter*. Cambridge, Mass.: Harvard University Press.

Novak, Michael. 1971. *The Rise of the Unmeltable Ethnics*. New York: Macmillan.

Paris, Peter J. 1985. *The Social Teaching of the Black Churches*. Philadelphia: Fortress Press.

Schlozman, Kay, and Sidney Verba. 1979. *Injury to Insult*. Cambridge, Mass.: Harvard University Press.

Schwartz, Sandra Kenyon, and David C. Schwartz. 1976. "Convergence and Divergence in Political Orientations between Blacks and Whites: 1960–1973." *Journal of Social Issues* 32:153–68.

Sidran, Ben. 1981. *Black Talk*. New York: Decapo Press.

Smallwood, James M. 1981. *Time of Hope, Time of Despair*. Port Washington, N.Y.: Kennikat Press.

Sowell, Thomas. 1981. *Ethnic America*. New York: Basic Books.

Stack, Carol B. 1975. *All Our Kin*. New York: Harper and Row.

Thompson, E. P. 1966. *The Making of the English Working Class*. New York: Vintage Books.

Tyack, David. 1974. *The One Best System*. Cambridge, Mass.: Harvard University Press.

Valentine, Charles A. 1971. "Deficit, Difference, and Bicultural Modes of A-A Behavior." *Harvard Educational Review* 41:137–57.

———. 1972. "Black Studies and Anthropology: Scholarly and Political Interests in Afro-American Culture." *Current Topics in Anthropology*, module 15, 3:15–53.

Vecoli, Rudolph J. 1984. "Comment on 'Socialism and Ethnicity.' " In *Failure of a Dream*, rev. ed., edited by John H. M. Haslett and Seymour Martin Lipset, pp. 269–84. Berkeley: University of California Press.

———. 1978. "Prelates and Peasants: Italian Immigrants and the Church." In *The Other Catholics*, edited by Keith Dyrud, Michael Novak, and Rudolph J. Vecoli. New York: Arno Press.

———. 1977. "Cult and Occult in Italian American Culture: The Persistence of a Religious Heritage." In *Immigrants and Religion in Urban America*, edited by Randall M. Miller and Thomas D. Marzik, pp. 25–47. Philadelphia: Temple University Press.

Weber, Max. 1958. *The Protestant Ethic and the Spirit of Capitalism*. Translated by Talcott Parsons. New York: Charles Scribner's Sons.

Williamson, Joel R. 1971. "Black Self Assertion before and after Emancipation."

In *Key Issues in the Afro-American Experience to 1877*, vol. I, edited by Nathaniel I. Huggins, Martin Kilson, and Daniel M. Fox. New York: Harcourt, Brace, Jovanovich.

Wilson, William Julius. 1980. *The Declining Significance of Race.* Chicago: University of Chicago Press.

Wolseley, Roland E. 1971. *The Black Press, USA.* Ames: Iowa State University Press.

Zangwill, Israel. 1909. *The Melting Pot.* New York: Macmillan.

8

Looking Upward

Calvin F. Exoo

Sisyphus was a subversive. Out of the Underworld on a weekend pass from his fate, he went AWOL. The best threats of the powers that used to be could not quell his rebellion. His punishment, although terrible, came naturally to a man who would not be resigned to the way things are.

The gods... condemned Sisyphus to ceaselessly rolling a rock to the top of a mountain, whence the stone would fall back of its own weight. They had thought with some reason that there is no more dreadful punishment than futile and hopeless labor.[1]

Today, those of us who are unresigned often ask what has gone wrong. Why is there no alternative, no democracy, no socialism? We hide our faces, for a moment, in the innocence of those questions. At our age, it is an innocence we probably should have outgrown. Our age being one in which individualism has become narcissism, and the "me" decade of self-absorption has given way to the "mine" decade of self-aggrandizement. Sisyphus would have known the meaning of that crashing declension. Its meaning is the divine irony. Human hearts that know of justice, in a world that probably never will.

One sees... the huge stone... the face screwed up, the cheek tight against the stone, the shoulder bracing the clay-covered mass, the foot wedging against it, the fresh start with arms outstretched, the wholly human security of two earth-clotted hands. At the very end of his long effort measured by skyless space and time without depth, the purpose is achieved. Then Sisyphus watches the stone rush down in a few moments toward that lower world whence he will have to push it up again toward the summit.

This book has been about some of what we are up against in the hard rock of hegemony. "Pessimism of the intellect," Gramsci might have called it; it was part of his motto. But for Gramsci, who also understood the divine irony, there was a more important part: "optimism of the will" (1971, p. 175).

He goes back down to the plain. It is during that return, that pause, that Sisyphus interests me. . . . I see that man going back down with a heavy yet measured step toward the torment of which he will never know the end. That hour like a breathing space which returns as surely as his suffering, that is the hour of consciousness. At each of those moments when he leaves the heights and gradually sinks toward the lairs of the gods, he is superior to his fate. He is stronger than his rock. . . . Sisyphus, proletarian of the gods, powerless and rebellious, knows the whole extent of his wretched condition; it is what he thinks of during his descent. The lucidity that was to constitute his torture at the same time crowns his victory. There is no fate that cannot be surmounted by scorn. . . . "I conclude that all is well," says Oedipus, and that remark is sacred. It echoes in the wild and limited universe of man. It teaches that all is not, has not been, exhausted. It drives out of this world a god . . . with a preference for futile sufferings. It makes of fate a human matter, which must be settled among men.

Today, the mountain before us seems more unyielding than ever. In spite of that, because of that, the men and women of the counterculture are all around us, drawing a last deep breath, rolling up shirt sleeves, *choosing* the rock, relishing its challenge.

They are there, in any recent issue of a paper like *Afterimage*—a chronicle of independent filmmaking, video production, photography. There are their efforts to string together a national television network of independent—usually countercultural—public access operations around the country. There, too, are reviews of the ongoing production of stylistically and politically critical films: one of them documents the direct and self-conscious attack on advertising in public places of a billboard graffiti artist; another, the day-to-day effects of U.S. foreign policy and corporate activity in the Third World; a third contrasts the message of Charlie Chaplin's films with the use being made of them by an IBM ad campaign.

Sisyphus' sons and daughters are there in journalism, challenging that profession with one of their own, challenging the notion that establishment mouthpieces and sensational pictures are all the news that's fit to print. They are there on the outside, in their own publications, in *Mother*

Jones, In These Times, The Guardian, the *Progressive,* the *Village Voice.* And they are there on the inside, alumni of the underground at work in the mainstream media, pushing out the boundaries of freedom of the press (Peck 1985).

They are there in the workplace. At bay for decades, the labor movement may at last be ready to do the only thing it can: fight back. Labor journals and newsletters are yeasty with radical departures from strategic business as usual: reporting and proposing "in-plant" strategies of non-cooperation; public campaigns against corporate goliaths; coalitions with the unemployed, with farmers, with women, and with blacks; the raising of the political unconsciousness of union members and the public; democratization of unions; democratization of the workplace through worker representation on corporate boards, worker self-management, employee ownership, and even nationalization of industry (see, for example, *Labor Research Review* or recent issues of *Labor Notes*). One way or another, all these departures and their bold proponents convey a common message: consumerism has been a bowl of pottage; workers want their birthright back. They want democracy. When one beleaguered organizer allowed that, for him, it was "no fun anymore," another replied, "Hell, it's just starting to get fun." It was his way of saying, "I conclude that all is well."

The unresigned are there in the schools. Some of them have joined forces to form the Committee on Correspondence for Public Schools. It is an information clearinghouse and political coalition of teachers, administrators, parents, academics, and others militating against the reactionary tendencies currently coursing through the ministries of education in Washington and the states. On another front, teachers' unions have renewed their call for "professionalization." Despite the pretensions of that word, theirs is a call for an end to top-down management of their teaching. It is a demand that a democratic people be put in charge of their own work lives; that critical thinking be allowed to come to its own conclusions; that, as Bryan used to say, "the people be allowed to make their own mistakes."

The rebellious are at work in politics. Having taken over city governments from Burlington, Vermont, to Santa Monica, California, they have come together in the Conference on Alternative State and Local Public Policies to nationally disseminate their call for less of the same, politics as unusual. Meanwhile the Association of Community Organizations for Reform Now (ACORN) has built itself into a national organization to wage its "protracted confrontation with the Democratic Party" (Delgado 1982). Electorally, the resistance has proven hydra-headed. Whether outside the major parties, as the Citizens Party usually was, or inside, as in the case of the Rainbow Coalition, their opposition is unstilled.

But often, the increasing cost of free speech is too high. When that happens, when the rebels literally cannot afford the election campaign, the film production costs, the price of newsprint, then they are there organizing in the free spaces of society. In the backyards, the storefronts, the churches, the ethnic halls. "In New York City alone, more than 3,000 block clubs developed from 1975 to 1978.... The ... National Commission on Neighborhoods listed more than 8,000 community organizations, almost all formed since 1970" (Boyte 1984, p. 27). Increasingly, these organizations are moving beyond the shallow soil of immediate, tangible concessions; they are sinking deep roots in communally-cultivated, communally-lived values (Boyte 1984, pp. 129–36).

All Sisyphus' silent joy is contained therein. His fate belongs to him. His rock is his thing. Likewise, the absurd man, when he contemplates his torment, silences all the idols. In the universe suddenly restored to its silence, the myriad wondering little voices of the earth rise up. Unconscious, secret calls, invitations from all the faces, they are the necessary reverse and price of victory.

Recently, a number of writers from far-flung fields have converged on a hopeful proposition: that the deep descent of the last decade is only a harbinger of higher peaks. Their argument is this: in the early 1970s, there began what Gramsci would have called an "organic crisis" of capitalism—one of its contradictions had matured (1971, p. 210). For one thing, foreign opportunities for profit making had been eagerly exploited with foreign investment, which meant home-front disinvestment, and the two together had produced foreign competition. U.S. productivity growth declined. So did real income. Suddenly, the hush money that labor had long accepted from business was drying up. Business deployed several strategies to keep its profits from doing likewise, while keeping the lid on labor.

One of them was the cultural campaign. It has been on view throughout this book. It is a catalyst of the recent sea change in all the cultural realms we have reviewed. The change that has brought us Rambo, the New Right, back to basics, Mario the Moderate, new friends for the contras at the New York *Times*, union-busting, neo-conservatism, and so on. It is a Sherman's march through the New Deal, a declaration of individualism of a more purely capitalist strain. In this time of crisis more than ever, it declares with renewed resolve, what's good for corporate America is what's good for America.

Concomitant with the attack on New Deal ideology came one on its programs. Government retrenched. Regulations were "trimmed." Welfare benefits were "limited." Capital was unbound. Workers were chastened. As the holes in the safety net grew larger, workers found themselves clinging to even lower and lower pay, fewer benefits, more and more dangerous work.

The final prong of the strategy was a massive reinvestment, out of those industries where competition was keenest, into new "growth opportunities." This caused a "sweeping change in the international division of labor," which left the United States a center of administrative, scientific, technical, and financial services (Aronowitz 1983). This, too, wonderfully focused the minds of working people, as it first swept them out of their jobs in unionized industries, and then threw some of them non-unionized, low-paying lifelines from the service sector.

So much for declension. Where, for goodness sake, is the hope in this bleak history? First, as the progress of earlier ascents came crashing down, "they left in their wake a profound transformation" (Piven and Cloward 1982, p. 118). For one thing, they created a new "moral economy"—suffer at least the disabled, the young, the old, the jobless to come to the state, it says. As we saw in Chapter 2, that charity has thus far not been withdrawn. For another, the agencies set up to administer those programs were the ballast of a new "iron triangle"—this one with poor and working class people at its apex. Those programs created an apparatus "staffed by millions of people who are civil servants and social workers and construction workers and teachers and doctors and mental health workers" (Piven and Cloward 1982, p. 120). They are organizers and lobbyists for the poor. Pushed hard enough by the new corporate offensive, they may become the resistance movement of a new class war.

By now, labor unions should be prepared to join them. The new order of things—increasing capital mobility and a shrinking American pie—has meant a decade of irrefutable ultimatums: take it or watch us leave. It is painfully clear that the salad days of the bargaining strategy are over. But that may be just the darkness needed to make a new dawn welcome. What may become clear is that all the alternatives to gun-to-the-head bargaining—alternatives like plant-closing legislation, government-assisted employee buyouts, nationalization—are declarations of class war. A war that must begin in the cultural trenches, winning the hearts and minds of workers away from capitalist individualism.

Then there are the "new workers," the ununionized, scientific, technical, clerical, and administrative workers. The growing white-collar leviathan. They have been given, some will argue, "too much" education for too little autonomy. Where earlier generations of workers "learned to labor" (Willis 1977), this one should learn to problem-solve, to think critically, creatively, said the education experts. They were wrong. Too many young people arrive at the job market to find too few of the jobs promised by an oversold technocratic revolution (Carnoy and Levin 1985, p. 161). And to find that the jobs there are being "de-skilled" for the convenience of employers, much as their grandfathers' jobs were, from craft to assembly-line labor (Aronowitz 1983, pp. 151–57). Their disillusions are rife with possibilities. Their response, so far, is an old and sad story in U.S. labor history: high rates of turnover, absenteeism, some sabotage, much drug use. But even that anarchic resistance has already forced some reform of the workplace—toward more employee autonomy (Carnoy and Levin 1985, ch. 7). Not surprisingly, workers who taste a little of that freedom often want more. And more? Who knows where it could lead.

All of these are important possibilities. But it is also important to add that that is all they are. So far, there is precious little evidence to support their sanguineness. In fact, recent auguries unsettle such optimism. In this country, political triangles with poor people at their apex have had more of tin about them than iron. That axiom has run true to form in the 1980s as a *novus ordo* cut through the lifelines of the poor like a hot knife through butter. Then, in 1984, the man who held the hot knife cantered his way to a hero's welcome at the voting booth, scarcely noticing the underfunded registration drive that the new triangle had tried to mount against him.

At the same time, a new survey of the union "movement" concluded that there hasn't been much lately: "As the 1980s opened there were few signs of impending changes in labor structure, ideology, and politics. The force that will spark a new labor left is not yet on the horizon as these words are written" (Lens 1985, p. 142).

And survey evidence suggests that the forces of hegemony have managed to make the answer to the crisis of capitalism—more capitalism. By a ratio of almost 2 to 1, Americans now see the party of supply-side, of trickle-down, of self-reliance as the one that can "make the economy strong and prosperous" (Ladd 1986, p. 27). The "newest workers," the cohort aged 18 to 29, is one of that party's strongest support groups (Ladd 1986, p. 11). At this moment, the theories of "organic crisis" remain not completely implausible fond hopes.

And still, this can be said with certainty of Sisyphus' stone: it will be moved. Those nascent, inchoate, struggling, failing, valiant resistances we see all around us will grow. Probably, the movement of the stone will not be rapid. Probably, it will not happen without reversals. Quite likely, somewhere near the top, years of struggle will fall down in failure. And then, just as surely, they will begin again.

I leave Sisyphus at the foot of the mountain! One always finds one's burden again. But Sisyphus teaches the higher fidelity that negates the gods and raises rocks. He too concludes that all is well. This universe henceforth without a master seems to him neither sterile nor futile. Each atom of that stone, each mineral flake of that night-filled mountain, in itself forms a world. The struggle itself toward the heights is enough to fill a man's heart. One must imagine Sisyphus happy.

NOTE

1. All the extracts in this chapter are from Camus (1955, pp. 88–91).

REFERENCES

Aronowitz, Stanley, 1983. *Working Class Hero*. New York: Pilgrim Press.

Boyte, Harry C. 1984. *Community Is Possible*. New York: Harper and Row.

Camus, Albert. 1955. *The Myth of Sisyphus and Other Essays*. Translated by Justin O'Brien. New York: Alfred A. Knopf.

Carnoy, Martin, and Henry M. Levin. 1985. *Schooling and Work in the Democratic State*. Stanford, Calif.: Stanford University Press.

Delgado, Gary. 1982. "Taking It to the Streets." *Socialist Review* 12:49–84.

Gramsci, Antonio. 1971. *Selections from the Prison Notebooks*. Edited and translated by Quintin Hoare and Geoffrey N. Smith. New York: International Publishers.

Ladd, Everett Carll. 1986. "Alignment and Realignment: Where Are All the Voters Going?" New York: W. W. Norton.

Lens, Sidney. 1985. "Labor and Capital Today and Tomorrow." In *Working for Democracy*, edited by Mari Jo Buhle and Alan Dawley, pp. 135–42. Chicago: University of Illinois Press.

Pateman, Carole. 1970. *Participation and Democratic Theory*. New York: Cambridge University Press.

Peck, Abe. 1985. *Uncovering the Sixties*. New York: Pantheon.

Piven, Frances Fox, and Richard A. Cloward. 1982. *The New Class War*. New York: Pantheon.

Willis, Paul. 1977. *Learning to Labor*. Lexington, Mass.: Heath.

Index

About the Authors

CALVIN F. EXOO received his Ph.D. in Political Science from the University of Wisconsin–Madison in 1979. He is Associate Professor of Government at St. Lawrence University in Canton, New York. His articles and reviews on the politics of the media and on the political behavior of journalists, policymakers, and ethnic groups have appeared in *Polity*, *The Journal of Ethnic Studies*, *The Journal of Politics*, *Policy and Administration Review*, and *The American Political Science Review*.

MICHAEL W. APPLE is Professor of Curriculum and Instruction and Educational Policy Studies at the University of Wisconsin–Madison. He received his Ph.D. from Columbia University in 1970. He is editor and author of numerous books and articles on the relationship between schooling and inequalities in the larger society. His recent books include *Ideology and Curriculum*, *Education and Power*, and *Teachers and Texts: A Political Economy of Class and Gender Relations in Education*.

ALAN DRAPER is Assistant Professor of Government at St. Lawrence University. He received his Ph.D. from Columbia University in 1982. His reviews and articles on economic policy and labor union politics have appeared in such journals as *Insurgent Sociologist*, *Economic and Industrial Democracy*, *Labor Studies Journal*, and the *American Political Science Review*.

RICHARD GUARASCI is Professor of Government at St. Lawrence University. He received his Ph.D. from Indiana University in 1977. He is author of *The Theory and Practice of American Marxism, 1957–1970*. His articles on the politics of workplace safety have appeared in *The Review of Radical Political*

Economics, *Humanity and Society*, *Workplace Democracy*, and *Insurgent Sociologist*.

DOUGLAS KELLNER is Associate Professor of Philosophy at the University of Texas at Austin. He received his Ph.D. from Columbia University in 1972. He is author or editor of four books and numerous articles on critical and Marxist theory and popular culture. His recent books include *Herbert Marcuse and the Crisis of Marxism* and (with Michael Ryan) *Camera Politica: The Politics and Ideology of Contemporary Hollywood Film*.

KENNETH TEITELBAUM is Assistant Professor of Education and Director of the Urban Teacher Preparation Program at Syracuse University. He received his Ph.D. from the University of Wisconsin–Madison in 1985. His articles on socialist education in the United States, changes in the work of teachers, and on teacher education have appeared in the *History of Education Quarterly*, *Journal of Curriculum Studies*, *Social Education*, *Journal of Education for Teachers*, and others.